Photo Finish:

The Digital Photographer's Guide to Printing, Showing, and Selling Images

Jon Canfield

Tim Grey

SYBEX®   San Francisco • London

Associate Publisher: DAN BRODNITZ
Acquisitions Editor: BONNIE BILLS
Developmental Editors: JIM COMPTON, PETE GAUGHAN
Production Editor: LESLIE E.H. LIGHT
Technical Editor: ELLEN ANON
Copyeditor: KATHY GRIDER-CARLYLE
Compositor: HAPPENSTANCE TYPE-O-RAMA
Graphic Illustrator: RAPPID RABBIT
Proofreaders: NANCY RIDDIOUGH, LAURIE O'CONNELL
Indexer: JACK LEWIS
Cover Designer: RICHARD MILLER, CALYX DESIGN
Photographers: JON CANFIELD, TIM GREY. JASON HAHN

Library of Congress Card Number: 2004108200

ISBN: 0-7821-4348-2

To Kathy—the love of my life.
—Jon

To Lisa, Miranda, and Riley—my trinity of joy.
—Tim

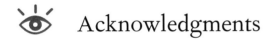 # Acknowledgments

Jon Canfield

Knowing where to start is easy. I want to thank my beautiful wife and best friend, Kathy. She's always believed in me (usually more than I believed in myself), encouraged me, and consoled me. Most of all, she's loved me for 25 years—even when I'm cranky.

My children, Ken and Erin, are out of the house now, but they still inspire me and make me proud to be their father. Both of you grew up to be fine adults and I love you.

Finally, I'd like to dedicate this to my other best friend, Bo. Bo was my constant companion and could always be found curled under my desk while I wrote. Part way through this book, we lost Bo to cancer. I miss him every day, and I hope that when my time comes, he'll be there waiting for me with his tennis ball, asking "What took you so long?"

My co-author, Tim Grey, deserves special thanks for taking a chance with the new guy and agreeing to help write this book. His advice and experience made this project come together, and his experience and talent made it possible.

Peter Burian is a fine author, friend, and mentor who coached my early attempts at writing, and I'm grateful for his support and help.

Charlotte Lowrie is another fine author and friend, and she is responsible for my first published articles. The opportunity and experience she provided helped lead to this book.

I also want to thank all the fine photographers who allowed us to use images from their websites, including John Shaw, Art Wolfe, Debbie Ferrell, Ellen Anon, Charlotte Lowrie, John Paul Caponigro, Mahesh Thapa, Fred Miranda, and Phil Askey.

Thomas Frizelle and Jay Kelbley at Kodak, Heather Hollaender at Macromedia, Amanda Sahliyeh at Photodex, Kathy Stuparyk at ACD Systems, and Joy Remuzzi at iView Multimedia all provided assistance and encouragement that were invaluable to the project.

I also want to thank everyone at Sybex who shepherded me through this book. This was my first book, and a learning experience with patient teachers. I hope we have the opportunity to work together again. A special thanks goes to acquisitions editor Bonnie Bills for giving a rookie the chance to take a concept and turn it into a reality. Thanks also go to developmental editors Jim Compton and Peter Gaughan, production editor Leslie Light, technical editor Ellen Anon, copyeditor Kathy Grider-Carlyle, compositor Maureen Forys and the rest of the staff at Happenstance Type-O-Rama, illustrator Tony Jonick, proofreaders Nancy Riddiough and Laurie O'Connell, and Thom Dyson for his assistance with the companion website.

Tim Grey

As I take on more and more projects doing the work that I absolutely love, my wonderful wife Lisa continues to be understanding about the demands placed on me by writing deadlines and keeps me focused on maintaining balance. I'm a lucky man to be married to my best friend, who is also a loving and supportive wife.

I'd also like to thank Miranda and Riley for the pride with which they fill me. My good friend Bruce Heller also continues to inspire me in writing and in life. I also appreciate Jeff Greene for his friendship, great images, and service as a sounding board on many ideas.

A special thanks also goes out to Marianne Wallace. She's been a major supporter from day one, and I value her friendship. She had to know I wouldn't forget to mention her this time! Check out her website at www.ezpixels.com.

For the support and assistance they provided for this project, I'd also like to thank Dave Metz at Canon USA; Dan Steinhardt at Epson; Jan Lederman, Mark Rezzonico, and Lorenzo Gasparini at MAC Group US; Brian Levey at ColorVision; and Marc Pawliger at Adobe. Thanks also to the photographers who continue to inspire me with their awesome talent, including Dewitt Jones, John Shaw, Art Morris, Art Wolfe, and George Lepp, as well as two excellent photographers I've recently become acquainted with, Teru Kuwayama and Matthew Jordan Smith.

Dear Reader,

Thank you for choosing *Photo Finish*. This book is part of the growing library of Sybex graphics books, all written by outstanding authors—artists and teachers who really know their stuff and have a clear vision of the audience they're writing for.

Founded in 1976, Sybex is the oldest independent computer book publisher. More than twenty-five years later, we're committed to producing a full line of consistently exceptional graphics books. With each title, we're working hard to set a new standard for the industry. From the paper we print on, to the writers and photographers we work with, our goal is to bring you the best graphics books available.

I hope you see all that reflected in these pages. I'd be very interested to hear your comments and get your feedback on how we're doing. To let us know what you think about this or any other Sybex book, please visit us at www.sybex.com. Once there, go to the book's page, click on Submit Feedback, and fill out the questionnaire. Your input is greatly appreciated.

Please also visit www.sybex.com to learn more about the rest of our graphics line.

Best regards,

DAN BRODNITZ
Associate Publisher—Graphics
Sybex Inc.

Foreword

In digital photography, taking the picture is only the first, albeit important, step in the process. Just as it was with film, a digital picture isn't "finished" until it's printed and displayed. And it's that second part—the printing and display—that has a lot of would-be digital photographers refusing to come down from the familiar hills of film photography. In fact, a recent survey shows that more than 50 percent of professional photographers are still shooting film. Doubtless they've heard that digital can be not only expensive but also difficult.

The knowledge and skills required for implementing a day-to-day color workflow, getting reliable output (whether printed or as a digital slideshow) and, of course, designing, publishing, and maintaining a website can feel intimidating. They seem to require that today's photographer not only pack around the latest and greatest digital SLR or digital pro back, but that he or she also wear the proverbial white plastic shirt-pocket protector to indicate his or her mastery of computer skills as well.

Digital photography shouldn't be this hard. And, if it must be this hard, then there should be a clear path through the maze of technology and product choices to the finished photo. That's what *Photo Finish* provides: A guide through bewildering terms, options, and technology to the final display, whether it is print, a slideshow, or the Web.

What better guides than Jon Canfield and Tim Grey to lead the way? Jon Canfield is an experienced and respected photographer and columnist with a solid background in digital photography. Teaming up with Jon is Tim Grey, who is not only a prolific and highly readable author, but also a respected instructor in all things related to digital input and output at the Lepp Institute in California. With a clear and easy writing style, both Jon and Tim provide welcome voices of experience for both new and seasoned digital photographers.

Together, Jon and Tim demystify the second part of digital photography—from color management through printing, website display, and slideshow presentation. I'm sure you'll enjoy, as I did, having experts to guide you to a photo finish.

CHARLOTTE K. LOWRIE
Managing editor, MSN Photos (http://photos.msn.com). *Writer, photographer, and author of* Teach Yourself Visually Digital Photography, Second Edition.
www.wordsandphotos.org

About the Authors

Jon Canfield

Jon Canfield is a landscape and nature photographer living in the Pacific Northwest, where he's blessed with some of North America's most scenic landscapes. He has been involved with digital imaging from the early days, and he spent several years at Microsoft working on digital photography products. Jon was the technical editor for Tim Grey's *Color Confidence* book. His articles have been published in several magazines, including *Shutterbug, Connected Photographer,* and *NANPA Currents.* He has a regular column on digital output in *eDigitalPhoto* magazine. Jon enjoys teaching digital imaging and learning from others. You can visit Jon on the Web at www.joncanfield.com.

Tim Grey

A lifetime of working with computers and a love of photography combine as the perfect passion for Tim Grey. He loves learning as much as he possibly can about digital imaging, and he loves sharing that information even more. He does so through his writing and speaking appearances. His articles have been published in *Outdoor Photographer, PC Photo,* and *Digital Photo Pro* magazines, among others. He recently wrote *Color Confidence: The Digital Photographer's Guide to Color Management,* also published by Sybex. He is a co-author of *Real World Digital Photography, 2nd Edition.* He teaches courses at the Lepp Institute of Digital Imaging (www.leppinstitute.com), and he lectures and appears at various other venues. Tim also publishes a regular "Digital Darkroom Questions" e-mail list where he answers questions related to digital imaging for photographers. To add your e-mail address to the list, visit www.timgrey.com.

Contents

Chapter 4   **Specialty Printing**   **59**

Part II   **Using Print Services**

Chapter 5   **Choosing the Output and Print Lab**   **87**

Chapter 6   **Using Online Print Services**   **103**

Part V   Showing and Selling Your Images

"It is easier than ever to share your photographic images with a large audience."

Introduction

Photography is about capturing your vision of the world, but more importantly it is about sharing that vision. You won't find too many photographers who take pictures and hide them where nobody will ever see them. Quite the contrary, most photographers want to share their images with as many people as possible.

We two authors are continually inspired by the images captured by our favorite photographers. Among those photographers are professionals whose work is represented in this book. But others are amateur photographers who simply love their craft and aren't trying to make a living at it. Today it is easier than ever to share your photographic images with a large audience, and for this we are truly grateful. Without this ability, we wouldn't have had the opportunity to view nearly as many wonderful images from such a wide variety of photographers.

Traditionally, the way to share photographic images has been through the print. This continues to be a popular way for many photographers to share their images. Producing the best possible print is important, and in the first section of this book we'll show you exactly how to do that. This includes choosing the best printer and media, preparing your images to achieve the best quality, using a proper color management workflow to ensure accurate colors in every print, and sending the images to the printer. We'll also show you how to take advantage of print labs and online print services when you want to leave the printing to someone else. To help you stretch your creativity, we'll also guide you through several methods for creating unique variations of your images. The presentation of the final print has a major impact on how it is perceived. The last chapters offer guidance on the best display methods, and provide tips on getting those images into galleries and making sales.

Breaking with traditions of the past and creating new traditions for the future, photographers are increasingly taking advantage of the latest technologies for sharing images. To reach a truly global audience at minimal expense, photographers are going to the Web. While you've no doubt spent plenty of time surfing the Web, you may not have tackled your desire to put a gallery online to share with the world. We'll show you how to create a site you'll be proud of without a steep learning curve. Whatever your purpose in launching a site, whether it's to sell your photography online or just to share a special interest that you've documented with digital shots, the chapters in Part II will show you how to plan and organize the site, how to build the pages using common web-authoring software like Dreamweaver MX 2004 and FrontPage 2003, how to optimize your photos for web display using common image-editing software like Photoshop or Photoshop Elements, and more.

Although a website lets you share your work with (potentially) anyone in the world, a digital slideshow is a much more intimate and focused presentation. Standing in front of a room and talking about your pictures as you display them on a screen can make a significant impact, whether you are telling a group of fellow photographers how you took some of your favorite shots or convincing your neighbors that a historic building is worth saving. Creating a show with high-quality images, smooth and impressive transitions, and music synchronized to the flow of images is remarkably easy. We'll show you how it's done so you can turn your best images into a dynamic presentation that will add to the power of your photographs.

Who Should Use This Book

This book is for any photographer who would like to create beautiful and professional displays of their photographic images, which pretty much means this book is for all photographers. With the widespread use of digital tools for photography, you've probably already started making prints. This book will show you how to ensure you are producing prints of optimal quality and how to display those prints for maximum appeal.

If you'd like to take your images beyond the print and learn how to create digital slideshows, you've come to the right book. You don't need to be a Photoshop expert or even a computer geek. If you have basic computer skills, we can show you the way to producing slideshows that will have your audience asking how in the world you created such a sophisticated presentation.

Of course, there's no audience bigger than the whole world, and that's the potential of the Web. People from just about any corner of the globe can view your images, but you'll need to build a site for your images to be seen. Again, you don't have to be a graphic designer or a Web expert. We'll show you how to create a basic site quickly, and then show you more advanced techniques for making a website that is easy to maintain and provides a professional presentation of your images.

In short, if you were enticed enough by the cover to pick up this book and open it, then this is the right book for you. Some of the topics we cover are advanced, but we've presented them in a clear and easy-to-follow manner so you won't be intimidated. If you're a photographer who wants to share your images, turn the page and we'll get started.

The *Photo Finish* Companion Website

We created a website to go along with this book. There you'll find links to our favorite software products and utilities, along with links to manufacturers and resellers of supplies. We've also included samples that you are free to download and either use in your own projects or take inspiration from as you design your print, website, or slideshow along with the templates created for use in Part II of the book. The companion site is www.photofinishbook.com, and we hope that you'll find that it's a valuable resource as you expand your horizons.

Contacting the Authors

We're very passionate about photography and digital imaging, and we enjoy sharing information to help you realize your photographic visions. We'd love to hear your comments about this book and your thoughts about future books you'd like to see. Jon can be contacted at jon@joncanfield.com, and Tim can be contacted at tim@timgrey.com.

When Jon shared his vision for this book, we both got excited about the possibilities. Beyond the nuts and bolts of specific techniques, our aim is to give photographers renewed enthusiasm for sharing their images. The methods and tips presented in this book are focused on helping you produce inspiring presentations of the highest quality possible. We look forward to seeing your images.

Printing on the Desktop

I

Digital imaging provides photographers with tremendous control over their images. In effect, it enables them to do everything they could do in the traditional wet darkroom—and then some— without the challenges and limitations inherent in that process. The cornerstone of the digital darkroom for serious photographers is the print-making process. This process involves making decisions about the printer and media, preparing the images, and producing accurate output. It also opens the door to new possibilities and flexibility in output.

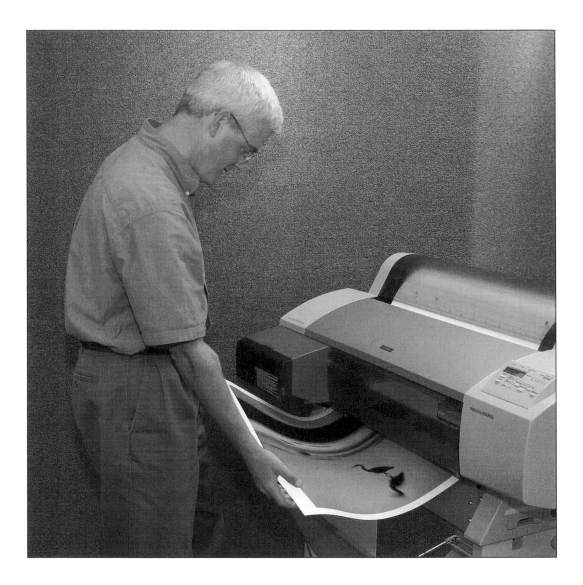

Choosing the Printer and Medium

1

For the vast majority of serious photographers, the final print defines the photograph. We put a tremendous amount of time, money, and effort into capturing and optimizing images, and most of these images are shared and enjoyed in the form of a print. Choosing the right printer and print medium for a particular image is a key step in producing a print you'll be proud of.

Chapter Contents
Choosing a Printer
Specialty Inksets
Setting the Mood
Media Options
Paper Properties

Choosing a Printer

When photographers think of output, the first thing that comes to mind is a print. The defining moment for photographers working in the digital darkroom is when the ink meets paper. To get the best results, make sure you use a printer that includes features that will make your workflow efficient and will produce the quality you demand.

Fortunately, there is no shortage of excellent printers capable of producing exceptional photo-quality output. Most photographers will want to use a photo inkjet printer because of the excellent quality and flexibility offered. Dye-sublimation printers have some advantages, such as durability and a highly "photographic" appearance. However, we don't consider them to be the best solution for most photographers because they tend to be more expensive and don't support a wide range of print media (papers). You should consider using a photo inkjet printer to produce prints of your images (see Figure 1.1). With a good inkjet printer, you can exercise greater control over the print-making process and save money. Generating your own prints is less expensive than using a high-quality print lab to produce them.

Figure 1.1 A photo inkjet printer, such as this Epson Stylus Photo 2200, allows you to produce prints of exceptional quality at a reasonable cost per print.

When choosing a photo inkjet printer there are quite a few issues to consider: the size of the output, the type of ink used, the number of inks, the size of the droplets of ink, the resolution of your output, the media supported by the printer, and the capabilities of your software. We cover each of these items in turn.

Output Size

Most photo inkjet printers fall into two categories of maximum output size: 8.5″×11″ and 13″×19″. There are also other printers that offer larger output options, including wide-format printers with widths up to 44″. When deciding on the right printer for you, consider how large you'll likely need to be able to print both now and in the future.

Ink Types

The basic choice here is between dye-based inks and pigment-based inks. Pigment-based inks last longer, but they have a narrower color gamut than dye-based inks. Still, the latest pigment-based inks, such as the UltraChrome inkset from Epson, provide vibrant colors that come close to matching dye-based inks. We recommend using pigment-based inks if you are producing prints for sale or for long-term display. If you don't need your images to last terribly long, and color vibrancy is more important, then dye-based inks might be an excellent choice. However, with the cost of pigment-based printers coming down nearly to the level of current dye-based printers, the choice to favor longevity in prints is even easier.

> **Note:** Just because pigment-based inks last longer than dye-based inks doesn't mean that dye-based inks will necessarily fade quickly. Many dye-based inks, when used in conjunction with appropriate papers, are able to produce prints that will last many decades. For details on print longevity estimates for a variety of printers, visit the Wilhelm Imaging Research website at www.wilhelm-research.com.

Number of Inks

Inkjet printers produce various tonal values for each color by adjusting how large the droplets are (if possible) and by adjusting the spacing between the droplets. The smaller and further apart the droplets are, the lighter the color will appear (see Figure 1.2).

To maintain the finest detail, many printers utilize "light" ink colors in addition to the standard cyan, magenta, yellow, and black (CMYK) inks so the droplets don't need to be spaced as far apart as would otherwise be necessary. These diluted inks (usually light cyan and light magenta, with some printers using a light black as well) provide for higher quality in the final print, while maintaining the ability to produce a wide range of color and tonal values. As a general rule, printers with six or more ink colors will produce the best results because the lighter inks provide broader tonal range while maintaining the ability to produce fine detail.

Note: Epson has a new UltraChrome Hi-Gloss inkset that uses red and blue inks instead of light cyan and light magenta. Because the ink droplets are so small, the diluted inks are no longer necessary to produce excellent quality. The red and blue inks help to expand the color gamut of the printer by offering additional hues that would otherwise be difficult to produce. Unfortunately, these new inks are not compatible with previous printers that use the original UltraChrome inks, and they are optimized specifically for glossy papers.

Ink Droplet Size

The smaller the ink droplets, the wider the range of tonal values and the finer the detail is that the printer is able to produce (see Figure 1.3).

Anything below 6 picoliters is very good, with 2 picoliters currently the smallest droplet size available.

Detail   Normal View

Figure 1.2 Inkjet printers simulate various tonal values by varying the size and spacing of individual ink droplets.

Resolution

For all practical purposes, you can pretty much ignore this specification. That's because any recent model photo inkjet printer will be able to produce output at 1,440 dpi or higher. In fact, even if your printer offers a higher quality setting, we recommend using the 1,440 dpi setting, which will still provide excellent quality indistinguishable from the higher settings. It will also print faster and use less ink. Keep in mind that this resolution specification is not the same as "image resolution." The printer resolution should be thought of only as an output quality setting.

Media Support

The variety of print media to which a printer is able to print to successfully isn't usually included in the specifications provided by the manufacturer. With some ink formulations, the types of paper you can print to with good results can be limited. We recommend checking reviews in magazines or on the Web to determine the range of papers and other print media supported by the printer.

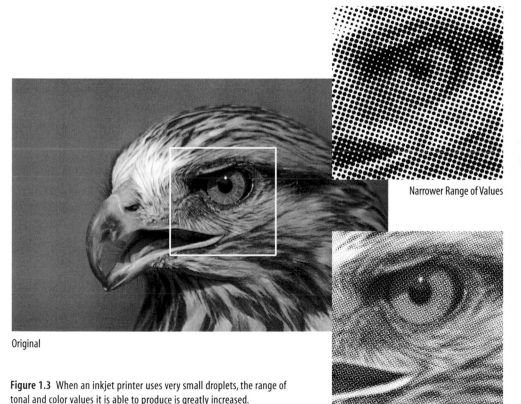

Narrower Range of Values

Original

Wider Range of Values

Figure 1.3 When an inkjet printer uses very small droplets, the range of tonal and color values it is able to produce is greatly increased.

The Truth About *dpi*

Resolution tends to be one of the most confusing topics for those who are new to digital imaging, and a tremendous amount of misinformation doesn't make it any easier to get a handle on it. Resolution relates to the quantity or density of pixels within an image. When you're talking about a digital camera, quantity is the normal unit of measure, such as megapixels. With a digital image file we refer to the number of pixels per inch (ppi), which is a measure of how the pixels within the image will be distributed. With a printed image, the density of the dots on paper is what matters. The more dots within an inch on paper, the more detail can be rendered and, therefore, the higher the quality. In this case, the number of dots per inch doesn't relate directly to image resolution, because more than one droplet of ink is used to create each pixel (dot) in the image file.

However, when it comes to ink on paper, there is a definite limit. In our experience, printers offering resolutions over about 1,440 dpi don't offer a real advantage. If your printer supports more than 1,440 dpi, it probably doesn't make any sense to use that higher setting, because you'll waste ink, require more time to produce a print, and the quality won't visibly improve.

When resizing the image, you need to specify an output resolution that is completely independent of the printer resolution. There are many theories regarding which image resolution is the best. Some say 240 dpi; others say 300, 360, or some other "magic number." We've done extensive testing, and we feel that any value between 240 and 360 dpi will produce excellent results. A setting of 360 dpi will generally ensure the very best quality, but this is a quality difference that is virtually impossible to distinguish from an image set to 240 dpi for printing. Therefore, as far as we're concerned you can use any value between 240 and 360 dpi. To us, 300 dpi makes sense because it still ensures excellent print quality while also matching the standard used by most offset press printers in the industry.

Software Capabilities

Getting information from manufacturers about the flexibility and ease-of-use of the dialog boxes you will use to configure their printer settings is difficult. Again, refer to reviews in magazines or on the Web for information on whether the printer settings allow you to adjust the output to get the most accurate colors and to see how easy a particular printer is to operate.

Specialty Inksets

The vast majority of photographers use the inks that were specifically designed for their printers. However, if you're willing to deal with the limitations and possible complications of using third-party inks, the results are often well worth the trouble, particularly when your goal is to produce perfectly neutral black-and-white prints.

Staying with the manufacturer's printer-specific inks is certainly the safest approach, as printer manufacturers develop inks for the printers that will produce optimal results and ensure compatibility. Using third-party inks does introduce concerns about clogging, and it voids the printer manufacturer's warranty. However, most of them are engineered to work well with a wide variety of inkjet printers. Although most specialty inks work with a relatively large number of printers, the list isn't exhaustive. You'll need to confirm that your printer is compatible with the inksets you plan to use. Many of the more recent printer models utilize special chipsets for their ink cartridges that make it difficult or impossible to use third-party inks with those printers. Check compatibility before you plan to use third-party inks.

> **Note:** Specialty inksets are available from a wide range of sources. Some of the most popular inksets include Lysonic from Lyson (www.lyson.com), Piezography from Cone Editions (www.piezography.com), Generations pigmented inks from Media Street (www.mediastreet.com), and a variety of inksets from MIS Associates (www.inksupply.com).

The most common type of specialty inksets are those known as "quadtone" inks. This name comes from the fact that these inks originally included four shades of black (tones) to replace the four colors of early printers. New printers have six or seven ink colors, and some of the newer specialty inksets include more than four inks.

> **Note:** Although most quadtone inks now include more than four shades of ink, the name has stuck.

Inkjet printers with standard inks create grayscale images by using only the black ink or by blending all of the ink colors. Using only the black ink means the printer won't be able to produce the wide range of tonal values we expect in an image, and the resulting print will lack smooth gradations of color. Blending all of the color inks ensures smooth gradations of tone; however, if the inks are not mixed in perfect balance, the result can be a grayscale print with a very strong color cast. In our experience, most printers are simply not capable of producing a perfectly neutral grayscale print.

Because quadtone inks have multiple inks of varying tonal values, they are able to solve both problems at once. Multiple shades in the inkset ensure smooth gradations of tonal values within the print, and the fact that all of the inks are perfectly neutral ensures the print won't exhibit any color cast.

Of course, there are situations where you want to produce a grayscale print that isn't perfectly neutral. This option is also available from most of the quadtone ink suppliers. The inks are offered in both warm and cool versions that provide a consistent print with a slight cast that adds an element of depth to the image. Inksets are also available to produce a realistic sepia-tone print on your inkjet printer, using a stronger color cast than the warm or cool quadtone inks.

Note: When using specialty inksets, you will generally need to flush the printer when changing inksets and periodically after certain usage intervals. To ensure optimal performance with your printer, be sure to carefully read and follow the instructions for using specialty inksets.

Pigmented ink is another type of specialty ink that provides archival capabilities for printers that are designed to work only with dye-based inks. A popular example is the Generations series of inks from Media Street (www.mediastreet.com). Some versions are designed to allow dye-based printers to use pigmented inks. Other versions replace the pigmented inks of certain printers with less expensive pigmented inks.

Note: Because of the challenges involved with switching between ink types on any inkjet printer, we strongly recommend that you purchase an additional printer to use exclusively with specialty inks if you are going to use them.

Setting the Mood

When you view a photographic image on display in an art gallery, the elements surrounding the image are often carefully planned. The walls are generally plain and neutral so that your attention is not drawn away from the image. The image itself is adorned in a frame that both complements the image and draws you into the photograph. The lighting isn't typically a harsh spotlight; it is usually a warm illumination source that glows as an aura around the image.

The photographic image itself stands at the center of this shrine, at the focus of attention. All the other elements such as mat, frame, and lighting are added to emphasize the photograph, not to draw your attention away from it. To be presented in such a manner, the image must be printed on some form of print medium.

Just as a painter can choose a canvas type for the specific image to be created, photographers have many options when it comes to the media on which an image is printed and displayed. The paper you use to print an image can make an amazing difference in the final presentation. Each paper has different properties of ink absorption, different color, and different texture. While this provides variety that appeals to many photographers, it is important to remember that the print medium sets the mood for the image. Therefore, rather than simply choosing a material that you like, the print medium should be matched to the image to complement it.

Glossy or Matte?

As you decide which paper types are best suited for a particular image, the first issue to consider is the surface type, which is generally categorized as glossy or matte finish. This is an obvious simplification of the wide range of possibilities, but these two basic categories provide some direction to begin the decision-making process.

With glossy papers, the inks tend to sit up on the surface of the paper rather than soaking into it. The result is that colors are more vibrant, the contrast is higher, and the final print contains more detail. Glossy papers are, therefore, appropriate when you want to emphasize those properties in an image.

Matte papers absorb the inks more, so that they don't stay at the surface (see Figure 1.4). Also, matte papers tend to cause more *dot gain,* which is the amount the inks spread once they come in contact with the paper (see Figure 1.5). Because matte papers are more absorbent, the inks are able to spread more easily. As a result, the colors are more muted, the contrast is lower, and some detail is lost. These characteristics can complement subtle or ethereal images and enhance images for which you are trying to achieve a more "painterly" appearance.

These general rules offer some guidance in determining the general type of paper that is most appropriate for a particular image. However, the distinction between the different types isn't quite so clear. Many new matte-surface papers now include special coatings to optimize them for inkjet printing. These coatings reduce dot gain and keep the inks on the surface, resulting in a matte surface without reflections that retains vibrant colors, high contrast, and excellent detail in the printed image.

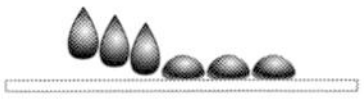

Glossy

Figure 1.4 Inks tend to sit on the surface of glossy papers. They are absorbed into matte papers, resulting in different tonal and color properties between the same colors printed to different paper types.

Matte

Figure 1.5 Matte papers, especially when they aren't coated, introduce much more dot gain than glossy paper types.

Media Options

If categorizing your basic print media options as either glossy or matte is a bit simplistic, the actual range of available options is mind-boggling. Each printer manufacturer offers a respectable selection of papers, and third parties offer a virtually unlimited variety.

We encourage you to experiment with different media types. While an image may seem perfectly suited to a particular paper, exploring other options is a good idea. You may be surprised to see how images look on different materials.

There's no such thing as the perfect medium for a given photographic image. Instead, each type of media allows you to present a particular interpretation of the image. It isn't a matter of deciding which media is the right one for a particular image, but rather which medium creates the intended interpretation for an image. When you match the right medium with the right image, the result is a print you'll be proud of (see Figure 1.6).

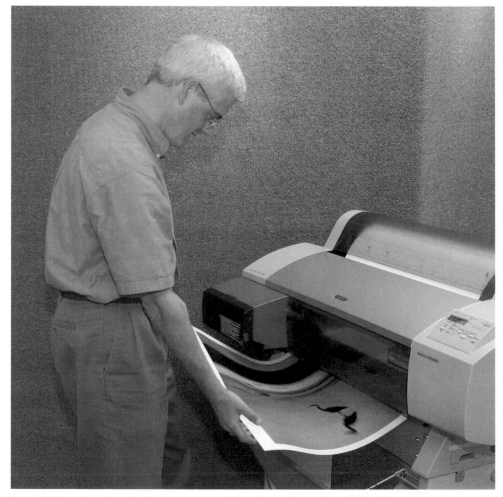

Figure 1.6 The wide variety of media options for photo inkjet printers gives you incredible flexibility for your images. (Photograph by Jeff Greene, ImageWest Photography.)

Note: Selecting the right media for your images is very subjective. We each have our own tastes and preferences. There is no "right answer" when it comes to choosing the right media for your images. Evaluate a wide range of options, and decide which achieves the look you prefer.

Traditional Papers

Many digital photographers started with film photography, and so they tend to think of the traditional papers when it comes time to make a print in their digital darkroom. The traditional papers are the basic options that you can find at any retailer that stocks photo inkjet supplies. These include the glossy, semi-gloss, and matte papers, all with a relatively smooth surface. Each of these categories of papers is best suited to a specific type of image:

- **Glossy** papers are best for images that require maximum impact. Because these papers maintain vibrant colors and high contrast, they are ideally suited for images with highly saturated colors. (However, the glare associated with the gloss may actually make it more difficult to see the detail within an image, depending on the lighting conditions where it will be viewed.)

- **Matte** papers work best with images with soft, muted colors, or where you don't want to emphasize detail. If the image contains muted colors to begin with or you want to tone down the colors in the image for effect, a matte paper is a good choice.

- **Semi-gloss** papers are a compromise between glossy and matte papers. They are well-suited for images that fall somewhere between the vibrant images that work best on glossy papers and the muted images that work best on matte papers. Semi-gloss is often the choice of photographers who would normally opt for a glossy paper, but who want to avoid the distracting glare and reflections that tend to occur with glossy papers.

Sampler Packs

Many paper manufacturers offer sampler packs at a nominal price. These sampler packs include a sheet or two of a variety of papers. Using these samples is an excellent way for you to test different papers and find the ones you like the most. Companies offering such sampler packs include paper manufacturers Red River Paper (www.redrivercatalog.com) and Legion Paper (www.legionpaper.com), and paper distributor Digital Art Supplies (www.digitalartsupplies.com).

These sampler packs offer excellent value, and they are frequently priced very competitively, in the hope you'll become a regular customer of the papers included in these packs. They are a low-risk and inexpensive way to try a wide variety of papers to see which you like the best.

Third-Party Papers

Some paper and ink combinations can produce very unsatisfactory results. Using papers produced by one printer manufacturer on a printer from a different manufacturer can cause compatibility problems. Some combinations do work, but be aware that compatibility problems do exist.

Many third-party papers from companies that don't manufacture printers have been specifically designed to work well with a wide range of printers, making them safe to use on virtually any printer. Printer manufacturers often recommend that you only use their brand of papers with their printers, but many third-party papers work exceptionally well with virtually all printers.

Be sure to check the website of third-party paper manufacturers for custom profiles for any third-party papers you plan to use. For one thing, those profiles will often ensure the most accurate prints possible. If profiles for a given paper are available for your model of printer, that is a good indication that the manufacturer has tested the paper for compatibility with that printer.

When you use third-party papers, the longevity of those prints may be an unknown because these combinations are not typically tested. In general, when using third-party papers you can expect the longevity to meet at least the level of the lowest-rated print medium from the same manufacturer as the printer, although that isn't guaranteed.

Fine Art Papers

Traditional print media are fine when you are simply sharing your images, such as with snapshot photos. Although many of the traditional print media provide beautiful ways to present your images, there are many other options that allow you to showcase your images in style.

You'll find that most of the papers considered worthy of the label "fine art" have a matte surface. Fine art images don't need to be flashy. In fact, any gloss on the surface can tend to detract from the image. The image should be able to stand on its own without the need for a glossy surface to add impact. Many of the current fine art papers are coated so that they don't behave the same way uncoated matte papers do. The coating keeps the inks near the surface of the paper and reduces dot gain, so colors remain vibrant and detail remains crisp.

Note: Keep in mind that even papers with a matte surface will tend to look slightly glossy when displayed under glass. We think of glass as a "surface equalizer" because most papers, when viewed through glass in a frame, tend to look somewhat glossy.

Many of the fine art papers also have a creamy color ranging from off-white to nearly beige. Although we tend to think of bright white paper as being the most desirable, the warm tone of many fine art papers adds richness to the printed image. When you first handle a fine art paper, you'll find that it feels substantial in your hands. These materials tend to be relatively heavy and thick. Of course, an image printed on fine art material will most likely end up matted and framed, so nobody will know how thick the medium is. Still, the heavier grade of these materials adds to their perceived value. While you may be the only one to hold a print before it gets matted and framed, you'll appreciate the durability and heft of the medium.

Of course, the increased weight and thickness of these fine art materials can be a problem. Many inkjet printers have a difficult time feeding these papers. In some cases, you can get the paper to feed through repeated attempts, but this can be frustrating. If your printer doesn't offer a special slot for feeding thicker papers, try to feed the paper into the printer before starting the print job by placing the paper in the input tray and pressing the paper feed button. Doing so will ensure the paper is properly loaded and ready for printing before the printer actually attempts to put ink onto the paper.

Note: Just because a printer is able to feed thick paper doesn't mean it will print reliably to it. Check the manual for your printer to determine the thickness limitations. Printing on thicker materials than your printer is designed for can result in damage to the prints *or your printer*.

There is considerable variation in surface texture for the many fine art papers available. Some, such as Epson's UltraSmooth Fine Art paper, are designed to be as smooth as possible with absolutely no texture. Others include a texture that adds depth to the printed image. Examples include Epson Textured Fine Art paper, Hahnemühle Torchon, Epson Canvas, and Lyson Rough Fine Art paper.

The various features of a fine art paper create an elegant material that feels good in the hands, displays well, is sturdy and rugged, protects the inks to stand the test of time, and maintains the vibrancy and accuracy of the colors in your images.

Fine Art Favorites

Many options are available to you when you are looking for a fine art paper to showcase your best images. Some of our favorites include the following:

- **Somerset Velvet** is a radiant white paper with a surface that is slightly textured. It is one of the most popular papers for fine art photo inkjet printing.
- **Hahnemühle Photo Rag** is a bright white cotton rag medium with a smooth surface. It maintains vibrant colors and a high dynamic range in the prints.

- **Hahnemühle Torchon** is a unique paper with a beautiful texture that resembles fluffy clouds. It maintains vibrant colors, but the texture is the real advantage. It works best with images that have areas of smooth texture that allow the paper's texture to really show through.
- **Epson Canvas** is a true canvas material with a coated printing surface. It works very well with deep tones and rich colors, adding a painterly look to the printed image.

Use this list as a basic guide to papers you may want to try, but research other options to find the materials you feel best accentuate your images.

 Note: Matte papers in general will offer less vibrant colors than their glossy counterparts. However, many matte papers (particularly fine art papers) utilize special coatings that result in colors that are nearly as vibrant as glossy papers without the reflections and glare that many photographers prefer to avoid in their prints.

Epson Canvas

Many print media options are promoted as "canvas." However, most of them are simply traditional papers with a faux canvas texture added to them for effect. These papers can be nice materials to print your images on, but they don't tend to achieve a fine art appearance.

We've tested a wide variety of canvas materials for inkjet printing. By far, our favorite is the Epson Canvas material. Rather than a traditional media type with texture added after the fact, the Epson Canvas is a genuine canvas material that has been coated so it will accept the inks from inkjet printers.

Epson Canvas is only offered in large rolls for the Epson Stylus Pro line of printers. It is recommended only for these printers because the fabric back of the material causes problems for printers utilizing standard rollers to feed the paper, especially when the printer doesn't support thick media. However, we've been successful in using the Epson Canvas in smaller desktop inkjet printers. Because the material only comes in large rolls, you'll need to cut custom sheets of the paper and then feed the material into the printer before starting the print job. If your printer offers a manual feed slot (such as the Epson Stylus Photo 2200), utilize that option to feed the canvas material more reliably.

The Epson Canvas print medium is a gorgeous material with a beautiful texture. It can even be mounted on a stretch frame as would be done with a painting on canvas, adding to the fine art appeal of this material. We find the Epson Canvas most appropriate for images with deep tones and rich colors, and it works very well with images containing smooth textures that allow the texture of the canvas surface to show through.

Specialty Media

Most photographers print their images to be shared through traditional means such as matting and framing them. However, there are many other ways to share a printed image, and specialty media provide the options. When you want to add a bit of flair to an image, specialty media may be the best choice. These media offer unconventional surfaces or materials designed for a specific purpose. Whatever their novelty, they add considerable variety to the available options in print media.

There are actually two basic categories of specialty media: those that are designed for specific predefined uses and those that are designed to help you create a unique presentation of an image.

As an example of a predefined use, prescored greeting cards that you can print on an inkjet printer provide a nice way to create your own cards to send to family and friends or offer for sale. Double-sided media are coated on both sides so you can create calendars or portfolio books. Websites such as Photographer's Edge at www.photographersedge.com offer such materials.

> **Note:** Besides simple double-sided media, some specialty media is specifically designed to assemble into bound portfolio books. For example, the Stone Editions products (www.stoneeditions.com) can be used to produce an elegant book to showcase your images.

Certain specialty media explore the limits of creativity. While many of the traditional and fine art materials are designed to appeal to a very wide audience, specialty media, as the name implies, are designed for maximum impact. By their nature, many photographers feel that these specialty media are too extravagant to be taken seriously. However, when matched with the right image, some of these unique materials can add to the appeal of the final print. For example, a variety of paper manufacturers offer magnetic papers. These sheets typically have a semi-gloss surface you print on, and a magnetic back that is protected with a film for printing. After printing to this media, you can peel the backing, cut out the picture, and post it on your refrigerator or other metallic surface. Other materials such as the Tyvek Brillion from Epson provide a durable material you can use to create outdoor displays. Pictorico makes a special printable silk media that could be used to sew an image into a pillow. You can even print to special iron-on transfer material and then use an iron to apply the image to a t-shirt or other fabric. If you can imagine a way you'd like to share your images, there's probably a specialty print media to make it possible.

Note: When you print on certain types of specialty media, your first reaction may be to dislike the media. However, it is important to remember that the more unique the material, the more likely you'll need to find just the right image for that media type. Keep in mind that some of these specialty media types require longer drying times, and the difference in appearance between wet and dry ink can be substantial.

In some cases, what makes a particular medium special isn't the surface you print on, but what's on the other side. An example of this is magnetic media. Often available in a semi-gloss finish, magnetic media can be printed to directly. When you've printed the image, you can cut it out and peel the backing material to reveal the magnetic back, ready to be stuck to any metal surface.

Note: Keep in mind that magnetic media have the potential to damage magnetic storage devices such as computer hard drives. Resist the temptation to put images printed to magnetic media on the case of your computer or other delicate electronic devices.

Regardless of how you want to share your printed images, a specialty medium is probably available to enable you to realize your vision. By exploring the range of available media options, you'll discover possibilities you may not have anticipated, inspiring you to create new interpretations for your photographic images.

Backlight

Photographers who have used slide film know the limitation of a printed image. When they examine the image through a loupe on a light table, the backlighting creates a luminous image that simply glows. A printed image simply can't produce this luminous appearance because it depends upon light reflected off the paper rather than light emitted through the image as is the case with a slide.

Even digital photographers who have never experienced a slide on a light table can appreciate the lack of luminosity in a print. Because a monitor produces an image by emitting light, it glows in much the same way that a slide on a light table does.

If you've ever experienced this frustration, you'll be amazed at the impact you can achieve by printing to backlight film material and displaying the image in a backlit display frame (see Figure 1.7; also see the version of this image in the color section). Instead of a print that depends upon reflected light for visibility, backlight film materials are designed to take advantage of emitted light to produce a luminous image that will attract attention.

Figure 1.7 Displaying an image printed on backlight film in a backlit frame adds tremendous impact to the final display.

Backlight film materials have a glossy front with a matte back. You print on the back of the image, producing a very flat image with inaccurate colors that are likely to make you wonder if you did something wrong. But when you turn the image around to view the glossy side with a light source behind it, you'll be impressed.

> **Note:** Although backlight film media typically offers longevity in line with other media types, these prints are exposed to bright light for much longer durations than normal, causing them to fade faster than you might otherwise expect.

Backlight film is certainly a specialty media type. That means there aren't a huge variety of backlight materials. Most printer manufacturers don't offer them. Epson had backlight film available in several sizes for a period of time, but they have since discontinued it. Fortunately, you can still find backlight film from a variety of sources. It may be difficult to find at retail outlets, but a variety of web-based stores, such as Digital Art Supplies (www.digitalartsupplies.com), carry several backlight film materials.

Once you have a beautiful image printed on backlight film, you'll have to find a way to display it. We'll talk about framing in Chapter 13, "Finishing Your Prints." Backlight materials require special consideration for framing, because they require a source of light behind them. That means buying a custom frame for the size print you want to display. Most frame shops don't have the resources to build a backlit frame, so you'll need to purchase a special backlit frame for these images.

> **Note:** For backlit frames that illuminate your images and allow you to change the image in the frame, take a look at the PhotoGlow products available at www.photoglow.com.

Shooting for the Medium

Once you've worked with a variety of different paper options, you can start to anticipate how an image will look on a particular type of paper and which materials are best suited for a given image. When you get to this point, you can start to anticipate the print medium you'll use for the final print while you're capturing the image.

For example, you may become more observant of textures in the scene as you are capturing an image, anticipating the print medium that will best accentuate or complement the textures. You may also consider which medium is the best match for the colors in your image, considering a semi-gloss or coated matte paper for images with vibrant colors, and uncoated matte papers for images with more subtle colors.

In short, thinking about the final print can influence how you photograph a scene. Rather than causing you to narrow your focus when photographing a particular subject, thinking about the range of available paper options will likely provide motivation to explore different ways to photograph a particular subject or scene.

Paper Properties

Selecting the print medium for an image based on surface type makes sense, because that surface is where the image will reside. However, in addition to the surface type, you'll want to consider other attributes of the paper when selecting print media. You'll also want to evaluate the properties of the paper itself, to ensure you're using the best print media possible for your images. The following properties should be considered when evaluating particular print media:

- **Thickness** is a direct measure of the actual thickness of the paper, and is most often measured in mils. One mil is equal to 1/1000th of an inch. Very thin papers are less than 5 mils thick, and they aren't what we consider photo-quality papers. Typical photo papers are around 10 mils thick, with very thick fine art papers topping out around 20 mils.

  Remember that just because a paper is thick doesn't mean it has a higher weight. Some thick papers aren't very dense, resulting in a lower weight. Although they will feel thick, they won't necessarily feel substantial.

- **Weight** is a measure of how heavy a paper weighs for a particular volume. The most common measurement is pounds, based on the weight of one ream (500 sheets) of the paper. However, the weight is based on 500 sheets at a standard size for the media type, which leads to confusion when comparing different papers because different papers come in different standard sizes. A more reliable unit of measure is grams per square meter (gsm) because it is based on paper weight for a fixed surface area. Lightweight photo papers are typically around 200 gsm, and heavy papers can range up to about 500 gsm.

Remember that just because a paper is relatively heavy doesn't mean it is thicker. Some heavy papers are simply very dense but still thin.

- **Brightness** is a measure of how close to pure white the print medium is. Brightness is expressed as a percentage of pure white based on reflectance. If brighteners are added to the paper, they can cause fluorescence, resulting in a brightness value greater than 100 percent. Although brightness gives you an idea of how white a particular medium type is, that doesn't necessarily translate into higher quality. For example, while many papers have brightness values of 95 percent or higher, some of the best fine art papers have brightness values in the low 80 percent range.

Although high brightness is usually desirable, many fine art materials actually have a creamy color to them. In fact, brighter papers can often have a cheaper look when compared to the richness of fine art media.

- **Base Material** indicates the type of material from which the print medium is made. Paper manufacturers don't usually indicate what base material is used for their papers, except in the case of fine art papers. The two major categories for base material are *fiber based,* in which some form of natural fiber is used as the base material, and *resin coated,* which includes a plastic coating on the surface. The base material does not affect the appearance of the printed image as much as the surface type does, so this choice is largely a matter of personal preference.

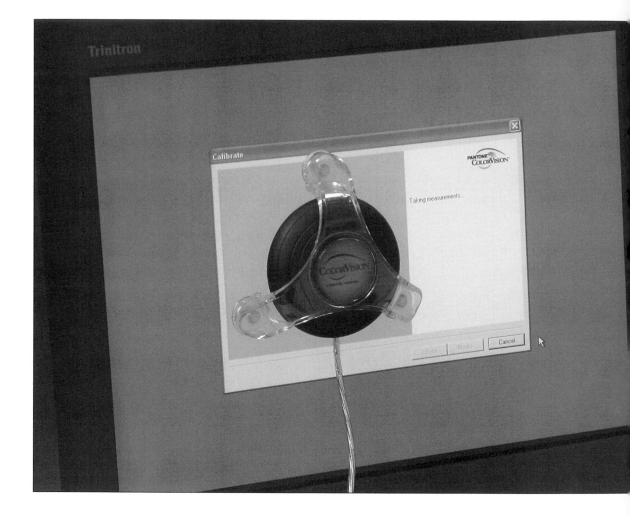

Preparing the Image

Before you can put ink to paper to produce the perfect print from your image file, you need to prepare that image file to ensure the most accurate output of the highest quality possible. Following a proper procedure for preparing the image will help ensure the best results.

Chapter Contents

The Optimized Image

For most photographers, the ultimate goal in the photographic process is to create a print that matches the vision from the moment the shutter release button was pressed. When that print is produced digitally, the key to making it perfect is an image file that has been optimized to produce the best result.

A Calibrated Monitor

If you aren't optimizing and evaluating your images on a calibrated monitor, you're really just rolling the proverbial dice when trying to get an accurate print. Monitor calibration is critical—especially if your images will ever be sent to someone else for printing or if you'll print them on more than one printer.

 Note: We can't stress enough how important it is to calibrate your monitor to ensure the most accurate prints possible. If you don't calibrate your monitor, start now.

The process of what we refer to as calibrating your monitor is actually two steps. The first step, calibration, involves adjusting the controls on your monitor so it is as close to established standards as possible. This is done based on special images displayed on your monitor by calibration software. By calibrating, the second step doesn't require as much adjustment. That second step is to characterize the display. This is often referred to as *profiling*, because the result is an International Color Consortium (ICC) profile that describes the color behavior of the monitor. With both steps complete, you can be assured of a consistent and accurate display of your images on the monitor.

 Note: While the process of creating an accurate display on your monitor involves both calibration and profiling, the full process is typically referred to as simply *monitor calibration*.

Some of the tools available for monitor calibration include:

- **ColorVision Spyder** (www.colorvision.com) includes the Monitor Spyder sensor (see Figure 2.1) and PhotoCAL software. This is currently the least expensive package available that includes a sensor at under $175.
- **MonacoOPTIX XR** (www.monacosys.com) includes the OPTIX XR sensor and MonacoEZcolor software. It isn't the most user-friendly option, but it does offer advanced options and produces highly accurate monitor profiles for around $300.

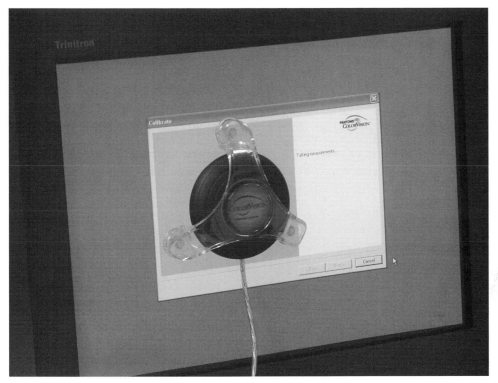

Figure 2.1 The Spyder package from ColorVision is an inexpensive and effective solution for calibrating your monitor.

- **GretagMacbeth Eye-One Display** (www.ilcolor.com) includes a compact colorimeter sensor and the Eye-One Match software. This package is easy to use and produces highly accurate profiles, selling for under $250.

> **Note:** Software-only solutions are available for monitor calibration, but we don't recommend them because they don't offer the accuracy provided by packages that include a sensor to read monitor display values.

Regardless of the monitor calibration package you use, calibrating your monitor on a regular basis is important. On CRT monitors, this is especially necessary because the electron guns that produce the image wear out over time. With three individual guns (one for red, green, and blue) wearing out at different rates, the result is a shift in color balance over time. LCD monitors are more stable, but the illumination source does lose power over time; therefore, regular calibration is still a good idea. As a general rule, we recommend calibrating at least once a month, but calibrating more frequently won't cause any problems and may even help ensure a more accurate display.

Scrutinize the Image

Once you are assured that the display you see on your monitor is accurate thanks to a monitor calibration package, carefully scrutinize the image to ensure it is indeed ready to be printed. Taking a close look at the image on your monitor will help you avoid wasting ink and paper by printing an image that has minor problems you could have solved before making the print.

To start, confirm that the image has been properly cropped to exclude areas you don't want included in the final image. This is particularly important with film scans, where it is possible to leave part of the slide frame around the outer edge of the image, appearing as black fringe areas (see Figure 2.2). Zoom in close on the image, and check the full perimeter of the image to be sure it has been cropped correctly.

Figure 2.2 Close examination of the edges of scanned images is important to confirm that all slide edges have been cropped out. If you don't catch problems such as this one before making the print, you'll waste ink and paper.

While you're taking a close look at the image, check for any dust, scratches, or other blemishes you may have missed during the image-optimization process. Large open areas, such as sky, in the image will make these blemishes easier to see, and you'll need to pay particular attention to such areas.

Check the overall tonal range of the image to ensure it has good brightness, appropriate contrast, adequate shadow and highlight detail, and no noise, which will most likely be found in dark shadow areas.

Next you want to take an overall look at the image to evaluate color. The color balance should be appropriate to the scene, without any undesired color casts. Objects within the scene should have accurate color based on the lighting under which the photograph was taken. Consider the saturation of colors in the image, making sure the colors aren't too muted. Also make sure that colors aren't over-saturated, resulting in colors that appear fake. The issues we've addressed here relate to typical quality considerations for photographic images. Obviously what defines a perfect image is incredibly subjective, and some of these factors may not apply in the traditional manner for every image.

If there are any problems with an image, take the time to get them resolved so the image on the monitor looks perfect before you attempt to make a print. Doing so will give you the best chance of producing a final print you'll be proud of.

Save the Master Image

Once you're satisfied that the image is perfect for printing, remember to save it as the master image file you'll use to produce all future prints or other output. This image should be saved with all layers intact so you can open the image to fine-tune it later. Changes may be required later either because you have discovered something that is less than optimal in the image or because you've changed your mind about how you want to interpret the image. Saving layers ensures the flexibility of modifying the image later without a loss of quality.

Saving the image with layers typically means saving it in the TIFF format, if your software supports layers in that format, or a proprietary format for your software. We're assuming you are using Adobe Photoshop to optimize your images, so that means you can save the image as a Photoshop PSD file. The choice between TIFF and PSD is largely a matter of preference. Both formats support all the features you need for optimizing your images with layers (see Figure 2.3), and both include some form of compression to help ensure that files, although still large, will be of a reasonable size for the amount of data included.

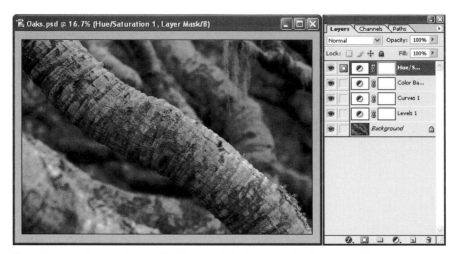

Figure 2.3 Saving the master image with all image and adjustment layers intact ensures you'll be able to fine-tune the image with maximum flexibility in the future.

Note: The master image file becomes your new original image, and it is as important as an original image on film. Therefore, you should protect this image as you would an original slide. One of the benefits of digital is that you can back up a perfect duplicate of the original, and we strongly encourage you to adopt a backup system to protect your images if you haven't already.

The master image file you save will be the image you should return to anytime you need to produce a print or process an image for inclusion on a website or in a digital slideshow. See Chapter 3, "Printing," Chapter 4, "Specialty Printing," and Chapter 8, "Going Live," for more information.

Soft Proofing and Gamut Warning

Adobe Photoshop includes two features that allow you to produce more accurate prints. They are the ability to soft proof your images to simulate the appearance of a particular printing method and a gamut warning display that identifies colors within an image that can't be printed.

Soft Proofing

Soft proofing is a powerful tool in Adobe Photoshop for previewing what your images will actually look like on the printed page. It uses a profile for a specific output process to determine the limits of color gamut and tonal range for the printer, ink, and paper combination for which the profile was created. The simulation is quite accurate, enabling you to get a very good idea of what the final print will look like.

> **Note:** For inkjet output, soft proofing and gamut warning aren't what we would consider to be critical tools for accurate output, because the color gamut of most photo inkjet printers comes very close to encompassing the range of colors available in the typical working spaces used by most photographers. It is still helpful for inkjet output, but is particularly useful for CMYK printing via offset press.

Before you can preview your image, you need to configure soft proofing with settings that match the intended output process. To do so, select View > Proof Setup > Custom from the menu (see Figure 2.4). We recommend that you turn off the Preview checkbox initially, because seeing the limitations of the output process you're using can be a bit disconcerting.

Select the specific profile from the Profile dropdown or the printer, ink, and paper combination you'll be using to print the image. The information in the profile specifies the capabilities of the output process so Photoshop can determine how the final print will appear.

> **Note:** Under no circumstances should you check the Preserve Color Numbers checkbox in the Proof Setup dialog box, as this will eliminate the actual simulation effect of soft proofing.

The Intent dropdown allows you to select the rendering intent you'll use to convert the color numbers in your image to ensure accurate results with the output profile. The two options that would typically be used for photographic output are Relative Colorimetric and Perceptual.

Relative Colorimetric This option causes colors in the image that can be reproduced with the output profile to remain unchanged. Colors outside the color gamut of the output profile will be clipped to the nearest reproducible color. This leaves most of the colors very accurate, with some changes in the most highly saturated colors that are out of gamut for the output device.

Perceptual This option compresses the full range of colors in the source image into the color gamut of the output profile. This generally means the saturation of the entire image will be reduced so no colors fall out of gamut. This maintains the relationship between colors in the image, but it results in less overall saturation.

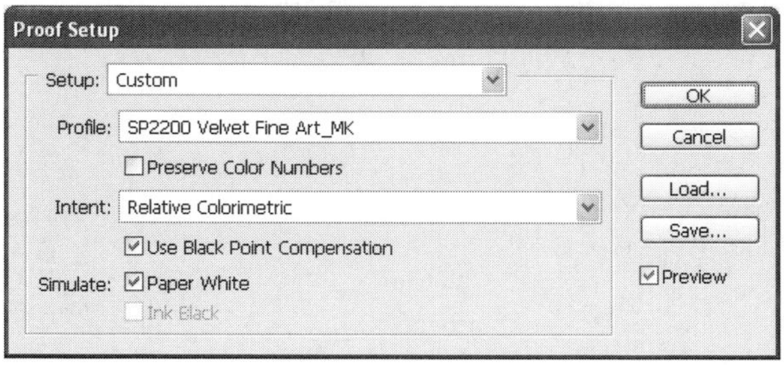

Figure 2.4 The Proof Setup dialog box allows you to configure the settings that will be used to simulate on your monitor display what the final print will look like.

The Absolute Colorimetric rendering intent behaves very similar to Relative Colorimetric, except that white in the source space is maintained in the destination space by adding ink, resulting in whites that don't appear true white when compared to the color of the paper. This causes ink to be laid down in pure white areas, so that the color of the paper the profile was built for will be simulated in the print. This rendering intent is designed to allow you to simulate the output of another printer on yours. For example, you can use your photo inkjet printer to simulate what an image will look like when reproduced on an offset press.

While there are situations where you might want to use the Absolute Colorimetric rendering intent, the Saturation rendering intent generally doesn't serve any benefit for photographic images. The Saturation rendering intent maintains the saturation of out-of-gamut colors without necessarily maintaining the actual color. Although photographers certainly like to maintain saturation in their images, they usually don't want to do so at the expense of color accuracy.

In our opinion, the Use Black Point Compensation checkbox should always be checked. This setting causes black in your image to be mapped to black in the output profile, so black will always be reproduced as accurately as possible based on the capabilities of the output process. Without checking this checkbox, the blacks in your image may not be rendered as true black in the print.

The final two checkboxes allow you to simulate Paper White and Ink Black. The Paper White option adjusts the preview display so the color of the paper is used in the place of white. This helps produce a more accurate simulation of the final output, rendering the whites at the brightness level of the paper you're using, as well as including any color cast introduced by the print medium. Whenever the Paper White checkbox is checked, the Ink Black checkbox will automatically be checked as well, unless the profile doesn't support this option. We recommend turning on both of these options when they are available for the profile you're using.

If you produce a large number of prints using the profile you've configured the Proof Setup for, and you will be using soft proofing to evaluate and optimize the images for print, it is a good idea to save the setup. To do so, click the Save button and save the setup with a name that will identify the printer and paper combination to which the settings apply. In the future, you can access the saved settings in one of three ways. You can select it from the bottom of the menu at View > Proof Setup, from the Setup dropdown in the Proof Setup dialog box, or by clicking the Load button in the Proof Setup dialog box.

Once you've configured the Proof Setup dialog box for the output process you'll be using, you're ready to click OK to apply the settings to your image.

Note: Although it seems counterintuitive, you may want to avoid looking at the preview image when you click OK. Seeing your image suddenly become duller with a possible color shift can be disconcerting. In many cases, the change in appearance is representative of a limitation of the output process you're using. When you see the image after the conversion is complete, it isn't usually too shocking.

Once you've clicked OK in the Proof Setup dialog box, the soft proofing display is automatically activated. It can be turned off (or on again) by selecting View > Proof Colors from the menu. When a checkmark appears in front of the option on the menu, the image is being displayed with soft proofing. Another indicator of the soft proofing is shown in the title bar for the image. After the color mode and bit-depth indication, the name of the saved Proof Setup settings or the profile being used for soft proofing will be shown. You can also toggle the soft proofing display by pressing Ctrl+Y (Command+Y on Macintosh) on your keyboard.

Gamut Warning

The gamut warning display is a perfect complement to the soft proofing display in Photoshop. While soft proofing allows you to get an idea of what the final output will look like, the gamut warning display shows you which colors in your image can't be reproduced at all. Before activating the gamut warning display, you'll want to configure the settings. This is done by selecting Edit > Preferences > Transparency & Gamut (Photoshop > Preferences > Transparency & Gamut on Macintosh) from the menu (see Figure 2.5).

The Color option allows you to select which color will be displayed over colors in the image that can't be reproduced with the output process you're using. We recommend using a highly saturated color that will stand out in your image, so it will be very obvious which areas of your image contain colors that can't be printed. The color you select for this should not appear elsewhere in the image. We typically use a highly saturated green or magenta, but you may need to select a different color for certain images.

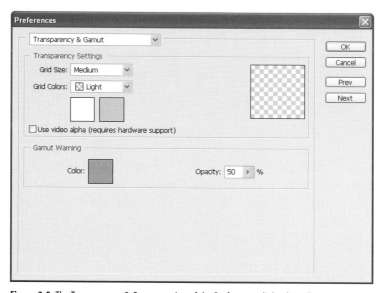

Figure 2.5 The Transparency & Gamut section of the Preferences dialog box allows you to specify how the gamut warning display will appear on your image.

The Opacity setting determines how much you'll be able to "see through" the color displayed by the gamut warning display. With a 100% Opacity setting, you won't be able to see the underlying image at all. We recommend using a slightly lower setting so you can see the texture in the image under the gamut warning display. We usually prefer to leave this setting at around 50%.

With the settings established, you can click OK in the Preferences dialog box and activate the gamut warning display by selecting View > Gamut Warning from the menu. You can also press Shift+Ctrl+Y (Shift+Command+Y on Macintosh) on the keyboard to toggle the gamut warning display on or off. As with the Proof Colors option, a checkmark in front of the Gamut Warning option on the View menu indicates this option is enabled. When it is enabled, the color selected in the Preferences for Transparency & Gamut will be overlayed on the image in the areas where the colors can't be reproduced in print based on the Proof Colors settings.

Preview Compensation

With the Proof Color and Gamut Warning options enabled, you'll have a good idea of what the image will look like when printed and which colors can't be reproduced in the print. The next step is to adjust the image to make it look as good as possible in the final print with no out-of-gamut colors remaining in the image. In other words, you'll want to adjust the image to produce the best print, compromising because of the printer limitations.

Chances are you'll want to print with the same printer, ink, and paper combination repeatedly. You'll want to save the adjustments that compensate for output limitations so you don't need to adjust the image every time you print it. We strongly recommend using adjustment layers to fine-tune the image for optimal output. To help keep the image even more organized, you can use a layer set to contain all of the adjustment layers for a specific output process.

To create a layer set, click the Add Layer Set button (with the folder icon) at the bottom of the Layers palette. This will create a new layer set you can use to hold all of the adjustments for the image. You can name the layer set to identify the output process its adjustments are for by double-clicking the name of the layer set on the Layers palette, typing a new name, and then pressing Enter on the keyboard.

With a layer set created, you can add adjustment layers into the set by first selecting the layer set and then clicking the Add Adjustment Layer button (the half-black and half-white circle) at the bottom of the Layers palette. Create adjustments for the image that produce the most desirable output with no colors that are out of gamut (see Figure 2.6). If you leave out-of-gamut colors in the image, they will be dealt with at the time of printing based on the rendering intent selected. However, by using the gamut warning display in conjunction with adjustment layers, you can exercise complete control over the process.

Figure 2.6 You can compensate for the limitations of the final printed output based on the Proof Colors and Gamut Warning displays. Place each required adjustment layer into a layer set named for the paper for which you're adjusting the image.

Once you have completed the process of adjusting the image by creating adjustment layers based on the Proof Colors and Gamut Warning displays, you can collapse the layer set to keep your Layers palette tidy and organized. To do so, click the triangle to the left of the folder. This allows you to expand or contract the layer set as needed.

Print Preparation Workflow

With an image that has been optimized and is ready to print, you're ready to follow the print preparation workflow to get the image ready to send to the printer. As we mentioned earlier in this chapter, the final image file should be preserved as the master image. The process of preparing the image for print results in changes to pixel values within the image, and we recommend that you avoid altering the master image. Therefore, the first step is to create a working copy of your image by selecting Image > Duplicate from the menu. You'll be prompted to enter a name for the working copy (see Figure 2.7), which by default will be the same as the master image file with the word "copy" appended. Once you've created a working copy of the image, you can close the original master image.

At this point we recommend flattening the image, which provides a couple of benefits. For one, it immediately reduces the image file size, which results in less memory consumption. This can help to improve overall system performance as you process the image for printing. Another benefit of flattening is that it ensures all pixels in the image will be sharpened equally when you reach that step. If you have used multiple image layers, or have used the Clone Stamp or Healing Brush tools on a separate layer, you will need to sharpen each of those layers individually with the same settings to be sure all pixels are sharpened to the same degree. By flattening the image, you can simply sharpen the image in its entirety.

Sizing and Resolution

To produce the perfect print, you'll need to size the image to fit on the paper you'll use at an appropriate resolution for optimal quality. In Photoshop, you can set the output size and resolution by selecting Image > Image Size from the menu (see Figure 2.8).

If you aren't completely familiar with resizing your images, you may find it helpful to first uncheck the Resample Image checkbox at the bottom of the Image Size dialog box. Then set the Resolution in the Document Size section of the dialog box to the value you want to use, such as 300 dpi.

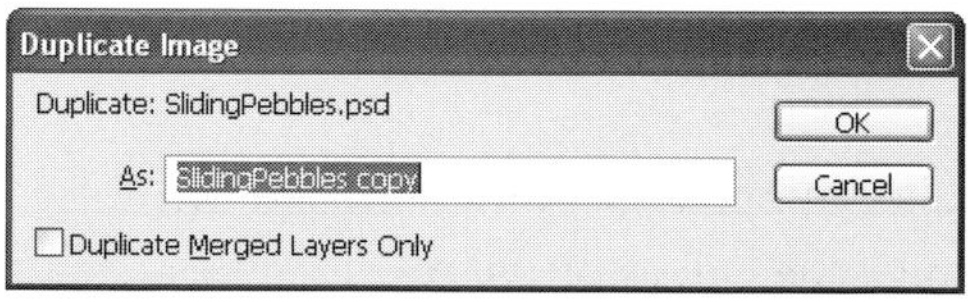

Duplicate Image

Duplicate: SlidingPebbles.psd

As: SlidingPebbles copy

☐ Duplicate Merged Layers Only

OK

Cancel

Figure 2.7 Creating a duplicate copy of your image before processing for printing helps ensure that you don't accidentally replace your master image file with a resized and flattened version.

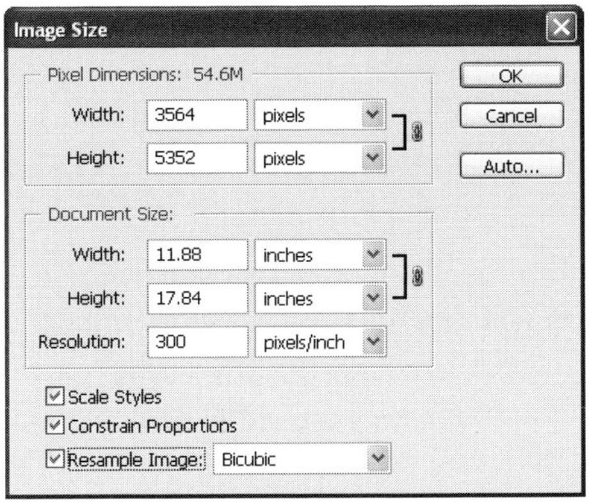

Figure 2.8 The Image Size dialog box enables you to resize your image for a specific output size.

With the Resample Image checkbox unchecked, you can't change the number of pixels in the image. Therefore, changing the output resolution requires that the output size be changed. As a result, when you set the output resolution, you will be able to see what the output size would be without any interpolation at that resolution. This gives you a better perspective on exactly how significantly you are enlarging the image if that is necessary for the desired output size. We recommend using an output resolution of 300 dpi for your images. This will ensure excellent quality for prints you produce, and it is the standard used for most printed output from offset press.

Note: You'd probably be surprised at just how much you can enlarge your images with Bicubic interpolation. Doubling the dimensions of height and width is certainly possible with high-quality images—and with your very best images, you could enlarge them even more.

With the Resolution set, you can recheck the Resample Image checkbox so you can actually adjust the final output size. Be sure the Constrain Proportions checkbox is checked, and enter a new value for Width or Height in the Document Size section, as desired. Be sure both dimensions fit within the constraints of the printable area for the paper size you'll be printing to.

Note: If you need to size the image to a specific aspect ratio, you can use the Crop tool with Height, Width, and Resolution values entered on the Options bar. The crop will then be constrained to those proportions. When you apply the crop, the image will be interpolated to the size entered.

Most likely, you'll be changing the number of pixels within the image, which means interpolation will be required to determine the values of the pixels to be added to the image, or to determine which pixels will be removed if you are reducing the size. You can specify what type of interpolation will be used to make these calculations using the dropdown to the right of the Resample Image checkbox (see Figure 2.9). The default value is determined by the Image Interpolation option selected in the General Preferences. Nearest Neighbor and Bilinear are not appropriate for photographic images, as they aren't sophisticated enough to produce high-quality results. Bicubic produces excellent results, and it is the best overall option. However, Photoshop CS has added two new interpolation algorithms you may want to consider. Bicubic Smoother helps to ensure smooth curves without any "jaggies" when you are enlarging an image. Our experience has been that this option produces better results than the standard Bicubic option with most images. Bicubic Sharper helps to retain image sharpness when reducing the size of an image. We feel it adds excessive sharpness to the image, so we prefer to use the standard Bicubic option instead, perhaps with an additional pass of Unsharp Mask after doing so if necessary.

With the options set in the Image Size dialog box, you can click OK and the image will be resized based on your settings.

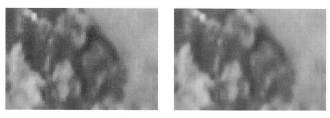

Nearest Neighbor   Bilinear

Bicubic   Bicubic Smoother   Bicubic Sharper

Figure 2.9 The different algorithms used by each interpolation method in Photoshop result in slightly different results, with the Bicubic options producing the best quality. You can see the different effects with these extreme close-ups of a portion of an image that has been enlarged using the various interpolation methods.

Sharpening for Print

Sharpening the image is saved for last, primarily because the sharpening settings used are specific to the size of the image. The size affects the sharpening settings needed to achieve the best results, and resizing the image can alter the sharpening applied to the image, either by minimizing the effect or exaggerating the edge halo effect resulting from the sharpening process.

As far as we're concerned, there's only one way to sharpen an image and that's to use the Unsharp Mask filter. The other sharpening filters don't offer the control you need. Once you understand how to use Unsharp Mask properly, the third-party plug-ins for sharpening don't offer a significant benefit.

Note: Sharpening doesn't allow you to take an out of focus image and make it look like it was captured with sharp focus. Instead, it creates the illusion of higher sharpness by enhancing edge contrast.

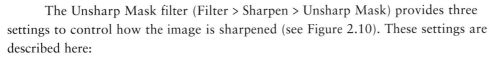

The Unsharp Mask filter (Filter > Sharpen > Unsharp Mask) provides three settings to control how the image is sharpened (see Figure 2.10). These settings are described here:

- **Amount** controls the intensity of the contrast added to edges within the image. This setting will vary inversely with the Radius setting. With high-detail images, you'll tend to use a high Amount setting (150% to 200%), while low detail images call for a lower setting (75% to 125%).

- **Radius** determines the width in pixels of the halos that will be added to edges within the image to enhance contrast. This is the most important setting within the Unsharp Mask dialog box. High-detail images are best sharpened with a low Radius setting (0.5 to 1.0), while low-detail images will benefit from a higher setting (1.0 to 2.0).

- **Threshold** helps to avoid sharpening areas of smooth texture. It functions by determining how much difference must exist between pixels before they are considered an edge. A setting of 0 effectively means that all pixels are considered edge pixels, so the entire image is sharpened. With high-detail images, this is often preferred, with settings between 0 and 4. For images with smooth textures you don't want to sharpen, a slightly higher Threshold setting (8 to 12) can be used. A common example of an image you would use a higher Threshold setting on would be a portrait, where you want to enhance the high contrast areas but don't want to exaggerate detail in the smooth skin tones.

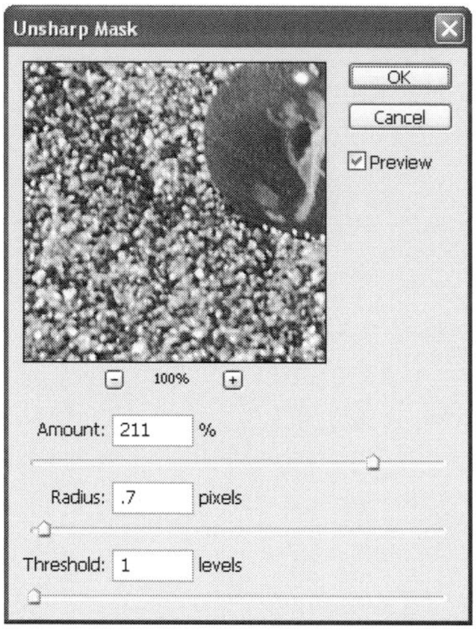

Figure 2.10 The Unsharp Mask filter provides the control needed to sharpen your images while avoiding artifacts or excessive halos at contrast edges. Sharpening is an important step to compensate for the loss of sharpness in the original digital capture or film scan, as well as the final print.

With the image properly sharpened, you're ready to actually send it to the printer with settings that will ensure accurate color and optimal quality.

Printing

An optimized master image file ensures that the pixel values in your image represent your vision of what the image should look like, and it provides an avenue for you to modify that image in the future. As important as that master image file is, for many photographers the real goal is a perfect print. Even when other output methods are used, photographers tend to think of an image in terms of the final print—that is the perceived final result, whether or not it's actually the final product.

3

Chapter Contents

Producing a print you're happy with and that faithfully reproduces the tone and color of the master image file requires careful attention to the settings used in the printing process.

Previewing Your Print Job

In Chapter 2, "Preparing the Image," we discussed the process of preparing the master image for printing and covered the steps necessary to create a print-ready file from your master image. Now, you're ready to print. Unfortunately, doing so isn't a simple matter of selecting File > Print from the menu and sitting back to wait for the print.

To start with, we need to select the correct print command so we can provide more details about how the image is to be printed. In Adobe Photoshop CS, that means selecting File > Print With Preview from the menu (in Photoshop Elements, start with File > Print Preview). The dialog box that appears is identical in both Photoshop versions, and it includes options for configuring the page layout and color management settings (see Figure 3.1). Other photo-editing software offers similar output options, allowing you to specify a printer profile. If you are using software that doesn't offer those options, you'll need to use the printer properties to control all aspects of the final output.

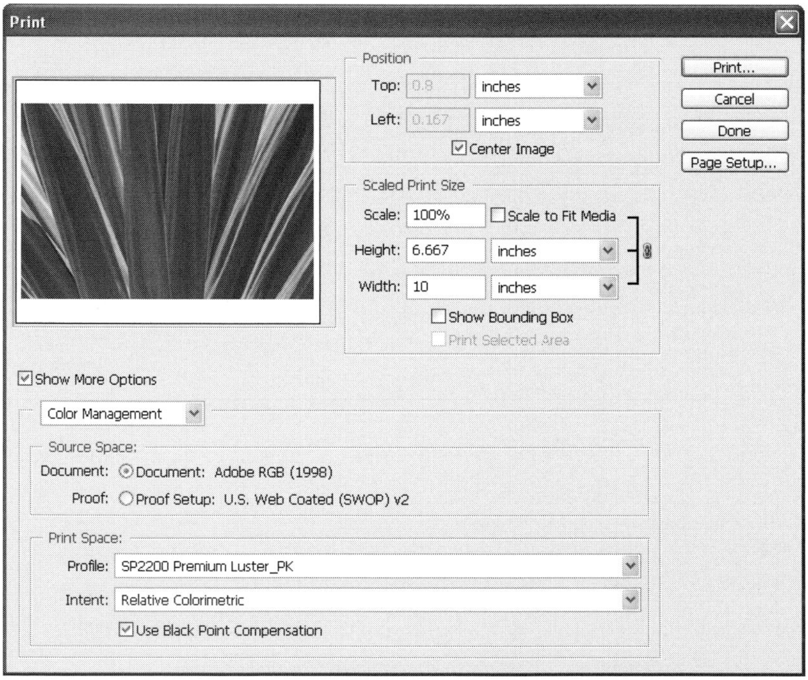

Figure 3.1 The Print With Preview dialog box in Photoshop allows you to establish the key settings for accurate output in a color-managed workflow.

Preview

The preview display in the Print With Preview dialog box shows you what the image will look like on the page. Don't focus on tone and color in the preview, because it is only intended to show you page layout and orientation. If the image doesn't fit the page properly in this initial preview, that doesn't mean that you won't be able to make the image fit; it just means that you need to configure the page layout settings. When working in Windows, we typically set those options in the Printer Properties rather than in the Print With Preview dialog box, so the preview display might not reflect the correct paper size and orientation settings you'll be setting later. (See "Setting Printer Properties" later in this chapter.)

Note: Setting the page layout options in Printer Properties gives Windows users the convenience of effectively setting all print parameters in the same place. Macintosh OS X users need to set those options in the Print With Preview dialog box, as discussed later in this chapter.

Position

The Position section of the dialog box allows you to specify exactly where on the page you'd like the image to print. The default is for the Center Image checkbox to be checked, so the image will be centered on the page. In most cases, we recommend leaving this option selected. However, there are certainly situations where you want to change the position of the image. For example, if you want to produce a folded greeting card with an image printed on the front cover, you could uncheck the Center Image checkbox and adjust the position to the top (or bottom) of the page (see Figure 3.2) as needed for your layout. Changing the position of the image is a simple matter of clicking and dragging the image on the Preview display, as long as the Show Bounding Box checkbox in the Scaled Print Size section is checked, as shown in the figure. You can also enter new values for the Top and Left position of the image to change the position. The default unit of measure is Inches, but you can change this to several other settings and then enter a value in the box to define where you want the image to appear on the paper.

Note: Selecting the Center Image option in the Print With Preview dialog box doesn't necessarily guarantee the image will appear in the *precise* center of the page. Often, you'll need to select an option in the printer properties to ensure a truly centered print.

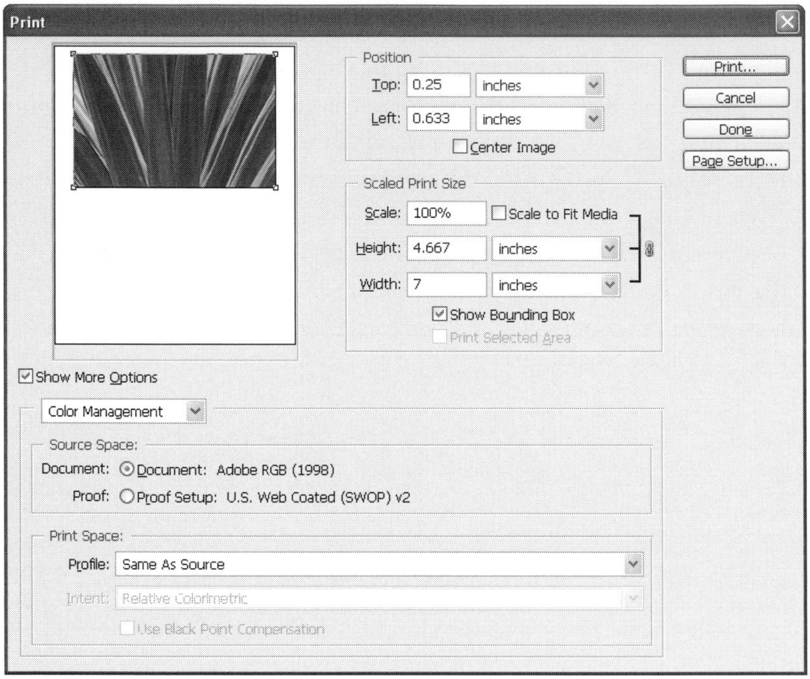

Figure 3.2 Normally, images are centered on the page and make full use of the printer paper. However, if you want to create a greeting card or other output that requires the image to be printed in a position other than the center of the page, you can adjust the position of the image in the Print With Preview dialog box.

Scaled Print Size

The Scaled Print Size section of the Print With Preview dialog box allows you to change the size of the image at the time of printing. We strongly recommend against using these options. Instead, if you want to change the size of the image, do so using Photoshop's Image Size dialog box, as discussed in Chapter 2, before you start the printing process. Image Size provides options to ensure better image quality in the resizing. It also allows you to sharpen the image after you have resized. Resizing after sharpening defeats much of the sharpening effect, and it risks over-emphasizing the halos that are created to improve perceived sharpness.

To print based on the specified image size, be sure the Scale option is set to 100%. If you check the Scale To Fit Media checkbox, the image will be resized based on the current media size. The Show Bounding Box option puts a sizing box around your image, so you can move it or drag the corners to resize.

If a selection is active when you select Print With Preview from the File menu, the Print Selected Area checkbox will be available. Checking this box will cause only the selected area of the image to be printed.

Show More Options

When you check the Show More Options checkbox, the Print With Preview dialog box will be expanded to reveal additional settings. Below this checkbox is a dropdown menu that allows you to choose whether you want to adjust the Output or Color Management settings. You can switch back and forth to adjust settings in each section, and all settings in both sections will apply to the final print.

The Output settings provide options to change the way the image is printed. For example, you can add a border around the print and select various print marks (such as Registration Marks, Corner Crop Marks, and other settings) to be included. Most of these options are geared toward making printing proofs for future offset press output, and they aren't typically desirable for producing fine-art prints—although the border and background options may be useful for certain output such as cards and promo sheets. However, the Color Management settings are critical for producing accurate output.

Color Management Settings

With the Color Management option selected from the dropdown, you'll have options to select the Source Space and Print Space settings to ensure accurate tone and color in the final print.

The Source Space section defines which color setup will be used to define the colors within the image itself. You'll want to select the Document setting, which will cause the colors in the image to be interpreted based on the profile embedded in the image (which is presumably the same as your RGB working space). Even if you're using soft proofing to fine-tune the appearance of the image for the output process you're using, you don't want to select the Proof option. This option would be used to simulate the output of a different printer using your printer. For example, if you are going to have some images printed in a catalog with an offset press, and you have a profile for that printing process, you can simulate what that final output will look like by utilizing the Proof option in the Source Space section.

The Print Space section allows you to specify the profile to be used to convert the color values in your image to those that will produce the intended colors in the print. Three basic options are available, and the choice is determined in part by whether you have a profile available for the specific printer and paper combination you're using, as well as the settings recommended for your particular printer. The available options are as follows:

- **A Custom Profile** for the printer and paper combination you are using is the best possible solution. It will typically ensure the most accurate colors in the final print, assuming the profile is accurate to begin with. Using a custom profile requires that you set the printer properties so no additional conversion will be applied, because the conversion is happening before the color information is being sent to the printer. You can build your own custom profiles with tools from Gretag-Macbeth (www.i1color.com), Monaco Systems (www.monacosys.com), and others. You can also purchase custom profiles from service providers such as Chromix (www.chromix.com/profilecity/).

 Note: For more details on custom profiles and other topics related to color management, see Tim Grey's book *Color Confidence: The Digital Photographer's Guide to Color Management* (Sybex, 2004).

- **A Generic Profile** for your printer can be selected if you don't have profiles available for the specific paper being used. Using this option requires that you specify settings in the printer properties that will cause the driver to compensate for the color values in the image automatically. This option functions in much the same way as the Same As Source option.

- **Same As Source** or **Printer Color Management** will cause the color values within the image to remain unchanged when sent to the printer driver. This will then require the printer to do the necessary conversion to ensure accurate color. This option should only be used if it is recommended for your printer and you don't have a profile available.

The Intent option allows you to select the rendering intent that will be used to deal with colors in your image that the printer can't actually reproduce on the paper type you are using. There are four options, but only two of them are appropriate for printing photographic images: Relative Colorimetric and Perceptual. These rendering intents perform as follows:

- **Relative Colorimetric** accurately reproduces colors that are within the color gamut of the printer. Out-of-gamut colors are shifted to the closest matching color that can be reproduced. This ensures that most colors will be printed exactly and that out-of-gamut colors will be rendered as accurately as possible. This is the most appropriate option for most photographic prints, particularly if there are very few colors outside the printer's color gamut.

- **Perceptual** compresses the range of colors in the image so all of them will fit within the color gamut of the printer. The advantage is that it maintains the relationships between colors in the image. However, it also results in an image with less overall saturation. It is a good choice for images with a large number of out-of-gamut colors. However, in most cases it would be better to deal with that issue in Photoshop using soft proofing and gamut warning, as discussed in Chapter 2, and printing with the Relative Colorimetric rendering intent.

Page Setup

The Page Setup button brings up an additional dialog box that allows you to set options for paper size, orientation, and feed source on the printer (see Figure 3.3). These options are convenient when you are configuring print settings in the Print With Preview dialog box. The settings you establish here will be reflected in the Printer Properties dialog box where you set your final print settings. Because you'll need to review the settings there, we suggest that you simply wait to establish your page setup settings in the Printer Properties dialog box.

The page setup options for Macintosh OS X users differ somewhat from the Windows options. In addition to setting standard page attributes including the default paper sizes, Page Setup also allows you to set the scale to print your image and create custom page sizes (see Figure 3.4). The most important difference, however, is that the Macintosh version of Photoshop does not include a Printer Properties dialog box; paper size and orientation need to be set in Page Setup first. See "Setting Printer Properties on a Macintosh" later in this chapter.

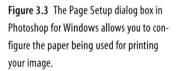

Figure 3.3 The Page Setup dialog box in Photoshop for Windows allows you to configure the paper being used for printing your image.

Print

When you have established all of the appropriate settings in the Print With Preview dialog box, you can click the Print button to proceed. This will bring up the Print dialog box, where you can select the printer you'll be using from the dropdown list (see Figure 3.5) and set the number of copies you want to make. With a Windows-based computer, select the correct printer, and click the Properties button to bring up the Printer Properties dialog box to set the final output settings. Macintosh OS X users access these settings by selecting the Settings dropdown list in the Print dialog box. In addition to the Layout options illustrated in Figure 3.6, Macintosh settings include job scheduling to allow you to print at a specific time and layout options that allow you to print multiple documents on a single page.

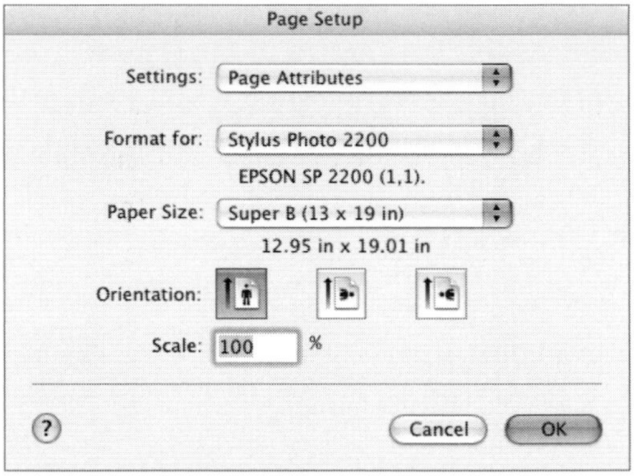

Figure 3.4 The Page Setup dialog for Macintosh OS X includes similar features and allows you to set custom page sizes and image orientation.

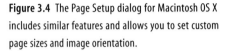

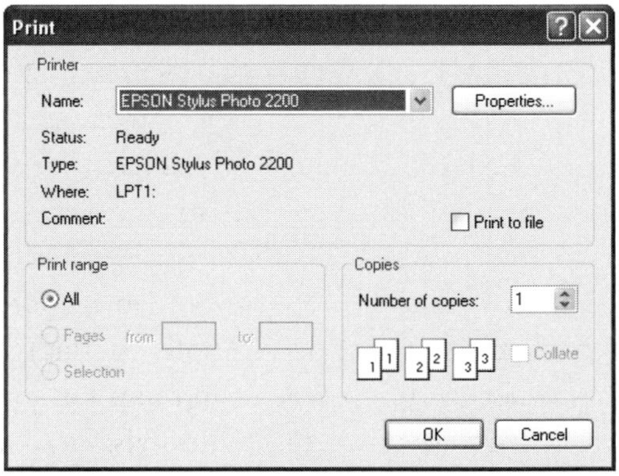

Figure 3.5 The Print dialog box allows you to select the printer to which you'll be printing. On a Windows-based PC, you can also access the printer properties.

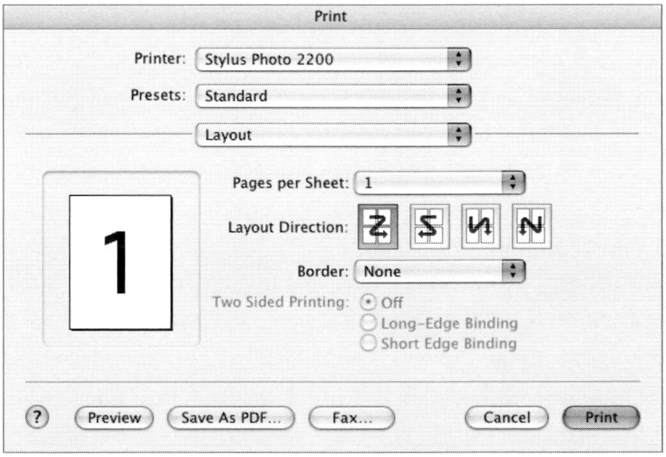

Figure 3.6 On Macintosh OS X, the Print dialog box offers access to additional features, including page layout options, job scheduling, and paper handling.

Setting Printer Properties

The Printer Properties dialog box allows you to establish settings specific to your model of printer (see Figure 3.7). The specific settings will vary from printer to printer, but the basic requirements are the same. The basic settings you'll need to establish are as follows:

- **The Paper Source** dropdown defines which paper feed slot in the printer will be used. This obviously doesn't affect the appearance of the print, but it is important to select the correct source so the printer will know where to feed the paper from. Most often you'll use the Sheet source, but if your printer includes support for roll paper or a manual feed slot, those options may apply.

- **Paper Type** lets the printer know what type of paper you are printing to, and it is arguably the most critical setting in the Printer Properties dialog box for producing accurate color. The absorption properties of the paper being used have a significant effect on the final color appearance, and using the correct setting is critical.

- **Print Quality** is used to determine how closely the ink droplets are laid down on paper, which affects final image quality. In this context, print quality is generally referred to as the number of dots of ink per inch (dpi) being put to paper. This setting is the result of much confusion among photographers in terms of which printer is best, how this number relates to actual image resolution, and what setting should be used. We recommend using the setting that corresponds to output resolution of around 1,440 dpi (which is often referred to as a "Photo" setting). Lower settings may result in banding or other quality problems in the print. Higher settings will result in slower prints that use more ink, but no visible improvement in print quality.

- **Paper Size** specifies what size paper you're printing on. This setting will obviously be determined by the size paper you feed into the printer, which in turn determines the size you set your image to before sending it to the printer. The correct setting is important to ensure the image is printed properly on the page.

- **Orientation** allows you to select between Portrait and Landscape orientation. This can be a confusing setting at times, particularly when using roll paper in a printer when you are printing a landscape image across the full width. Think of this setting as determining whether the image needs to be rotated by 90 degrees to fit properly on the paper. Cut-sheet paper is typically fed into the printer in a vertical (portrait) orientation. Therefore, when printing a vertical image, the Portrait orientation option should be selected, and when printing a horizontal image, the Landscape option should be used.

- **Color Management Settings** allow you to determine how the printer processes color information. If you are using a custom profile for the printer and paper combination you're using, you'll want to select the option that causes no processing of the color information being sent to the printer. This option is often called "No Color Adjustment" or something similar. If you are using a generic printer profile or the Same As Source option in the Print with Preview dialog box, you'll want to use the options provided in the Printer Properties dialog box that allow the printer to optimize the image data for the printer. This option is often called "Color Controls" or something similar, and it includes options for optimizing the image based on the capabilities of the printer. For example, you may decide to adjust the color balance, brightness, or contrast for the print to provide a better match with the monitor display.

- **Print Preview** is an option that will present a preview of the page layout settings before committing to putting ink on paper. Using this setting will help avoid wasting paper and ink.

Once you click OK in the Printer Properties dialog box, it will close and you'll again see the Print dialog box. Click OK, and the print process will begin. If you selected the Print Preview option in the Printer Properties dialog box, the preview will be displayed. In most cases, you'll want to ignore tone and color in this preview, because it will likely not take into account the custom profile if you are using one. Instead, confirm the page layout, image size, and orientation to confirm the image will fit properly on the page before clicking the Print button to actually send the image data to the printer.

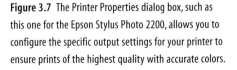

Figure 3.7 The Printer Properties dialog box, such as this one for the Epson Stylus Photo 2200, allows you to configure the specific output settings for your printer to ensure prints of the highest quality with accurate colors.

Setting Printer Properties on the Macintosh

The process for Macintosh OS X users is similar, as are the final settings, although the dialog boxes are very different. After setting the Page Setup, including paper size and orientation, in the Print With Preview dialog box, select Print to access the options shown in Figure 3.8.

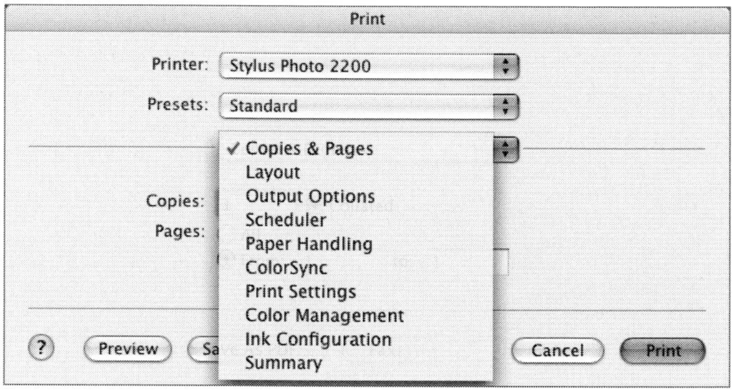

Figure 3.8 Choosing which printer options to configure in Macintosh OS X

- **Copies & Pages** allows you to select the printer and choose how many copies of a photo you want to print. The other options on this setting typically don't apply to images and can be safely ignored.

- **Layout** allows you to specify how many pages will fit on a single sheet of paper. It has options for 1, 2, 4, 6, 9, and 16 pages per sheet. Direction settings specify how the pages will be laid out on the sheet, and Border has options for single, double, or no lines around the pages. These settings can be useful, particularly when printing on roll paper with wider format printers.

- **Output Options** allows you to specify whether to save the page to a file or send it to the printer. This adds the ability to save to a Postscript file in addition to the PDF file available at the bottom of the dialog box at all times.

- **Scheduler** allows you to specify whether to print immediately or save the print job for a specific time. This is useful if you have a number of images to print and want to delay the printing until you're done with other tasks.

- **Paper Handling** options allow you to select which pages to print. It is similar to Copies & Pages, but rather than selecting a range of pages, such as page 3 to 5, you can select all, even, or odd pages. This can be useful when printing double-sided. It allows you to print, for example, the inside of a card and then run the job again for the outside of the card.

- **ColorSync** allows you to specify whether to use the built-in color management system on the Macintosh, or, if the printer supports it, the printer's color management system. Quartz Filter options allow you to specify color conversion options such as Sepia, Black & White, and Blue or Gray tones. Unless you have a specific need, we suggest doing your color conversion work within Photoshop where you have control over the amount of effect applied.

- **Print Settings** is where you'll select your paper type, which as mentioned earlier is the most important setting to have correct in order to obtain an accurate print (see Figure 3.9).

- **Color Management** allows you to select whether to use the printer color controls, ColorSync, or No Color Adjustment. As with the Windows configuration, if you're using custom profiles or printer supplied profiles for a specific paper, you'll want to set this to No Color Adjustment.

- **Ink Configuration** allows you to select color density and drying time per page on high-end Epson printers.

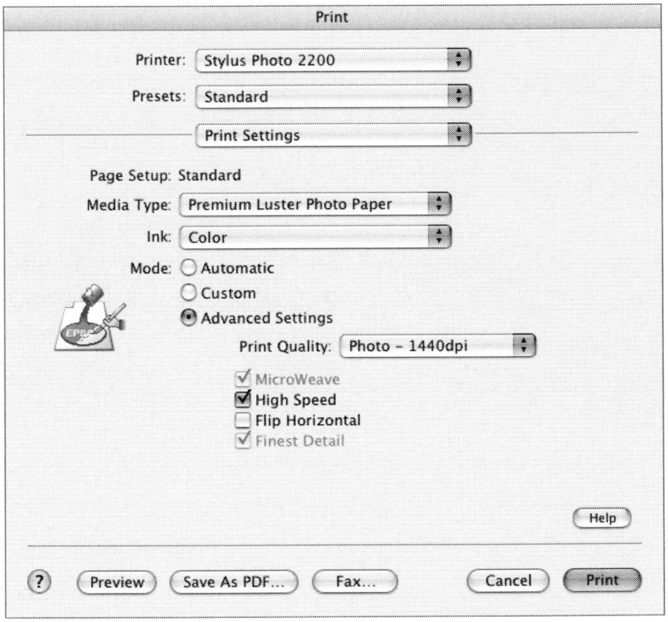

Figure 3.9 The Print Settings dialog box in Photoshop CS for the Macintosh

Choosing and Using a RIP

Earlier in this chapter, we emphasized the importance of printer profiles as a tool for color management. If you are producing a particularly large volume of prints and accurate color is critical to your work, but you don't have access to a good custom profile for your combination of printer, inks, and paper, you may want to consider purchasing a RIP to help process your images. RIP stands for Rasterized Image Processor. The name may be a little misleading for photographic output. Unlike the vector-based font information in text destined for printing, a photograph is already raster data. But rasterizing is only part of the processing that a RIP does, converting (pixel-based) image data and processing it into a form the printer can understand. A RIP talks directly to the printer.

Traditionally, a RIP was a piece of hardware (effectively a small and specialized computer) that would manage print jobs for you, helping to automate the process and ensure more accurate and consistent prints. They were often quite expensive and specialized, making them a less than ideal solution for most photographers. However, software RIPs are now available, and they offer much of the functionality of a hardware RIP at a fraction of the price.

Choosing a Software RIP

One of the major advantages of a software RIP is that it typically includes profiles (or a way to create them) for specific printer, ink, and paper combinations that are very accurate. In fact, the appeal for many photographers is that a RIP provides profiles that are much more accurate than those provided by the printer manufacturer. If you use a variety of different papers, the cost of a software RIP might be less than you would spend for the hardware required to build your own printer profiles and possibly even less than you would pay a service to build profiles for you.

Note: Although the profiles included with a software RIP are typically much more accurate than those included with your printer, a profile for every possible paper your printer can utilize won't be included. If you print on a wide variety of third-party papers, you may still need tools for creating your own printer profiles, or you may need to purchase them from a third-party service.

Other advantages of a RIP include the print job management features. As with printing images directly, each job goes into a queue. However, with a RIP you have much more control over the process. You can change the order of jobs in the queue, cancel or suspend print jobs, and view the status of all pending jobs. This can be a significant advantage for the photographer printing a large number of images.

Note: Macintosh users will note that some of this functionality is built into the OS X print engine, allowing you to set print times and priorities. Although the ability to change the order of jobs is not supported, you can work around this somewhat by setting the priority of a print job in Photoshop; the options are Low, Medium, High, and Urgent.

If you feel the advantages of a RIP will benefit your print processing, consider the features of various software RIPs, including:

- **Printer support** is a key consideration when choosing a RIP. If a RIP doesn't support the printer you will be using, it isn't of any use to you.

- **A broad range of profiles** for many different types of paper will help ensure you're able to print to the papers you prefer to use, rather than choosing papers based on what your RIP supports. One of the major side benefits of these profiles is the ability to produce perfectly neutral grayscale prints with many printers.

- **Flexible job management** features will help you control the output, prioritize particular print jobs, suspend a job when necessary, and perform other tasks to manage the jobs as they are printed.

- **Page layout control** can help you save money on paper by automatically placing multiple images onto a single sheet or optimizing the use of roll papers. This can be much more efficient than trying to create your own print layouts in Photoshop.

Note: As with scheduling, there is built-in support for page layout in Photoshop on the Macintosh, but you are much more limited in your options compared to using a RIP.

- **Price** is always a consideration with any purchase, and software RIPs aren't exactly cheap.

Note: Make sure the software RIP you're considering supports the specific printer model you plan to use it with.

As you're considering which software RIP is best for you, consider the following as good options to choose from:

- **ImagePrint** from ColorByte Software (www.colorbytesoftware.com, Windows and Macintosh) supports primarily Epson printers, with prices starting at under $500.

- **StudioPrint** from ErgoSoft (www.ergosoftus.com, Windows only) offers broad support for printers from many major manufacturers including Canon, Epson, and Hewlett-Packard, with prices starting at about $1,300.

- **EFI Photo Edition** from EFI Proofing Solutions (www.bestcolor.com, Macintosh only) is offered in various versions supporting printers from Canon, Epson, Hewlett-Packard and others, with prices starting at around $750.

Using a Software RIP

Once you've selected a software RIP, you'll want to become familiar with the specific features it offers to help optimize your printing workflow. To help you get a better idea of the printing workflow process when using a RIP, we'll use the ImagePrint RIP from ColorByte Software to present a typical workflow (see Figure 3.10).

Before you even start using the RIP to print your images, you'll need to optimize your images so they are actually ready for printing. Optimization is part of the normal workflow with your images, and it will typically result in a "master" image file you'll use for all printed output. Chapter 2 shows how to do this in Photoshop.

Figure 3.10 ImagePrint from ColorByte Software is a software RIP that allows you to manage the process of printing your images with great flexibility and high accuracy.

Using the RIP software, open the master image file you want to print. Then select the color management settings (see Figure 3.11) to specify which printer you'll be using, along with the specific profile for the type of paper you're using. Some RIPs even include various profiles for prints that will be displayed under particular lighting or printed at specific output quality settings. This is what allows you to produce output with highly accurate color by utilizing the profiles bundled with the RIP software.

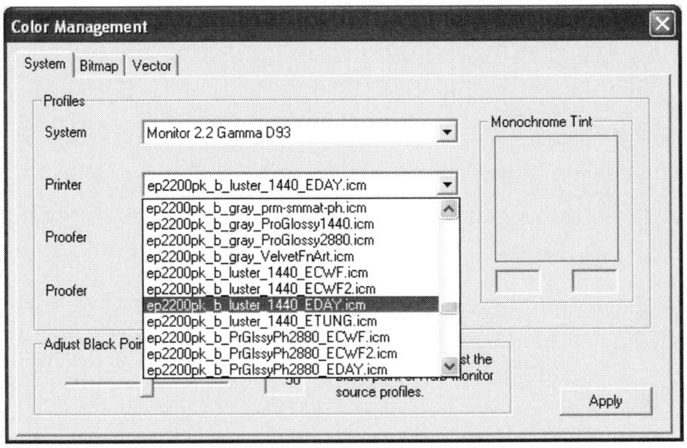

Figure 3.11 The Color Management dialog box in ImagePrint allows you to select from a wide range of available printer profiles, ensuring the most accurate colors possible in the final print.

With the settings established, you can send the image to the print queue, where it will be placed at the end of the list of images to be printed (see Figure 3.12). You can then manage all print jobs in the queue, suspend or cancel jobs, change the print order based on current priorities, and view the status of all pending print jobs. This aspect of a software RIP can be of significant benefit to professional photographers printing a large number of images on a regular basis with varying degrees of urgency for the prints.

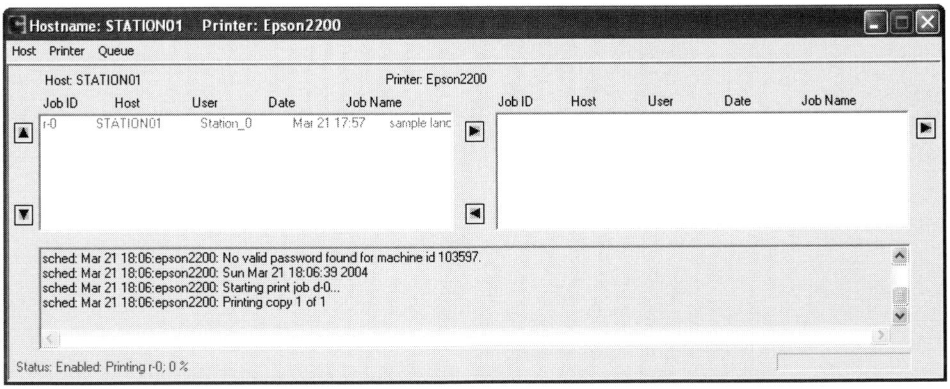

Figure 3.12 After you send an image to the print queue, you can manage the images waiting to be printed, change the print order, and cancel print jobs.

Specialty Printing

Making "traditional" prints of a single image on a single sheet of paper is the primary goal of most photographers working in a digital darkroom. However, there are many other ways to put ink on paper. This flexibility allows you to create a variety of printing products. You can create proof (or contact) sheets with many images on a page, creative album pages, and prints with artistic border treatments that complement the subject of the photo.

4

Chapter Contents
Creating Proof Sheets
Designing Albums
Creative Border Treatments

Creating Proof Sheets

A framed and matted print is certainly a beautiful way to share your images, but sometimes you need to share a large number of images with a client (or a potential client) where the beauty of the presentation is less important than the ability to view many images quickly and easily. Whether you're sharing photos of a recent vacation, presenting proofs to a client, or creating a portfolio of images, a proof sheet provides a quick and easy way to present a collection of images (see Figure 4.1).

cayucos beach rocks.psd   IMG_4447.JPG   IMG_4448.JPG

IMG_4449.JPG   IMG_4450.JPG   IMG_4451.JPG

IMG_4452.JPG   IMG_4453.JPG   IMG_4454.JPG

IMG_4455.JPG   IMG_4456.JPG   IMG_4457.JPG

Figure 4.1 Proof sheets provide an effective way to share a series of images with others.

Creating a Contact Sheet in Photoshop

Photoshop CS and Photoshop Elements include a built-in feature called Contact Sheet II (or simply Contact Sheet in Elements) that allows you to quickly generate contact sheets from a selection of images. You can control how many rows and columns of images will be printed on paper of a size you specify, allowing you to exercise reasonable control over the final result.

To create a proof sheet with the Contact Sheet feature, select File > Automate > Contact Sheet II from the menu (File > Print Layouts > Contact Sheet in Photoshop Elements). This will bring up the Contact Sheet II dialog box (see Figure 4.2).

In the Contact Sheet II dialog box, you can configure the settings desired for your proof sheets with the following steps:

1. Select the source location for images from the Use dropdown list. (Click the Browse button in the Source Directory section if you're using Elements.)

   The Current Open Documents option will use all of the images currently open in Photoshop as the basis for the contact sheet. The Folder option allows you to select a folder, with all of the images in that folder used to create the contact sheet. Finally, the Selected Images From File Browser option will create a contact sheet that includes the images currently selected in the Photoshop File Browser.

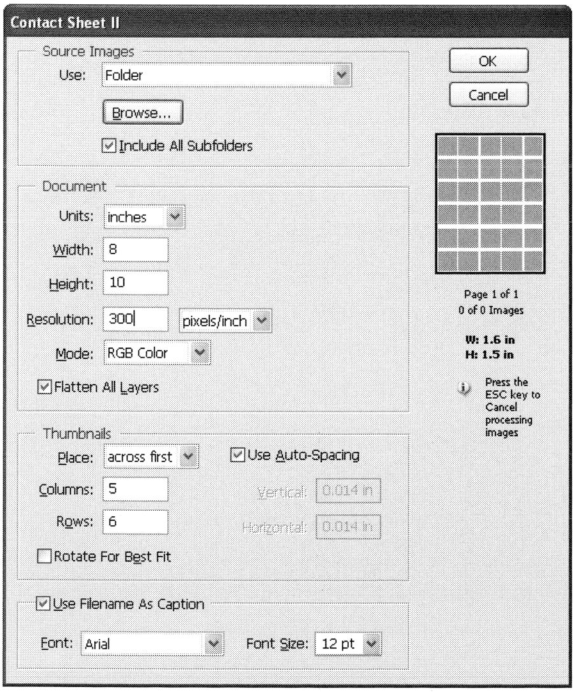

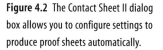

Figure 4.2 The Contact Sheet II dialog box allows you to configure settings to produce proof sheets automatically.

2. If you've selected the Folder option as the source of images in Photoshop, click the Browse button and select the folder containing the images you'd like to use to create a contact sheet. You can also check the Include All Subfolders checkbox so images in any folders within the selected folder will be included.

Note: Create a separate folder for your contact sheet, and then copy the images you want to print into that folder. This will allow you to organize the images before you create your proof sheets.

3. In the Document section of the dialog box, select the unit of measure for the page from the Units dropdown list, and enter the desired Width, Height, and Resolution for the contact sheet. You can also select a color mode to use for the documents, but the mode should be left at RGB if you're making your own prints on a desktop printer.

Note: We recommend making the document dimensions slightly smaller than the paper you'll be printing to, just to ensure that the final contact sheet will fit on the page without any clipping because of printer limitations.

4. By default, the Flatten All Layers checkbox is checked, so that the final result will be a flattened document without individual layers. This is typically the best option, because you only need to print the final result. However, in some situations you may want to uncheck this checkbox so you can fine-tune the position of the individual images after the contact sheet is created.

5. The Thumbnails section allows you to define the arrangement of the images on the page. The Place dropdown list provides the option to specify whether images should be placed going across in rows or down in columns in order by filename. You can determine how many images will appear on a page by setting values for Columns and Rows.

Note: The Columns and Rows settings determine how many images are placed on a page, which in turn affects how large the images are. The images need to be large enough to see clearly, so we recommend keeping these settings relatively low. For a typical 8.5"×11" sheet, using a value of **3** for Columns and **4** for Rows will result in 12 images on the page that are large enough to see clearly. However, you might want smaller thumbnails for a contact sheet with an accompanying CD. For example, you could have up to 16 or even 20 thumbnails on the 4.75"×4.75" page. These thumbnails, despite their small size and lack of detail, will allow you to quickly recognize which pictures are on a CD.

6. You can use the Rotate For Best Fit checkbox (Photoshop CS only) to help make the best use of the paper. This will cause vertical images, for example, to be rotated to horizontal if that fits best within the layout defined by the Columns and Rows settings.

> **Note:** Keep in mind that if you set the images to rotate automatically for the best fit, vertical images may be rotated to horizontal, causing them to be more difficult to view without rotating the page for certain images.

7. We recommend using the Use Auto-Spacing option (Photoshop CS only) to automatically determine how much space is left between images on the page. If you prefer to control this setting, uncheck the checkbox to enable Vertical and Horizontal fields for spacing between images.

8. Normally, you'll need some way to identify the specific images on the contact sheets created, and the Use Filename As Caption checkbox allows you to do just that. When the box is checked, you will have options for the Font Face and Font Size to be used for these captions.

As you're adjusting the settings for the Contact Sheet, the preview display in the top-right corner of the dialog box will show you what the layout looks like so you have a general idea of how it will fit on the page. Once you're satisfied with the settings, click OK. Photoshop will generate the contact sheets. If there are too many images for a single page, multiple documents will be created to contain all of the images.

The fact that multiple pages are created as individual documents in Photoshop makes it a bit inefficient to print contact sheets with a large number of images. After the pages have been created, you still need to print them. With many images, the collection of documents can consume a considerable amount of memory. We, therefore, recommend limiting the number of images used to create these contact sheets so only a few pages will be created at a time.

Photoshop Picture Package

For those who want a bit more control over the layout of their proof sheets, including the ability to place images of varying sizes on a single sheet, Photoshop offers an additional option, the Picture Package automation tool. It includes reasonable flexibility and has been updated in Photoshop CS with the ability to edit layouts to customize the size and number of pictures included in the final package.

The primary intent of the Picture Package tool is to place the same image multiple times on the page, possibly with varying sizes, much as you would see from the prints offered as photo packages from many portrait studios. However, you can also create layouts that include different images at various sizes. (For example, you might choose to have two 4×5s of one image and four 2.5×3.5s of a different image, like the package illustrated in Figure 4.3.)

The Picture Package feature is started by selecting File > Automate > Picture Package from the menu (see Figure 4.4).

Figure 4.3 The Picture Package provides a way to share multiple images on a single page.

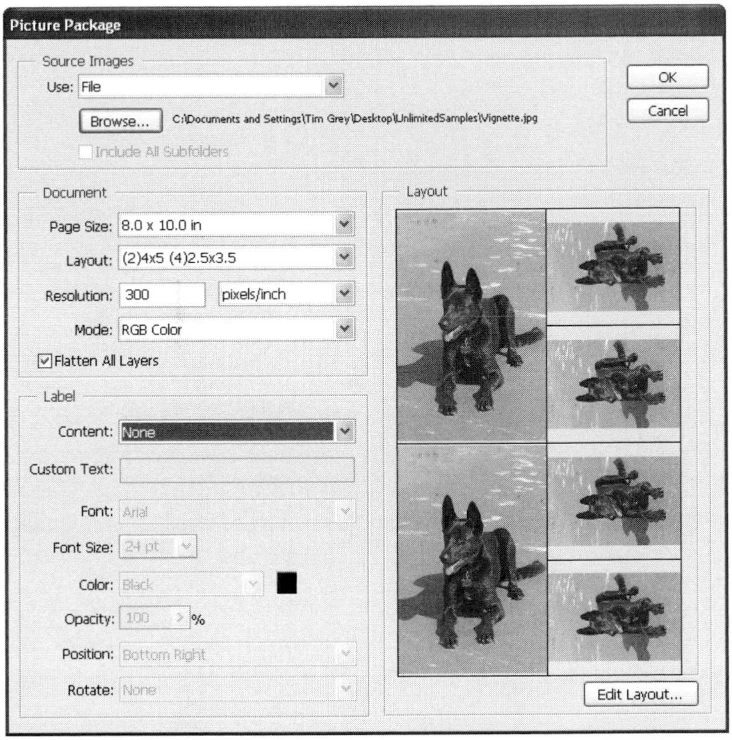

Figure 4.4 The wide range of options in the Picture Package dialog box allows you to create customized packages including one or more images at various sizes.

Use the following steps to configure the available options:

1. From the Use dropdown list in the Source Images section, select the file to be included in the package. The File option will use a single file for the package you create. If you select Folder, each page will include a single image in the package, with an individual page created for every image in the folder. Frontmost Document will create a package from the currently active document in Photoshop. Finally, the Selected Images From File Browser option will utilize the files you have selected in the File Browser, putting each image on a page with the package settings you've established.

Note: If you want only one page with several different images on it, select the File option and select a single file to begin. You can then modify the individual images on the page separately by clicking on each image in the Layout preview and selecting a different image from the dialog box that appears.

2. If you've selected File or Folder from the Use dropdown list, click the Browse button to select a specific file or folder to use. The Include All Subfolders checkbox can be checked so that all folders within the selected folder are included as well.

3. In the Document section of the dialog box, select the unit of measure for the page from the Units dropdown list, and enter the desired Width, Height, and Resolution for the final print. You can also select a color mode to use for the documents, but the mode should be left at RGB if you're making your own prints on a desktop printer.

Note: We recommend making the document dimensions slightly smaller than the paper to which you'll be printing, just to ensure the final contact sheet will fit on the page without being clipped because of printer limitations.

4. A Layout dropdown list is in the Document section. With it you can select from preset package options the quantity and size of the images to be included. The picture quantity is represented by a number in parentheses, and the size is listed after it. So, for example, (2)5×7 would place two 5″×7″ images on the page, and (2)4×5 (4)2.5×3.5 would place two 4″×5″ images and four 2.5×″3.5″ images.

5. By default, the Flatten All Layers checkbox is checked, so that the final result will be a flattened document without individual layers. This is typically the best option, because you only need to print the final result. However, in some situations you may want to uncheck this checkbox so you can fine-tune the position of the individual images after the contact sheet is created.

6. The Label section allows you to place text over the top of each image within the package. If you want to produce a package of images that can be cut out and used to frame or otherwise display, you may not want any text at all. In which case, you can select None from the Content dropdown list. If you would like to include text, select the source of that text from the Content dropdown list. If you select Custom Text, you can enter that text into the field by the same name. Select the various attributes for the text to determine the font, opacity, and position on the image. You can also select an option to rotate the text in preset increments. Because of the lack of flexibility here, you may prefer to set the Label option to None and simply add text later in Photoshop or Elements.

7. If you'd like to change an image used on the page layout for your picture package, simply click on that image in the preview. This will bring up a dialog box where you can select a specific file to use in that position of the package.

With your settings established, you can click OK and the package will be assembled, creating a new document in Photoshop. If more than one page is required based on your settings, each of those pages will be created as a separate document. You can then print the package as you would any other photographic image.

Custom Packages

Photoshop CS includes a user-friendly way to customize your own picture package (previously you could only adjust the packages by editing a text file). Within the Picture Package dialog box, click the Edit Layout button in the bottom-right corner. This will bring up the Picture Package Edit Layout dialog box, where you can modify the existing package or create a new one (see Figure 4.5).

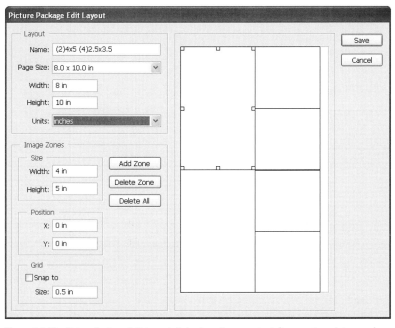

Figure 4.5 The Picture Package Edit Layout dialog box allows you to define a custom picture package with any number of images at various sizes to fit onto a particular paper size.

If you are changing an existing package, the specific image layout will change. Therefore, your first step should be to provide a new name for the custom package you're creating, such as "(1)5×7 (2)4×5." Be sure the name you use will clearly define the structure of the package, so you can easily select it by name in the future.

Once you're ready to modify the layout, we strongly recommend changing the Units dropdown list to inches (or centimeters) rather than the default of pixels. When you are preparing a picture package that will be printed, thinking in pixels isn't intuitive. With the unit of measure set as you prefer, select a Page Size from the dropdown list. Besides the presets available, you can select Custom and then enter any values you like for Width and Height. To help ensure the final picture package fits within the printable area of the printer you'll ultimately use to print this package, we recommend selecting a Page Size that fits within the paper size you'll be using. For example, for 8.5″×11″ paper, we would recommend choosing the 8×10 option.

Layouts in the picture package tool are defined based on image zones. Each zone has a specific size and location. When you create a picture package, each image is fit into each zone. Therefore, the process of editing the layout is really just a matter of defining each of the image zones.

If you want to start with a completely empty canvas for your picture package, you can click the Delete All button to clear all image zones. You then must add one or more zones to the layout to define where images will be placed and at what maximum size. To add a zone, click the Add Zone button. A new zone box will be added to the preview display. Then click the zone to adjust the settings for it.

To adjust the settings for a particular image zone, click on that zone in the preview display. You can change the position of the image zone by either dragging the box in the preview or by setting the X (horizontal) and Y (vertical) values in the Position section. Likewise, you can adjust the size of the image zone either by dragging the boxes along the border of the zone box, or by entering values for Width and Height in the Size section. In general, we find it best to enter values to start with, because you typically have an idea of what size images you want in the final package. As you get close to finishing the layout, you may find minor issues with image zones not fitting on the page. You can then use the mouse to drag any of the boxes around the edge of the image zone box to fine-tune the size of each image so they will all fit. If you find that a particular zone simply won't fit, or you otherwise don't want to include it in the layout, simply click on it in the preview display to select it, and then click the Delete Zone button.

Another option available in the layout editor is the ability to force each image zone to "snap" to a preset grid. When the Snap To checkbox is checked in the Grid section, a grid will appear in the preview display. If you click on (or drag) any image zone box, it will snap to the grid lines. This can help ensure even alignment of images within the layout. With the Snap To checkbox checked, a Size field will become active. It defaults to a 0.5″ spacing between gridlines, but you can set this to any value to define the distance between each of the lines to which the image zones will snap.

When you are finished defining the layout, click Save to commit the changes. You'll then be prompted for a name with which to save the layout. Giving it a name that identifies the layout for you is a good idea. After entering a name, click Save. The layout will be saved for future use. You can then select the saved layout from the Layout dropdown list in the Document section of the Picture Package dialog box.

Image Browsers

Many image browser software packages include the ability to print thumbnail reports, which serve very nicely as proof sheets. One of the major advantages of using this feature is that the proof sheet is sent directly to the printer rather than creating a new document in Photoshop. This makes it faster and easier to create a basic proof sheet of your images. Image browsers also offer a variety of options including header information that can be printed at the top of the page, caption details including a variety of options for what information is used for the caption, and other printing options.

All of the image browser software applications we've seen include the ability to print proof sheets, often referred to as a *thumbnail report*. In this section, we'll use Ulead's Photo Explorer 8 software, (www.ulead.com, Windows only) to show you how a thumbnail report can be used to create proof sheets. We're using Ulead Photo Explorer 8 for this particular example; however, you can use a similar process with many other image browser software applications.

The following steps will allow you to create proof sheets with this software:

1. Navigate to the folder containing the images you'd like to print, and select all of the images you want to include in your proof sheets.

2. Select File > Print > Thumbnails from the menu. This will bring up the Print Thumbnails dialog box where you can select the printing options (see Figure 4.6).

3. In the Thumbnail Arrangement section, select how many images you would like to appear Across and Down. This will set the total number of images on each page, which in turn determines how large each image will be.

Note: We recommend limiting the total number of images on the page to about 12 to allow for individual images of a reasonable size.

4. In the Print Text With Thumbnails section, check the boxes to select the text details you want to print below each thumbnail image.

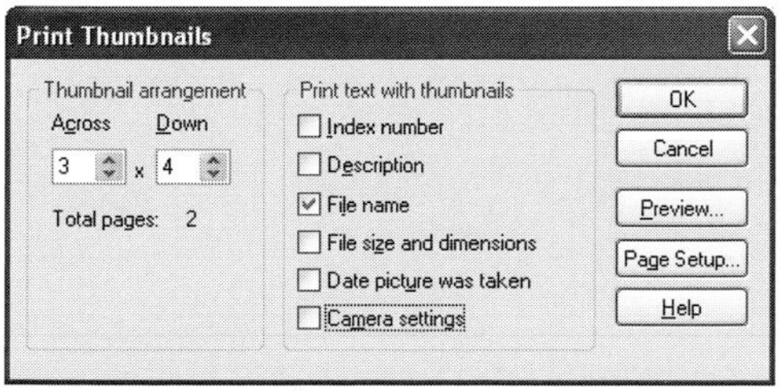

Figure 4.6 The Print Thumbnails dialog box in Ulead Photo Explorer 8 allows you to define the page layout for proof sheets from this image browser.

is not present.

5. Click the Page Setup button to bring up the Page Setup dialog box (see Figure 4.7). This dialog box includes options to specify margins for all four sides of the page. We recommend leaving these options alone unless your printer is unable to print close enough to the edge or you simply want to have some additional white space around one or more edges.

6. At the bottom of the Page Setup dialog box, check the appropriate box if you would like header or footer text printed on each page. With the box checked for either, you can enter text that will appear at the top or bottom of the page. Click OK to close the Page Setup dialog box.

7. If you'd like to verify your print settings, click the Preview checkbox. This will present a preview of the page as it will be printed based on your current settings. Click Print from this window to start the print job, or click Close to return to the Print Thumbnails dialog box, where you can click OK to start the print job.

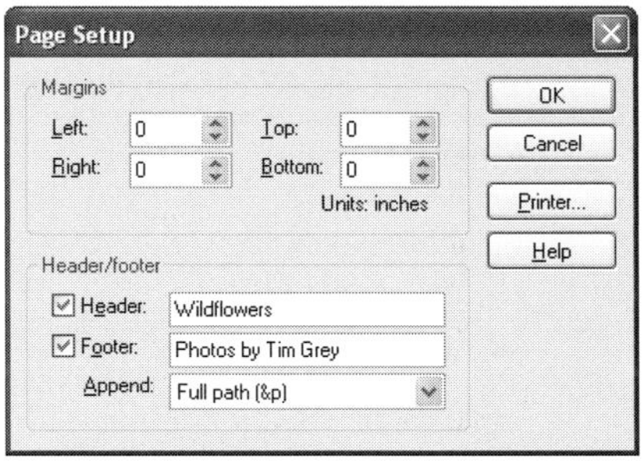

Figure 4.7 The Page Setup dialog box accessed from the Print Thumbnails dialog box in Ulead Photo Explorer provides options to apply a header and footer to the printed page and define a margin around the paper's edge.

Designing Albums

Although proof sheets provide an effective way to share a large number of images, they tend to be a rather utilitarian solution without much aesthetic appeal. When you want to share images in a more artistic manner, creating your own album pages provides the flexibility to create a beautiful presentation of a collection of images.

Album Materials

Before you start creating album pages, you need to give some thought to the final product. This includes considering how the pages will be assembled. However, the most important consideration relating to design and printing is the type of paper you'll be using. Although virtually any type of paper can be assembled into an album in some form, most photographers want to have the option to print on both sides of the paper. Therefore, you'll need to consider which double-sided papers are available for the size output you'd like to produce.

A number of options are available that provide double-sided printing support as well as a convenient method of assembling the pages into a beautiful presentation album. One of our favorite solutions is the variety of inkjet-printable pages and album covers available in the StoneHinge system from Stone Editions (www.stoneeditions.com). They are available in several sizes and several paper surfaces. Translucent interleaves are also available to help prevent burnishing or other damage to the printed pages.

This solution is particularly efficient because you can print to both sides of the paper, directly onto the album pages. These pages can then be assembled into an attractive album using the album covers utilizing a three-post binding system (see Figure 4.8).

Page Design

Creating custom albums provides tremendous flexibility in the way your images are presented on the page. However, it also places the responsibility on you to create layouts that will add appeal to the images rather than detract from them. Although placing a single image on a page certainly puts it in the spotlight, placing multiple images on a page helps build the story you're telling with your images, and it can add an artistic element that complements your images.

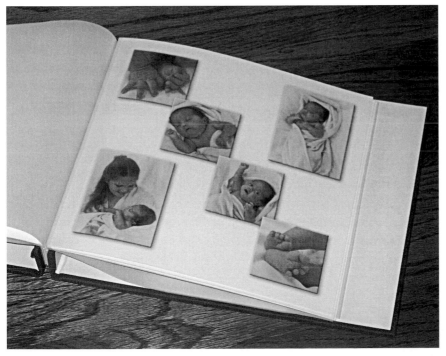

Figure 4.8 Printing directly on album pages that can be assembled into an attractive book is an excellent way to share your images in a beautiful package.

Consider the following tips as you are creating design layouts for each page in your album:

- **Use a grid layout**, with images aligning to an imaginary grid. This will create a sense of symmetry and organization on the page. When images are slightly out of alignment, the image may seem chaotic to the viewer.

- **Create visual balance on the page** with the arrangement of images. A page with balance is more pleasing to the eye and helps guide the viewer along a path through all of the images.

- **Utilize white space** to give the viewer a chance to "rest" within the layout. Many photographers make the mistake of feeling they need to fill every available space on the page with images. Including white space without images is an important component of good design.

- **Maintain consistency** in the design for each page. This doesn't mean that every page should look exactly the same. In fact, you'll want to have variety among the pages to keep the viewer interested. However, maintaining some consistency throughout the album, such as repeating the same basic layout on multiple (though not consecutive) pages, will result in an album where all pages seem to belong together.

- **Break the rules** to help add emphasis to an image on the page. For example, placing a single image on a page and putting it near one edge of the page can help add interest to the page and focus the viewer's eye on the image. You can even rotate some of the images on the page to add more variety to the layout.

Creating Page Layouts

Once you have a page layout in mind for a particular page, you're ready to start creating that page layout. The following steps in Photoshop will guide you through the process:

1. Select File > New from the menu to create a new document. In the dropdown list, set the unit of measure for Width and Height to Inches, and set the values for each text box to the dimensions of the paper to which you'll be printing. Set the Resolution to the value you use for normal photographic prints (typically, 300 dpi), make sure the mode is set to RGB, and set the Background Contents to White. Then click OK to create the new document, which will serve as your canvas for the album page.

2. Open the images you'd like to include on the current page of the album.

3. Displaying rulers along the edge of the images can be helpful. You can use them as a basic guide to spacing and sizing on the page. To activate the rulers, select View > Rulers from the menu for each image.

Note: Keep in mind that you'll want the edge of the page that will be bound to have extra space to accommodate the binding. This empty space is referred to as the gutter, and it will be on the left side of odd-numbered pages and the right side of even-numbered pages.

4. With most inkjet-printable album pages, you can't print all the way to the edges, primarily because you need to leave room for the binding area of the page. Many printers can't print all the way to the edge of the paper either. Creating guides around the edges of the document can help ensure you don't encroach on the margins with your images. To create these guides, you can either click and drag from the ruler around your images if you have them turned on, or you can select View > New Guide from the menu and enter the appropriate details for the guide line you'd like to create (see Figure 4.9).

5. If you are using a grid structure to define the arrangement of images on the page, you can also create guides to mark where the images should align.

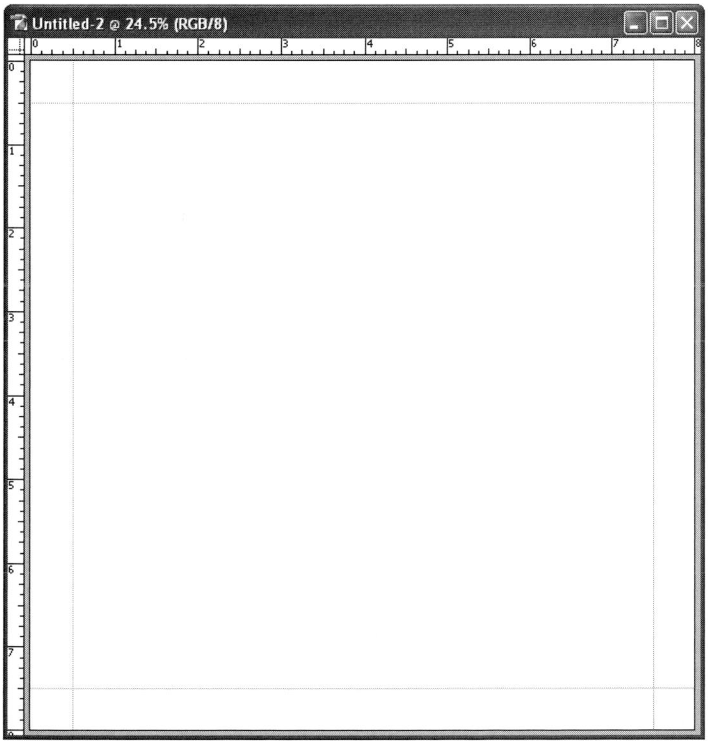

Figure 4.9 Guides can help you define the margin around the page layout and the layout of images within the page.

6. Open each of the images you'd like to include in the layout, and create a working copy for each of them by selecting each image in turn and choosing Image > Duplicate from the menu. You can then close the original master images.

7. Flatten each of these duplicate images by selecting each image in turn and choosing Layer > Flatten Image from the menu.

8. If you already have an idea of how large each image will be on the page, resize the images before bringing them into the album layout. Select each image in turn and choose Image > Image Size from the menu. Set the Width or Height in the Document Size section to establish the size of the image (the other dimension will adjust automatically if you have the Constrain Proportions checkbox checked, which we recommend). The Resolution should be set to the same output resolution value used for the new document you created. Be sure the Resample checkbox is checked when resizing the image. Click OK when all parameters have been established.

9. Apply sharpening to each image by selecting Filter > Sharpen > Unsharp Mask from the menu.

10. Use the Move tool to click and drag each image in turn onto the new document you created. Be sure that you drag all the way into the new document so the image will be copied correctly.

11. Once you have brought the images into the layout, use the Move tool to adjust their positions. During this process, check the Auto Select Layer checkbox on the Options bar so that you don't need to select a layer on the Layers palette in order to move it. Instead, simply point the mouse to the image you want to move, and click and drag to move it. You can also use the arrow keys on the keyboard to nudge the image by one pixel at a time into precise position. Adding Shift to the arrow keys will cause the image to move by 10 pixels at a time.

12. As you're adjusting the layout for your album pages, you'll likely need to fine-tune the sizing of individual images. To do so, be sure the image layer you want to resize is the currently active layer on the Layers palette and select Edit > Transform > Scale from the menu. This will place a bounding box around the image, with boxes along the edges and at each corner. To resize the image, hold the Shift key (to preserve the proportions of the image) as you click and drag one of the corner boxes on the bounding box.

13.	You can block out portions of the images in your layout by clicking the Add Layer Mask button at the bottom of the Layers palette and then painting in black with a soft-edged brush on the areas of the image you'd like to block. If you make a mistake, you can paint with white to "unhide" pixels. For example, if you are creating a layout with a series of images of people, you may want to block out the background from each image. This helps to focus attention on the intended subject of the images and also adds an artistic edge to the photos.

14.	If you'd like to add an effect to the image, such as a drop shadow or a stroke (a fine line around the edge of the image), you can select an image layer, click the Add Layer Style button at the bottom of the Layers palette, and choose the type of effect you'd like to add. Adjust the settings in the Layer Style dialog box and click OK to apply the effect. You can copy the same styles with the same settings to other image layers by clicking the Effects item under the layer they apply to on the Layers palette and dragging it onto another layer.

Once you've fine-tuned the layout to perfection (see Figure 4.10), you can print it onto your special album pages and assemble the images into a presentation portfolio.

Figure 4.10 The finished page layout for your album is ready to be printed and assembled into an album to share with friends or clients. (Photography by Chris Greene, ImageWest Photography)

Creative Border Treatments

Another way to produce a creative presentation of your images is to apply a border treatment to them, adding texture around the edge of the image for a unique appearance. Whether you're printing a single image or assembling multiple images into album pages, this is a great way to make your images stand out (see Figure 4.11).

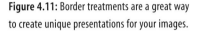

Figure 4.11: Border treatments are a great way to create unique presentations for your images.

Extensis PhotoFrame

For an automated method to create a border treatment on your images, the PhotoFrame plug-in from Extensis (www.extensis.com, Windows and Macintosh) is an excellent tool. It is priced at under $200 and includes thousands of border masks. (A free 30-day trial version was also available for download as this book went to press.) You can apply one or more borders to an image, which will cause pixels to be blocked from the image to create the border effect selected.

Note: The frame effects are stored on the installation CD, and they are not copied to your hard drive by default. We recommend copying the Frame Files folder from the installation CD onto your hard drive to make them more easily accessible.

If you decide to try PhotoFrame, you can use the following steps to apply a border effect:

1. Review the PDF document included on the installation CD for PhotoFrame. This PDF includes previews of all the edge effects included with PhotoFrame, divided into sections. Select a border effect that complements the texture or subject matter of the image you're applying it to for the best results.

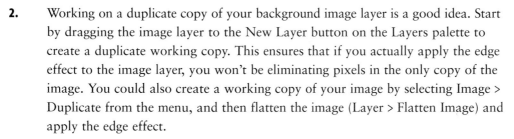

Note: A PDF document that includes samples of all the border effects available in PhotoFrame is included on the installation CD. We recommend making a printout of it. Doing so makes it much easier to find the frame you'd like to use for a particular image.

2. Working on a duplicate copy of your background image layer is a good idea. Start by dragging the image layer to the New Layer button on the Layers palette to create a duplicate working copy. This ensures that if you actually apply the edge effect to the image layer, you won't be eliminating pixels in the only copy of the image. You could also create a working copy of your image by selecting Image > Duplicate from the menu, and then flatten the image (Layer > Flatten Image) and apply the edge effect.

3. Select Filter > Extensis > PhotoFrame from the menu to bring up the PhotoFrame dialog box (see Figure 4.12).

4. If there are already frame templates selected, you can remove them by selecting them and clicking the Delete Frame button on the Frame palette.

Figure 4.12 The PhotoFrame dialog box allows you to select one or more frames to apply to an image and adjust the area of your image to be affected.

5. Click the Add Frame File button and navigate to the location where the frame files are stored. Select the specific frame file you want to apply as a border effect to the current image, and click OK.

6. In the preview display, adjust the bounding box of the border effect by clicking and dragging the boxes around the edge. Be sure not to drag the box out so far that sections of the image are left with a straight edge.

7. If you'd like to stack multiple border effects on the same image, click the Add Frame File button and select an additional frame file.

Note: To help you decide whether you want to include an effect in your final border, turn off the visibility of that border effect by clicking the eyeball icon to the left of each frame file you add to the list. When you apply the border effect to your image, only the frame files that are visible on the list will be applied to the image.

8. When you're happy with the border effect you've created, click the Apply button to apply the effect to the currently active layer, or click the Apply To New Layer button to apply the effect onto a separate layer above the image layer. The latter option will cause a transparent layer with white pixels around the edge in the shape of the border effect you've selected to be added above the currently active image layer.

Note: Photo/Graphic Edges from Auto FX (www.autofx.com, Windows and Macintosh) is another plug-in that offers the same basic functionality as Extensis PhotoFrame. However, it uses an unorthodox interface and consumes considerable memory resources, which causes us to favor PhotoFrame.

Photoshop Masking

The automated approach of plug-ins such as Extensis PhotoFrame or AutoFX Photo/Graphic Edges is convenient, but you can apply similar effects to your images manually in Photoshop without the need to buy any additional plug-in software. This can be accomplished with two basic methods: filtered selections and painted masks.

Filtered Selections

Many filters are available in Photoshop that create distorted effects in your images. These filters can be used to modify a selection, which in turn can be used to mask out an image as a border effect. The key is to use Quick Mask mode to apply filters to your selections. The mask defines the area where the filter effect will apply.

The following steps will allow you to utilize this method to create border treatments for your images:

1. Select most of your image using the Rectangular Marquee tool (see Figure 4.13). The edge of the selection should define the inner boundary of the area where you'd like the border treatment to appear; that is, the pixels outside the selection will form the mask, the area to be filtered and partially hidden.

2. Switch to Quick Mask mode by pressing Q on the keyboard or by clicking the Edit In Quick Mask Mode button below the Color Picker on the Tools palette (see Figure 4.14).

3. Apply a filter to the Quick Mask by selecting a filter from the Filter menu. We find that the filters in the Artistic, Brush Strokes, and Distort sections of the Filter menu work best. Using the preview for the filter, adjust the settings to create the border treatment shape you'd like to apply to the image, and click OK (see Figure 4.15).

Note: You can apply multiple filters to the Quick Mask to create a more complicated edge effect.

Figure 4.13 The first step in creating a border treatment using a filtered selection is to create a selection such as this one done with the Rectangular Marquee tool.

Figure 4.14 Switching to Quick Mask mode allows you to apply filters to the shape defined by your selection.

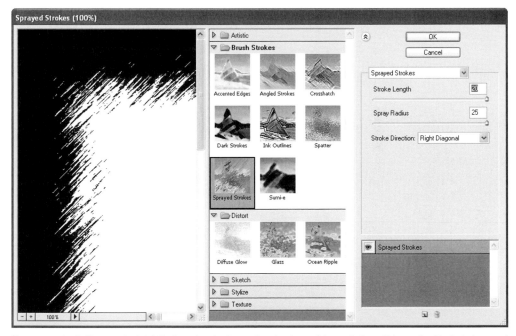

Figure 4.15 Apply filters to the Quick Mask mode selection to alter the shape of the mask that will be used to block pixels around the edge of an image.

4. Return to Standard mode for the selection by again pressing **Q** on the keyboard or by clicking the Edit In Standard Mode button below the Color Picker on the Tools palette. This will display the modified selection as the typical "marching ants" outline.

5. If you're applying the border treatment to a background image layer, you'll need to convert the background layer to a normal image layer by double-clicking its thumbnail on the Layers palette and clicking OK in the New Layer dialog box that will be displayed.

6. Be sure the image layer to which you are adding the border effect is active on the Layers palette. Click the Add Layer Mask button (with an icon of a circle in a square) at the bottom of the Layers palette to create a layer mask from the selection you've created. This will block the pixels outside the selection so that only the pixels within the selection are visible. Because filters were applied to the selection while in Quick Mask mode, the result is a unique border treatment (see Figure 4.16).

Note: It can be helpful to create a new layer filled with white below the image layer you're applying the border treatment to so you can see the result more clearly. You can do so by holding Ctrl (Command on Macintosh) while clicking the New Layer button at the bottom of the Layers palette while the bottom-most layer is active. Then select Edit > Fill from the menu, set the color to White, and click OK.

Figure 4.16 The filtered selection method of creating border treatments allows you to quickly alter the edge of your images with tools readily available in Photoshop.

Painted Masks

With the ability to create brushes of any shape, you can use a layer mask to paint away areas around the edge of the image to create a border treatment. This provides a more artistic approach with greater flexibility. Use the following steps to create a painted mask border treatment:

1.   If you're applying the border treatment to a background image layer, you'll need to convert the background layer to a normal image layer by double-clicking its thumbnail on the Layers palette and clicking OK in the New Layer dialog box that will be displayed.

2.   Create a layer mask for this layer by clicking the Add Layer Mask button at the bottom of the Layers palette.

3.   Select the Brush tool by pressing **B** on the keyboard or by selecting it from the Tools palette.

4.   On the Options bar, click the Brush dropdown list and select a brush with a very random shape. These brushes can be found near the bottom of the list of available brushes. In addition, more brush shapes can be added by clicking the side menu button (triangle on a circular button) on the dropdown brushes list and selecting the group of brushes by name (such as Natural Brushes). Be sure to select the Append option from the dialog box displayed, so you add brushes to the available options rather than replace all existing brushes.

5.   Set the foreground color to black with the Color Picker on the Tools palette. You can set the colors to the defaults of black and white by pressing **D** on your keyboard. If you need to swap the foreground and background colors to get black as the foreground color, press **X** on your keyboard.

6.   Move your mouse over the image to determine if the brush size is appropriate for the border treatment you want to apply. You can reduce the brush size with the left bracket key ([) and increase the brush size with the right bracket key (]).

7. With the layer mask created in Step 2 active, paint along the edge of the image to block pixels (see Figure 4.17). Because you have selected a brush with a random shape, the edge you create will be rough and textured.

8. Continue painting around the edge of the image until you've created a border treatment around the full perimeter (see Figure 4.18).

Note: Keep in mind that this border treatment effect is usually best applied with a certain amount of randomness. Therefore, feel free to paint along a jagged line as you move along the border of the image.

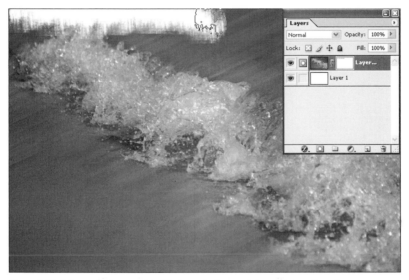

Figure 4.17 Paint on the layer mask to block out pixels around the perimeter of your image.

Figure 4.18 After painting around the entire edge of your image, the result is a custom border treatment that can add to the visual appeal of your image.

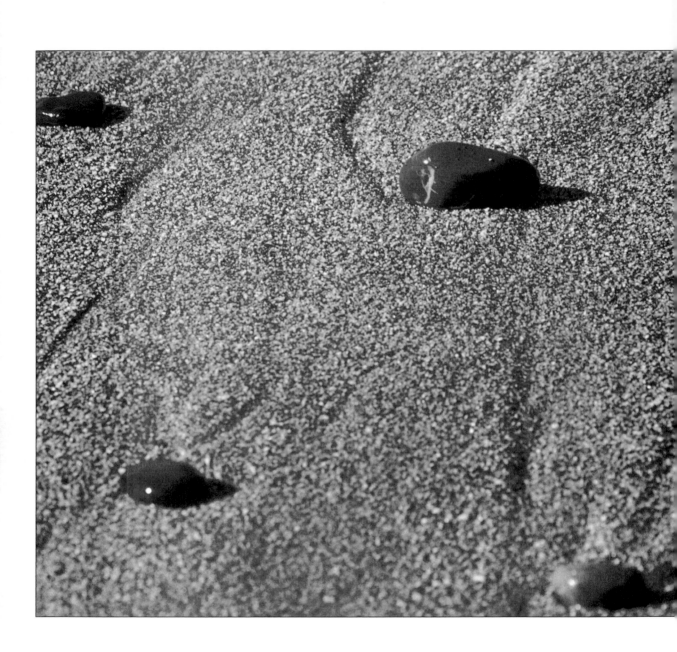

Using Print Services

Some photographers might take pictures only for themselves; however, most of us can't resist the desire to share our images with others. More often than not, we share those images through prints. In Part I, we covered output on your own printer. However, you may need to use a print lab or online print service to produce your prints, whether you make that choice based on cost, output size, or convenience. In this section, we'll take a look at some of your options for having prints made from your images.

Choosing the Output and Print Lab

5

There are a variety of reasons why you may opt to have a digital lab print your images for you. Whether it is to benefit from an expert's experience in producing high-quality prints or to obtain prints larger than you are able to produce on your own printer, many labs can offer prints of the utmost quality at very reasonable prices. When someone else will be printing your image for you, you need to consider the type of output to be created and the print lab that will offer that service.

Chapter Contents
Choosing the Output
Selecting a Print Lab
Preparing the File

Choosing the Output

The choice of output type is a personal decision for each photographer. The decision typically revolves around what the photographer is familiar and comfortable with, as well as what is available from the print lab with which the photographer already has a relationship. Regardless, it is important to consider the reasons for making a decision about a particular output type, so you'll have a better understanding of what to expect in the final print.

Here are the three major options available from a variety of print labs:

- Photo inkjet output using printers similar to those used by most photographers using digital tools
- Dye sublimation printers that produce prints with a very "photographic" feel
- Digital-to-photo-paper printers that blend digital technology with traditional chemical processing to produce a true photographic print

Inkjet

Many photographers have embraced inkjet printing for their images, as we recommended in Chapter 1, "Choosing the Printer and Medium," and even produce their own prints for sale utilizing such a printer. Today's photo inkjet printers are capable of producing beautiful fine-art prints worthy of framing for display. The inkjet printing process offers a high degree of control over image optimization and output, allowing the photographer to produce prints that perfectly match their original vision for the image.

You may feel that purchasing a print from a lab using the same (or similar) output process to what you're using at home doesn't make much sense. Why pay someone else to produce a print that you could produce yourself with the same printer? There are a couple of good reasons, depending on your needs.

Size

Although a photographer who has embraced digital imaging typically works with an inkjet printer in their own digital darkroom, one particular printer isn't necessarily appropriate for every print job. In particular, output size limitations can be an issue. Unless you're selling a relatively large number of prints, you may not be able to fit one of the largest inkjet printers into your budget. Most photographers are likely able to justify a desktop inkjet printer capable of printing to cut sheet media up to 13″ ×19″. However, wide-format printers capable of printing to roll paper or cut sheets with typical widths of 24 to 44 inches can cost thousands of dollars. If you only need to produce a relatively small number of large prints, purchasing those prints from a lab that offers inkjet printing services may be more appropriate than finding the money in your budget—and space in your digital darkroom—for such a large printer.

Giclée—Just a Fancy Name

You may have heard fine-art prints of photographic images referred to as "giclée" prints. Giclée is a French word that means "squirt," and it is really just a fancy way of referring to an inkjet print. The term does not refer to a specific output device or process.

Traditionally, a giclée print refers to a photographic print with a high-end inkjet printer using water-color or canvas print media. However, many companies offering giclée prints use a wide variety of photo inkjet printers and will print to any available print media of your choosing.

Just because a print is offered as a fine-art giclée doesn't necessarily mean it is an archival print using pigmented inks, so we strongly recommend asking which printer and inkset will be used for your prints. Common printers used are Iris, Roland, Epson, Canon, Hewlett-Packard, and others. The specific inks used will vary from printer to printer, and they can be inks from the original manufacturer or third parties.

If you're looking for a high-quality fine-art print, you probably want it to last as long as possible. We, therefore, recommend specifying pigment-based inks for any giclée prints you have prepared from your images.

Service

Many photographers feel that if they are hiring a lab to produce a print, they should use some sort of high-quality, high-end printer capable of producing particularly exceptional output. Professional-quality wide-format inkjet printers offer exactly that type of output. You don't need to have a print produced from an exotic printer to ensure the best quality. In effect, when purchasing an inkjet print from a print lab, you're really paying for the printmaking service. The lab is likely producing the print on equipment you could otherwise purchase yourself. Utilizing a lab allows you to obtain the same high-quality results you could produce yourself, without the investment of printer and materials. You can obtain prints on demand, as you need them at a very modest price per print.

The advantages of selecting inkjet output from a print lab include:

- **Reasonable prices** because the print labs are able to purchase materials whole-sale and because they produce enough volume to justify investing in bigger machines.

- **No upfront investment** in wide-format printers and supplies.

- **Additional media options** because some inkjet print media is available only in wide rolls.

- **Excellent quality** based on the technological advances in photo inkjet printing.

In short, purchasing photo inkjet prints from a print lab is a good choice for the same reasons that producing your own photo inkjet prints in your digital darkroom is an excellent solution for high-quality output, with the added advantage that you don't need to purchase a special printer if you need extra-large prints.

What to Ask the Inkjet Print Lab

When choosing a lab to provide you with inkjet prints, discuss the following questions, with the lab before making a final decision. Later in the chapter, we'll discuss the issues you should go over with any lab as you evaluate whether to use them, but these questions pertain specifically to the inkjet process:

- **Which printer is available?** Inkjet printing technology has developed at a rapid rate over the past few years, so you'll get the best results if the print lab is using a recent model inkjet printer. Once you know which models are being used by a particular lab, you can also research and read reviews about those printers to determine which will most likely meet your needs.

- **Which inkset will be used?** We strongly recommend purchasing prints made with pigment-based inks. Besides inks from the printer manufacturers, many print labs offer output using third-party inks, many of which are pigment-based. Although we have some concerns about using third-party inks (as discussed in Chapter 1), those issues don't affect the quality of the final output, so you shouldn't have any reservations about using a lab producing prints with third-party pigment-based inks.

- **Which print media are available?** The more options available, the more flexibility you'll have in selecting the best media for a particular image. If you've developed a strong preference for a particular media type for your own inkjet printing, finding a lab that offers output to that same media may improve your level of satisfaction with the final print.

- **What profiles are used?** A highly accurate output profile will help ensure the most accurate colors in the final print. A lab that takes color management very seriously, and has custom profiles created for each output process, is most likely to produce impressive prints. Ideally, you'll be able to obtain those profiles so you can soft proof your images before submission.

- **What is the cost per print?** Inkjet printers are relatively economical to operate, so you should find the price of inkjet output to be very reasonable relative to the output size you are ordering.

The bottom line is that inkjet prints from a print lab are the most appropriate choice for photographers looking for maximum flexibility in output size and print media at a reasonable price.

Comparing Continuous Tone

Print labs promoting output with processes other than inkjet printers often tout the benefits of *continuous tone* output as an advantage over inkjet prints. Continuous tone refers to prints that are made of continuous smooth transitions of tone and color, rather than being composed of individual dots. Inkjet printers produce the image on paper with a series of tiny dots. Therefore, they are technically not considered continuous tone output devices.

However, today's inkjet printers utilize droplets of ink that are so small, and that can be placed with such close spacing, that for all intents and purposes they can now be considered continuous tone devices. At normal viewing distances, it is impossible to see any patterns that would indicate the printer was anything other than a continuous tone device. Under close examination with a loupe or magnifying glass, you can certainly see that the image is made up of many tiny dots, but those dots are so small that they aren't evident when the print is viewed at a normal distance with the unaided eye. When comparing an inkjet print with a true continuous tone print at normal viewing distances, the quality of the prints will be comparable.

Dye Sublimation

Dye sublimation printers produce true continuous tone output with excellent quality. The name "dye sublimation" refers to the fact that the color is produced using dyes and that those dyes are directly changed (sublimated) from solid dye embedded in a film to a gaseous form. Each of the CMYK color channels is added in a separate pass (see Figure 5.1). By impregnating the gaseous dyes into the surface of the paper, the image is created without any dots, but rather as continuous tone with smooth transitions between tones and colors.

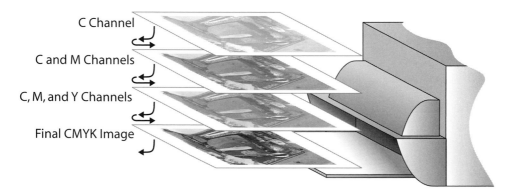

C Channel

C and M Channels

C, M, and Y Channels

Final CMYK Image

Figure 5.1 A dye sublimation printer creates a print in several passes by impregnating dyes into the paper. This produces a continuous-tone print that is very durable.

Most commercial print labs don't typically offer dye sublimation prints. This isn't an indication of less-than excellent quality in dye sublimation prints. It is a result of the fact that dye sublimation prints are generally not as economical as inkjet prints and they don't offer the flexibility of print media available with inkjet printers.

However, that doesn't mean that dye sublimation prints aren't a worthwhile consideration. In fact, dye sublimation prints very closely match the high quality and durability many people have become accustomed to with traditional photographic prints. You will most often find dye sublimation prints offered by small print labs or online printing services (see Chapter 6, "Using Online Print Services").

The advantages of selecting dye sublimation output from a print lab include:

- **High durability** because the laminate coating that is typically applied to these prints in the printing process. Dye sublimation prints are not easily damaged by water or handling.

- **Excellent quality** with true continuous tone output and photographic quality.

- **Reasonable prices** because the labs offering these print services often focus on high-volume production, though the pricing tends to be higher than for inkjet output.

- **No upfront investment** in a printer and supplies.

The bottom line is that dye sublimation prints are most appropriate for photographers looking for durable prints that have the look and feel of traditional glossy photo prints.

Digital to Photo Paper

While some photographers have quickly converted to a completely digital workflow from capture to the final print, other photographers have preferred to take more of a hybrid approach to producing their images. For example, many photographers continue to capture images on film, but then scan the film into a digital image and optimize the images using the best digital tools and techniques. When it comes to the final print, some digital photographers feel more comfortable using traditional print processes simply because they don't yet feel comfortable trusting digital, and some still consider film photography superior.

Printing digital images to photo paper provides a way to utilize traditional printing without giving up the advantages and control afforded by a digital workflow. A digital file is sent to a special printer such as the Durst Lambda, Chromira, and LightJet. Rather than applying ink or dyes onto a paper, these printers expose photographic paper to the image using lasers or LEDs. The exposed paper is then processed with a traditional silver-halide process (see Figure 5.2). The result is a true photographic print produced from a digital image file.

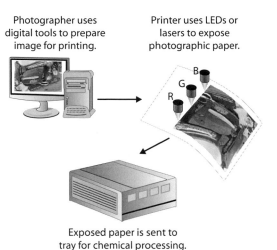

Photographer uses digital tools to prepare image for printing.

Printer uses LEDs or lasers to expose photographic paper.

B
G
R

Exposed paper is sent to tray for chemical processing.

Figure 5.2 Direct photo printers use a digital file as the basis for exposing light-sensitive photographic paper using lasers or LEDs. The exposed paper is then processed using a traditional silver-halide process.

The advantages of selecting digital-to-photo-paper output from a print lab include:

- **Higher comfort level for many photographers** because traditional silver-halide photographic processing is used for the prints. For photographers uneasy about digital prints because they don't yet feel comfortable with digital, this process provides prints they can feel confident about based on their experience with traditional photography.

- **Excellent quality** with true continuous tone output and photographic quality.

- **Reasonable prices** despite the high cost of the printers, because most labs offering these prints are well established and have a high volume of print production.

- **No upfront investment** in a printer and supplies.

The bottom line is that digital prints to photo paper are most appropriate for photographers who want high-quality output on traditional materials and who feel more comfortable using silver-based processes while still taking advantage of digital optimization.

Fuji Pictography

The Fuji Pictography series of printers use an exclusive process that combines laser exposure, thermal development, and dye transfer to produce the image on special donor paper. The result, through a slightly different printing process, is a print with properties and quality very similar to a digital print on photo paper. This process is a more environmentally friendly printing process because traditional development chemicals are not required. However, accelerated testing has shown that these prints have a shorter life, estimated at about ten years or more.

Comparing Output Methods

Table 5.1 summarizes the advantages and disadvantages of the three output methods.

▶ **Table 5.1:** Output Methods at a Glance

	Inkjet	Dye-Sublimation	Direct-To-Photo
Price	Excellent	Very Good	Good
Media Options	Excellent	Fair	Good
Print Quality	Excellent	Excellent	Excellent
Print Durability	Fair	Excellent	Good

Selecting a Print Lab

Selecting a print lab to produce your prints is a critically important process. Photographers tend to be very picky about the final appearance of their prints, and with good reason. Their images are their artistic expression, and they put a great deal of effort into getting to the best location, choosing the right camera equipment, determining optimal camera settings, capturing just the right image at just the right moment, and then optimizing that image in a digital darkroom. For many photographers, the final print is the ultimate vision in mind when the shutter release button is pressed and the image is recorded.

Feeling totally comfortable with the print lab you use is important, and you should build a good working relationship with them. This will help ensure a smooth process of obtaining high-quality prints of your images. Having a good relationship with your print lab will make it easier to find a solution when you aren't happy with a particular print.

What to Ask

Think of the process of finding just the right print lab as though you were in the process of hiring a photographic assistant. You'll need to ask questions to determine if a particular lab is the right one for you and if you'll be able to trust the lab to produce the best possible prints from your images. You might want to ask the following questions during the "interview" process as you try to find the right lab for you:

- **"What type of output do you offer?"** You probably figured out what type of output you actually want in the first section of this chapter, so this question may be more about finding out if they offer the output type you want. However, knowing all of a particular lab's options is helpful. When you have different needs for different images, you will have a sense of how much flexibility the lab offers.

- **"What output sizes are available?"** Chances are you're using a print lab to produce the prints that are larger than you're able to produce yourself, so it is a good idea to work with a lab that can produce larger output than you think you'll need. The maximum output size will depend on the printer being used, so there will be some variability here even when talking about the same output type for several different labs. Make sure the lab can produce at least the largest (or larger) print you think you'll typically need.

- **"Do you have custom profiles?"** This is largely a way to find out how serious the lab is about accurate color. If the lab doesn't know what a custom profile is, hang up and call a different lab. If they offer custom profiles and assure you they are highly accurate and that they calibrate their monitors on a regular basis, chances are you can be assured of accurate color. If they don't offer custom profiles, don't dismiss them automatically. Discuss their color-managed workflow, and ask them how they ensure the most accurate output possible without custom profiles. Perhaps they simply ask you to save your images in a particular color space, preferring to handle all color management tasks within the lab. This can certainly be an effective process, and it puts the responsibility on the lab for accurate color. In any event, discuss color management with the lab and get a sense of what they'll do to produce prints with the most accurate colors possible.

- **"Do you offer proof prints?"** Chapter 2, "Preparing the Image," discussed the importance of soft proofing when you are inkjet printing at home. Many photographers think of proof prints as a standard part of the printing process, but many print labs (even many of the best) don't offer proof prints. Instead they may offer some form of guarantee. If they do offer proof prints, it may be an optional service at an additional charge. In many cases, the proof print would be produced on a different printer than the final print, making it less than ideal for evaluating color for the final print. If proof prints are available, ask if they'll be produced using the same output process as the final print—otherwise the evaluation won't be as effective. In other words, the question of proof prints may not be as important as the next question.

- **"Do you offer a satisfaction guarantee?"** Knowing what the process will be if you aren't satisfied with a particular print is important. If the print lab has an advanced color-managed workflow they may not offer a free replacement, perhaps offering a discount on the reprint. Chances are you won't find a satisfaction guarantee without any limits, so discuss what options will be available if a print doesn't meet your expectations. Keep in mind if a print isn't what you expected, it may have to do with how you prepared the image, so discuss the likely cause with the lab as you describe what you feel is wrong with the print.

- **"Where is the lab located?"** In this day of instant electronic communication and highly reliable shipping methods, the location may not be an issue at all. However, if you ever want to stop by and see how the prints are produced, you'll obviously want to work with a lab that is relatively close to you. Using a local print lab also eliminates (or minimizes) the risk of damage in shipping and the delays involved. If there is a problem with a print, having the lab nearby will also make it easier to find a solution while reviewing the print together. If the lab is nearby, ask if you can stop by to look "behind the scenes" at how a print is produced.

- **"How do you ship prints?"** You'll want to concern yourself with two issues here. The first is how the prints get packaged. It doesn't matter how good the original print was if it gets damaged in shipping to you. Proper packaging is the key, and a print lab that takes packaging very seriously will be more likely to deliver prints in perfect condition. The other consideration is the speed of delivery. The longer a print spends in transit, the more chance of damage. Labs that use second day shipping as a standard method, for example, will usually have less chance of having prints damaged during shipping.

- **"What is your pricing structure?"** Making a lot of prints can get expensive, so while print quality should be your first concern, you'll certainly want to consider how much your prints will cost. We've found that most print labs offer a very similar pricing structure, this is certainly an issue to consider when comparing various print labs.

- **"Do you offer a volume discount?"** This is part of the issue of pricing structure, but it relates specifically to pricing for multiple prints. Because setup costs involve a large part of the total cost, there is typically a discount for multiple prints. However, these discounts are often only offered for multiple prints of the same image. If you'll be purchasing a large number of prints for a major show, for example, do they offer discounted pricing for that large volume?

- **"Do you produce prints for any photographers that I know?"** In effect, this is asking for a testimonial. If photographers you respect and trust are willing to trust the print lab you're considering, that says a great deal about the quality and service you can likely expect from that lab.

- **"Can I view samples of your output?"** One of the best ways to determine if a lab is able to produce prints with the quality you desire is to view some of those prints for yourself. If the lab allows you to scrutinize a sample print, you can make a better determination of how happy you'll likely be when they produce prints for you. If you're asking these questions over the phone, this also provides a good reason to stop by the lab and see how they operate for yourself—provided they're located close by. If not, see if they can ship you a small sample print for evaluation, or if you can get a discount on your first print job for the purposes of evaluating their services.

As you're discussing these issues with each lab, you'll find out if they can meet your needs and you'll start to get a sense of what the working relationship will be like. If they're friendly, helpful, and eager to answer your questions, chances are you'll continue to have a good working relationship. If they don't seem too interested in answering your questions, they may not be too interested in making sure you're happy with their final prints. Your comfort level with a lab is very important. With so many variables affecting a final print, you'll want to work with a lab that will help ensure you're preparing the files properly and that will be easy to talk to when you aren't completely satisfied.

Preparing the File

Much of the responsibility for getting the best prints possible from a print lab lies squarely with you. Fortunately, with an understanding of how to best prepare images, you can ensure accurate color in your prints.

The first step in preparing your image file is to contact the print lab and find out how they want the file prepared. They should be able to provide a custom profile for the output process to be used, as well as offer advice on other setup considerations. Talk to the person who will be processing your images for print, and discuss what you can do to prepare the best possible image for the best possible print, as well as what you can do to make the process as smooth as possible for the print lab. They'll appreciate your efforts, and you'll be helping to ensure prints you'll be happy with.

Note: We can't remind you too many times that calibrating your monitor is absolutely critical. Without a calibrated monitor, you can't expect accurate prints from a print lab. Refer to Chapter 2, for more details on monitor calibration.

Soft Proofing with Custom Profiles

If the print lab is able to provide you with a custom profile, you'll want to proof the image based on that profile to ensure the most accurate color possible. Discuss the availability of custom profiles with your print lab, and ask if they have recommendations about the settings to be used.

To configure soft proofing in Photoshop CS, follow the steps below.

To configure soft proofing in Photoshop CS, follow these steps:

1. Select View > Proof Setup > Custom (see Figure 5.3).

2. In the Proof Setup dialog box, select the custom profile from the Profile dropdown list. Unless the print lab recommends something to the contrary, set the Intent to Relative Colorimetric, check the Use Black Point Compensation checkbox, and check the Paper White checkbox (which will generally cause the Ink Black checkbox to be checked as well, which we also recommend).

3. Click OK and the Proof Colors view will automatically be turned on. You can toggle the soft proof preview on and off by selecting View > Proof Colors from the menu. When the checkmark is displayed in front of the Proof Colors option, the image is being displayed with soft proofing.

As discussed in Chapter 2, you can make adjustments to the image to optimize it based on the soft proof display. We recommend using adjustment layers in a separate layer set to fine-tune the image for the specific output process being used. Be sure to name the layer set to identify the output process for which the adjustments are designed.

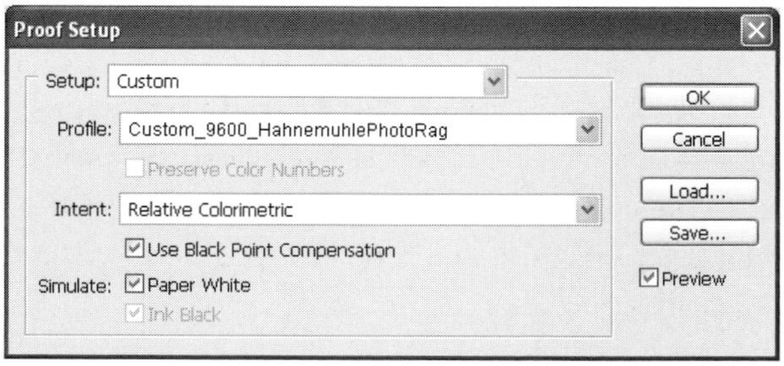

Figure 5.3 The Proof Setup dialog box allows you to configure soft proofing so you can preview what the image will look like in the final print.

Output Preparation

Once the image has been optimized to perfection for the output process that will be used for the image, you're ready to finalize the preparation so the image can be sent to the print lab. This process is essentially the same as we presented in "Print Preparation Workflow" in Chapter 2; here's a quick summary:

> **Note:** We're using Photoshop CS for this workflow, but similar options are available in most photo-editing software packages.

1. Save your master image file with layers intact. The master file will be used for all output processing, and saving this file with all pixels intact is important.

2. Create a duplicate working copy. Do this by selecting Image > Duplicate from the menu and clicking OK in the Duplicate dialog box (see Figure 5.4). You can then close your master image file.

Figure 5.4 Creating a duplicate copy of your image ensures you won't damage your master image file while preparing the image file to be sent to the print lab

3. Flatten the image. Do this by selecting Layer > Flatten Image from the menu, or by selecting Flatten Image from the palette menu on the Layers palette.

4. Resize the image to the final output dimensions. Select Image > Image Size from the menu (see Figure 5.5), set the output resolution as recommended by the print lab you're using, and set the output dimensions with the Resample checkbox checked. In general, we recommend the Bicubic Resampling option; however, if you are enlarging the image significantly the Bicubic Smoother option may produce a higher-quality enlargement.

5. Sharpen the image. Select Filter > Sharpen > Unsharp Mask from the menu (see Figure 5.6). We strongly recommend discussing the best settings with the print lab. You may want to do two sharpening passes: one to optimize the image to the desired sharpness and another to compensate for the loss of sharpness inherent in the output process being used. The first pass should be with a very small Radius setting, and the second pass should be targeted to the output process, likely using a higher Radius setting.

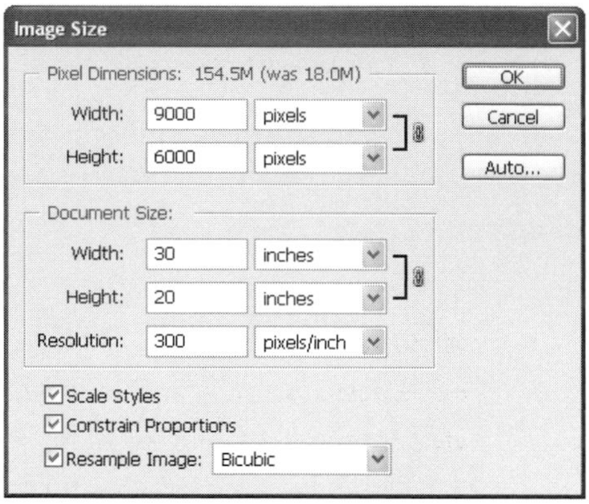

Figure 5.5 Resize the image to the final output dimensions using the Image Size dialog box.

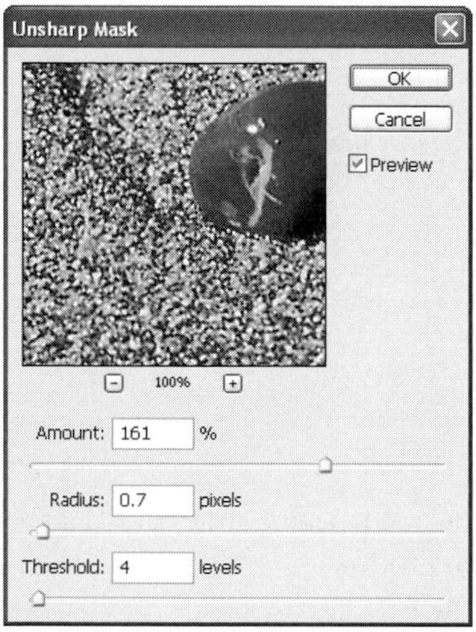

Figure 5.6 The Unsharp Mask filter allows you to exercise great control over the process of sharpening the image. Be sure to discuss optimal sharpening settings with your lab.

Note: In most cases, a print lab will request that you keep the image in your working space, such as Adobe RGB, rather than converting it to the output profile. However, discuss this issue with your print lab to see what they recommend.

6. Save the image. In most cases, you'll want to save the image in the TIFF format without any layers. Some labs may request that no compression be used on the file, including the lossless LZW compression available for TIFF files.

7. Copy the image to an appropriate media format for delivery. In most cases this will be a CD, and DVD may be a possibility. Again, discuss this issue with your print lab to confirm the media types they'll be able to read. In some cases, you may even be able to upload the image directly to the print lab's server using a high-speed Internet connection.

Editing from the Proof

If the print lab you are working with offers a proof print, this provides an additional opportunity to fine-tune the image file to produce the best output possible. If you've followed an appropriate workflow (with a calibrated monitor), you should be happy with the image on your monitor, which introduces a challenge when you want to adjust the final output based on the proof. If you aren't using an appropriate workflow, a proof print you're unhappy with should convince you it is time to get your color management house in order.

The first step in dealing with a less-than-perfect proof when you are using a color-managed workflow is to contact the lab and ask them why they feel the print doesn't match your image file. Explain the process you're using for color management, and be sure you understand the process they are using. Try to determine, with their help, where the weak link is. If the lab is using a calibrated monitor (as they should be) to view and process the image, ask them to review the image to confirm the accuracy of the colors (to the extent they are able). Chances are they don't have a proof print on hand, because they sent it to you. You may need to send the proof print back to the lab with an explanation of your concerns. If they are nearby, we recommend taking the proof print to them and comparing it to the image on their monitor. Then discuss with the lab what is wrong with the print and what solutions are available for getting more accurate results. In some cases, the problem with the print may simply be representative of a limitation of the output process. It may also point to less-than-accurate profiles, improper file handling, poor calibration of the printer, or other issues. Discuss the results with the lab to find a solution. Also, be sure you have adjusted the image using a calibrated monitor with appropriate soft proof settings.

As a last resort, you could modify the file on your own computer and resubmit it, but this isn't something we recommend because you would be chasing the print and producing an inaccurate image file based on your calibrated monitor. Instead, ask the print lab what options are available for correcting the print. With most print processes, they'll have control over the final output, and they can fine-tune it based on your feedback.

In most cases, you'll find the output is very accurate if you are using a proper color-managed workflow. When a print doesn't impress, contact the lab and discuss solutions. This is a perfect example of the importance of a good working relationship with your print lab, so you can effectively solve problems when they surface, resulting in the best prints possible from your images.

Using Online Print Services

Online print services provide an alternative to making your own prints or having a local "brick and mortar" print lab prepare them for you (although many local print labs now offer online services as well). Besides offering convenience and potential cost savings, online print services typically offer a wide variety of specialty print items, allowing you to quickly and easily produce gifts and other items for sharing your favorite pictures. They are geared toward "snapshot" prints rather than those you'll have matted and framed to hang on a wall.

Chapter Contents

Why Online?

An online print service is a business that offers prints from digital images, with an online interface available on the Web. You can visit their website, upload images using a user-friendly interface, and order prints of your favorite images (see Figure 6.1). Most even offer specialty items with your images on them, such as t-shirts, mugs, mousepads, calendars, and other items that make great gifts and excellent promotional items for photographers.

Figure 6.1 Online print services provide a convenient way to obtain prints of your favorite images to share with family and friends. (Photograph by Chris Greene, ImageWest Photography)

You may be asking yourself why you should even consider an online print service. After all, you certainly can't exercise the degree of control you're able to achieve when producing your own prints, and you can't really expect the attention to detail and quality you could otherwise obtain when using a specialized print lab. Using an online print service could represent a compromise in quality, but that's a little beside the point, as these online print services aren't trying to compete with the alternatives we've already discussed in previous chapters. An online print service isn't the best choice when you are looking for the best quality. However, we prefer to think of these services not as having a disadvantage when compared to other alternatives, but rather as offering different advantages.

We consider the most significant advantage of using an online print service to be convenience. Any hour of the day, any day of the week, you can get online and add images to your collection, place an order for prints, or review the status of an existing order (see Figure 6.2). You can stay at home in your pajamas, order prints of your favorite images, and have them delivered to your door in just a few days. You can also share image galleries in online albums, so that friends and relatives can also view the images, or even order prints for themselves.

Figure 6.2 The biggest benefit of using an online print service is convenience. You can order prints any time of the day or night from your own home.

Competitive pricing is another advantage of online print services. Prints can be purchased at prices competitive with or below what you would otherwise pay for prints at a traditional lab. The specialty items offered at most online print services are also very reasonably priced, offering creative ways to share images without breaking the bank. As online printing becomes more popular, the various services are competing to win you as a customer. This competition helps ensure that quality services are offered at the best possible prices, as the sites work to maintain customer loyalty.

Speed is another reason to choose an online print service for some of your printing. If you've ever tried to produce a batch of 4×6 prints from a vacation or special event, perhaps making duplicate prints to share with friends or family, you can appreciate how much effort is involved. You need to prepare each image for printing, and then actually print a large number of images. If you want to save money on printing, you'll want to print multiple images to larger sheets, and then cut those images down to size. Producing such prints in any volume can be very time consuming. You might be able to buy the materials for less than it would cost to have the prints made at an online print service (although we doubt it), but you'll also need to invest considerably more time into the process. By contrast, ordering a batch of images from an online print service can be done very quickly. Upload your images, choose the ones you want, set size and quantity options, and place your order. In a few days, the prints will arrive at your door. You'll have high-quality prints at a reasonable price and without putting significant time into the process.

Do-It-Yourself Convenience

Although it doesn't match the convenience of ordering photos from home in your pajamas, another excellent alternative can be found at many local camera shops and convenience stores. Kiosks at these locations allow you to insert a media card from your digital camera and review your photos. You can then order prints of your images and even apply creative treatments or quick fixes to the images.

The major advantage of using such a kiosk is that you are able to get the prints almost immediately. With some kiosks, the images are printed immediately, so you can have your images in minutes. In other cases, the images are printed elsewhere, with prints ready in about an hour. At the end of the process, you can burn a CD of your images so you have them safely stored and are ready to use the media card again for more pictures. The CD can then be used in the future for ordering additional prints.

These kiosks are a great solution for those looking to replace the film experience when using a digital camera, but who want to exercise greater control than is possible when having film processed at a local lab. For those who don't know how to transfer images onto the computer and then upload them to an online photo service, kiosks offer a solution.

An Author's Experience

Many of the advantages of using online print services presented in this chapter were experienced firsthand by Tim. When his wife Lisa gave birth to their daughter, the digital photos accumulated very quickly. Of course, Lisa wanted to get prints of those images to assemble albums and scrapbooks, but she isn't a "computer person" and couldn't make her own prints. Tim found it very difficult to find the time in his busy schedule to sit down and produce dozens (OK, hundreds) of prints. This, of course, frustrated Lisa. She even threatened to start using a film camera so she could easily get prints processed at the local drug store.

This served as a wake-up call for Tim, and he quickly set up an account on Shutterfly. All he had to do was upload the best images, and show Lisa how to log in and order prints. A few days later, a huge box of prints showed up in the mail. The quality was great, the speed was wonderful, and Tim was off the hook. They were convinced that when you're looking for snapshot prints, an online print service is the perfect solution.

Of course, Lisa soon figured out you could order t-shirts, coffee mugs, mini-albums, calendars, and other gift items emblazoned with a favorite photo. Gift buying for friends and family suddenly became a fun and creative process.

Ease-of-use is one of the most attractive benefits for some users, especially if they want to allow other "nondigital" friends or family members to make prints. While you may feel right at home in the digital darkroom, and are able to produce excellent prints from your images (with some help from the first five chapters of this book), other members of your family might not be so comfortable with the process. With an online print service, anyone who is comfortable surfing the Web can order prints.

Online print services allow you to customize your images before ordering prints. Some of the customization is simple optimization, correcting exposure or color problems, repairing red eye, and cropping (see Figure 6.3). These corrections can obviously be performed in photo-editing software, but for novice users the online interface is a simpler approach. In addition to these basic adjustment options, you can often add printed captions, fancy borders, and other effects to the images to help add some creative flair.

Even better, these advantages aren't available only to you. Once you've uploaded images to your account with an online print service, you can usually share a selection of images and invite friends or family to view these images. They can even order their own prints and specialty items. If you have distant friends and family, this provides a wonderful opportunity to share images with them. Doing so can also help you save money, because you can let others pay for their own prints rather than paying for all of them yourself.

Figure 6.3 Online print services allow you to perform a variety of photo-optimization tasks on your images before ordering prints.

Although online print services offer a number of advantages over alternative methods of obtaining prints, that doesn't mean you should use an online print service for every print. We don't consider these services to be a replacement for other options, but rather a supplement to them, filling a specific need for convenience. We wouldn't order an image intended as a fine art display from an online print service because we wouldn't expect the quality to be high enough. However, for snapshot prints and gift items featuring photos, online print services are an excellent choice.

Types of Prints

Most online print services use direct photo printers, which expose traditional photographic papers using lasers or LED lights. The exposed paper is then processed using a standard chemical process. Considering the fact that these services tend to be used for "snapshot" printing as opposed to prints you intend to have matted and frame to hang for sale in a gallery, the specific output process needn't be a cause for concern.

> **Note:** Don't get the impression that we consider family snapshots to be unimportant, and that you don't need to worry about longevity for those images. On the contrary, we consider such photos to be the most important. However, longevity tends to be more of a concern for images that will be displayed in a gallery and sold than for snapshots that will stay in an album.

In most cases, an online service won't emphasize what type of print processing they are using. If you really want to find out what process they use, you may need to dig deep on their website (typically in the help section) or contact their customer service department. All of the online print services we're familiar with use print processes that result in longevity of a couple decades or more with excellent photographic quality. When stored in dark storage—which is often the case for the types of images you would have printed online—the prints will last even longer.

The primary print type offered by online print services is the standard glossy print we've all become familiar with from local film processing labs. The standard size is a 4"×6" snapshot, but you can also order other sizes including wallet, 5"×7", 8"×10", and other custom sizes. In other words, these online print services have very much matched the traditional film-processing lab for digital images.

> **Note:** Most of the services offered by online print services are also available at a growing number of local photo shops and labs, as discussed in Chapter 5, "Choosing the Output and Print Lab." If you aren't online, prefer to support local businesses, or simply prefer person-to-person dealings, look for a local option for digital printing that offers similar services to those offered by online print services.

Specialty Items

One of the most fun aspects of using an online print service is the wide range of specialty items available, all with an image imprinted on them (see Figure 6.4). Frankly, some of these items will seem pretty corny to anyone who thinks of them as media for fine art photography—but that would be missing the point. T-shirts, coffee mugs, and the like are intended to portray and share people and events; the images are just a means to an end. Although the specific items available from each online photo service vary, the following items are offered by most of these services:

- **T-shirts.** What better way to celebrate your daughter's graduation than to wear a photograph of it around town? The t-shirts offered by online print services provide better longevity and durability than you can achieve with inkjet-printable iron-on transfer material. The price is also very reasonable, costing not much more than you would otherwise spend to purchase a shirt and the materials to iron on the image yourself.

- **Coffee Mugs.** Remind the gang how much fun that fishing trip was by sending everyone a coffee mug with their picture on it. This is an excellent example of a creative project you couldn't really do on your own.

- **Mouse Pads.** You probably don't spend much time looking at your mouse pad, but no doubt you spend a lot of time at your computer, and you know others who do as well. Having a mouse pad with a memorable photo on it can provide an opportunity to escape from your work and deadlines for a few moments.

- **Calendars.** Creating your own calendar allows you to share images all year round. Whether it's family photos, images of your pet, or some of your best artistic images, calendars are a great way to display your images, and they make a great gifts for family and friends. If you've ever dreamed of having your images published in a calendar, this is your chance to make it happen yourself.

- **Greeting Cards.** For any special occasion, a custom photo-greeting card is a great way to share your feelings with a great photo. Rather than going to a store and trying to pick out the card that has the most appropriate image and message for the occasion and person you're giving it to, you can create your own cards with the perfect image and your own text.

- **Photo Albums.** Some online print services offer special photo albums, often spiral bound into a small book. These are typically produced from the same type of print available for snapshots, spiral bound together. However, in most cases you can customize the presentation of the images, including your own caption on each page. This is a great way to create pocket-sized album you can easily carry with you, give as a gift, or use as a casual portfolio of your favorite images.

- **Posters.** For those who believe bigger is better, a large poster print might be just the thing. These extra-large prints are produced with relatively thin paper, as you would normally expect for posters, and result in a very reasonable price for a very large image. They can be a great way to create a large casual image on the wall, or to display an image at a special event such as a birthday party.

Figure 6.4 The specialty items available from many online photo services provide fun-filled ways to share your favorite images.

> **Note:** Keep in mind that you can further customize all of these specialty print items by creating your own artistic image using your photo-editing software. You aren't limited to sending only images right out of the camera. You can also create artistic variations, collages, or other creative departures from the typical image.

How It Works

As we mentioned earlier in this chapter, one of the major advantages of using an online print service is that it is very easy even for inexperienced users to order prints. Although each service has its own specific interface process, the basic steps are as follows:

1. Create an account, provide your personal information, and include a mailing address for the prints you'll order. Most sites also have you provide credit card information up front, which helps to streamline the order process later. Having a personal account allows you to password-protect your images so you don't have to worry about unauthorized users viewing or ordering prints from your images. Note that all of the major online print services utilize secured servers to keep your credit card information safe.

2. Upload images to your online album so they can be printed. Most sites provide a simple interface, even incorporating drag-and-drop support so you can select images on your computer and drag them into an area of the browser window to automatically start the upload process (see Figure 6.5). Most services can accept any image file format (TIF, JPEG, etc.) except RAW, which you aren't likely to use for this purpose anyway.

3. Optimize the images using the available tools. This can include rotating, cropping, adding special borders or text captions, and using other enhancements.

4. Select the images you'd like to print, and add them to your order using the appropriate option.

5. Set the quantity and sizing for each image you are ordering, or select the specialty items to have an image printed on (see Figure 6.6).

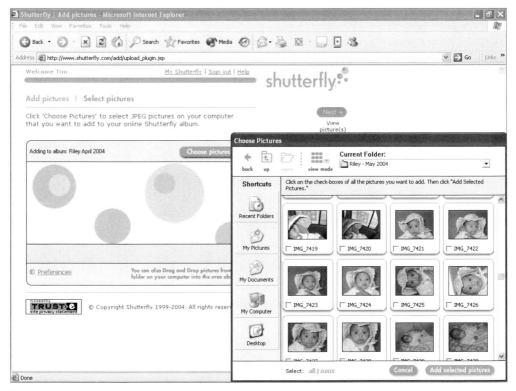

Figure 6.5 Convenient drag-and-drop interfaces make it easy to upload images to an online photo service.

Figure 6.6 You can customize the quantity and size for each image in your order.

6. Complete your order, filling out any additional details for shipping or payment options.

7. Wait a few days for the prints and specialty items to be delivered to your door.

Once you've gone through the process a few times, you'll be comfortable using the interface, and you will be able to quickly and easily upload your latest images and place an order for prints or specialty items.

Choosing a Service

If you compare the various options available at the different online print services, you'll find there are more similarities than differences. Quite honestly, no matter which service you choose, we expect you'll find the experience fun and simple, and you'll probably be happy with the resulting prints. When trying to decide on a specific print service, consider the following issues:

- **Price.** Although the prices offered by each of the online print services are subject to change at any time, price is certainly a factor you'll want to consider. Besides the basic price of particular prints and specialty items, review shipping charges and any other fees that may apply to your orders. Many services offer special bulk pricing, which result can lower the cost per print if you pay for a set number of prints up front.

- **Selection of Specialty Items.** Even if you only plan to purchase prints of your images, at some point we think you'll want to try out the specialty items available from most online print services. They are fun to create and even more fun to share. The greater the variety of options available from a particular print service, the happier you're likely to be in the long run.

- **Ease of Use.** Whether you're a novice or a computer expert, the easier it is to upload and order your images, the better. Look for a service that offers an automated way to upload your images, such as a simple drag-and-drop option. Many online print services offer a small number of free prints as an incentive to establish an account. Taking advantage of such an offer from several different services provides a perfect opportunity to test each one without obligation and decide which works best for you.

- **Sharing Options.** If you enjoy ordering prints and specialty items, you know your friends and family will also enjoy the opportunity. Sites that offer sharing options make it easy for you to make images available to others by invitation only. Your visitors can then purchase their own prints, so you don't have to handle the process yourself. This is a wonderful way to share family photos with distant relatives. Note, however, that in some cases you won't be able to link to the photo-sharing site from other websites.

As you're trying to decide on a specific online print service, we recommend considering some of the well-established services with a reputation for providing excellent quality and service at reasonable prices. The two we recommend the most are Shutterfly (www.shutterfly.com) and Kodak's Ofoto service (www.ofoto.com). Others you might want to explore include Snapfish (www.snapfish.com), Sony ImageStation (www.imagestation.com), and WalMart's Photo Center (www.walmart.com).

Printing Your Own Book

If you like the specialty items available from many of the online print services, you'll probably love the opportunity to produce your own photo book. Many photographers have dreamed of having their images published in a book, and with the cost efficiency of digital printing, that is now possible at prices that won't break the bank.

Several online services allow you to assemble your own book to be printed. One of the most popular is MyPublisher (www.mypublisher.com). You won't have the flexibility of a typical page-layout program, but you'll be able to assemble a hardbound photo book with a basic layout, suitable for sharing images in a fun, yet professional manner (see Figure 6.7). Starting packages for a 20-page book are often available for around $20. Specific pricing and volume discounts will vary. MyPublisher is for Windows users only, but Macintosh users can obtain the same printing capabilities with iPhoto, as discussed later in this section.

Figure 6.7 Producing a hardbound book featuring your photos is an excellent way to share your images.

In the case of MyPublisher, the process of creating a book is relatively simple, and it isn't much more complicated than creating specialty printing items with an online print service. One significant difference is that the book is not created online. Instead, you will need to download their BookMaker software, which you can use to import images into a book project and then adjust the layout and captions for the images.

The following basic steps can be used to create your own book using the Book-Maker software from MyPublisher:

1. Launch the BookMaker software.

2. Navigate to the folder where you've saved your images using the folder view on the left side of the window.

3. On the right side of the window, select the images you'd like to include in your book project.

4. Drag the selected images to the bottom bar in the window, which holds the images currently included in the project (see Figure 6.8).

5. Click the Organize button at the bottom of the window. Drag and drop the images to change the order you would like them to appear in the book (see Figure 6.9). If you want to remove an image from the project, click the small X button at the top-right corner of the thumbnail.

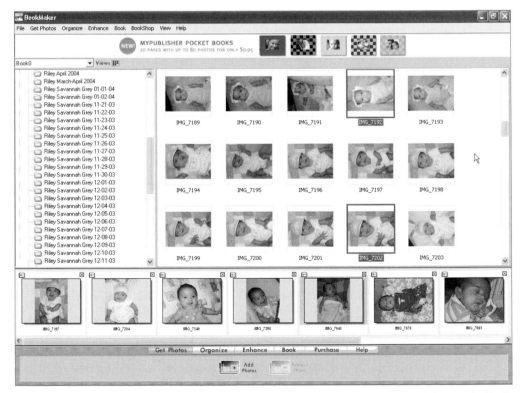

Figure 6.8 Using the browser interface in the BookMaker software, you can select the images you'd like to include in your final book. (Image courtesy of MyPublisher.com.)

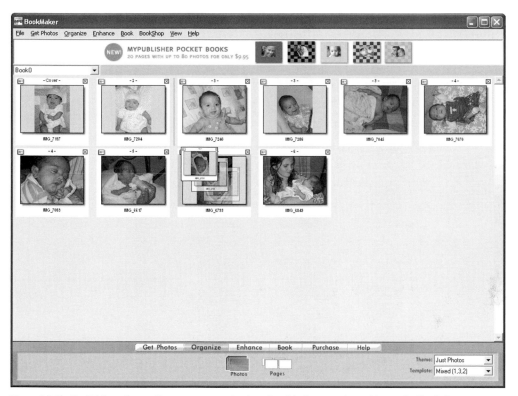

Figure 6.9 The BookMaker software allows you to customize the order of the images to be used in your final book. (Image courtesy of MyPublisher.com.)

6. If you would like to fine-tune any of the images, click the Enhance button or double-click on the thumbnail for the image. You can then use the tools available at the bottom of the window to optimize the images, although these are relatively limited.

7. Click the Book button at the bottom of the window. This will display the book layout options (see Figure 6.10). Along the top, you can change the way you want to view the page layouts. The left side of the window includes all of the images you have selected for the project; the right side shows you the available layout options for pages, and the bottom provides a thumbnail preview of all the pages so you can select the page you want to work on. The center area of the window shows a large preview of the currently active page. This is where you are able to add text and captions to your pages.

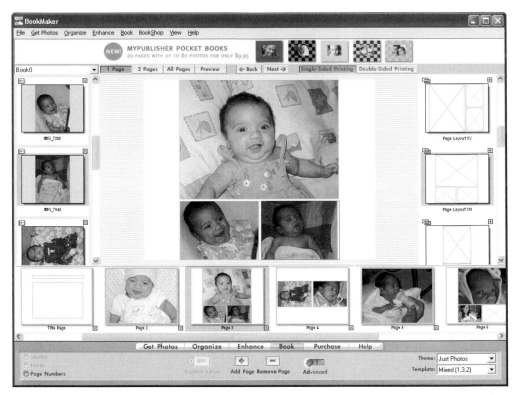

Figure 6.10 The Book options in BookMaker allow you to adjust the layout for each page within your book. (Image courtesy of MyPublisher.com.)

8. You can adjust the overall layout for the book by changing the Theme option in the bottom-right corner. You can also specify the number of images you want on a page, with fixed values or with mixed options that provide some variation in the overall appearance of the book.

9. For each page, you can change the layout by double-clicking on one of the options on the right side of the window. The images included on each page will change based on the options selected.

10. When you're happy with the layout of your book, click the Purchase button. This will take you through the step-by-step process of establishing an account with MyPublisher (or logging in if you already have an account) and placing an order for the book you've created.

Macintosh users have an even easier method of creating an online book using iPhoto at the same pricing structure. Start with an existing album of images (or create a new one), and iPhoto can automatically create an album for you. Select from a variety of themes, which define the style and layout of the book. You can then customize the book with captions, titles, comments, and page numbers. When you've finalized the layout, you can order automatically through iPhoto, and your books will arrive in a few days.

The quality of the books available from these services won't rival the high-quality you enjoy with the best photo books; however, the price is quite reasonable. This is a great way to produce an attractive bound book as a way to share your images with friends or family, or to use as a portfolio of your images to share with prospective clients. If you've always dreamed of having your images published in a photo book, these services offer an excellent way to achieve that dream.

Displaying Images on the Web

The Internet has changed the way many photographers do business. We now have a global market for our work to be seen and enjoyed by others. Although many books are available on web design, many of the guidelines they offer do not apply to photographers. As photographers, we are all about visual impact. After all, photography is a recording of our vision. This section of the book will guide you through the process of planning your website to accomplish the goals you have for it, making it easier for others to find you on the Web, setting it up, and maintaining a fresh look that will keep visitors coming back.

Planning Your Site

Having a website certainly increases the exposure to our work. Many photographers now have a means to be seen and to sell their work. However, for every successful photography site on the Web, there are countless others that fail due to poor planning. Careful planning for your website will improve its chance of success—just as it does when you're shooting an assignment.

7

What Do You Want Your Site to Accomplish?

Why have your own website? Because you want as many people as possible to see your work. Other chapters in this book help you create the best possible print or slideshow, but the number of people exposed to your photographs through those media is limited. When you have a website, you have a potential audience of millions.

If you simply want to share your images with friends or family, you don't need your own site (or this chapter). One of the many photo-sharing websites, such as Yahoo!, MSN, AOL, and Ofoto, or Apple's HomePage product (for Macintosh users) will meet your needs. However, if you're a professional who wants to sell photographs or promote your business, you will probably find it hard to resist the lure of the Internet with its worldwide audience of viewers and buyers and its 24-hour-a-day availability. Even if you are just a serious amateur who wants your work to be seen by anyone interested in photography (or in the subject matter of your photographs), you might determine that creating your own website is well worth the effort.

Before taking the plunge into the world of website creation and management, you need to consider some basic points. First and foremost, you need to know what you want from a website. Are you looking for a new venue to share your love of photography on a worldwide stage, or are you planning to set up a store front for your studio? (If you're planning to sell anything on your site, you'll need to provide a way for visitors to place orders, and you'll need a secure way for them to pay you. Fortunately, you don't need to build those capabilities yourself; the Internet provides ready-made tools for your site, and you'll learn about them in Chapter 8, "Going Live.")

For a professional photographer, your website is your resume and your portfolio, and it needs to show your work in the best possible light (pardon the pun). You'll want to select your best work, and you'll want to optimize the images for the Web's sRGB color space. (Chapter 2, "Preparing the Image," shows how to do that.) In addition, you may want the "look and feel" of your site to reflect the character of your photography practice. Potential clients for a wedding or portrait photographer, for example, may find that a formal, elegant site design looks appropriate for the occasion.

Once you've decided on the goals for your website, you'll need to take the time to do some careful preparation: deciding where you will host your site, deciding on the navigation and the overall look and feel for your online showcase, and selecting and preparing your photographs.

Realistic Expectations

Establishing your presence on the Web is relatively easy, but building, promoting, and maintaining your website will take time and effort. Don't expect your new site to generate hundreds or thousands of visitors a day (or week, or month) initially. By the same token, you shouldn't allow yourself to become discouraged either. With proper planning, and content that appeals to your intended audience, you'll begin to build traffic and customers, as the Fred Miranda site shown here has done (`www.fredmiranda.com`).

Note: Many sites use hit counters to show how popular they are. If your site has a lot of visitor traffic, a hit counter can look pretty impressive. When you're starting out though, a hit counter showing a few dozen or even a hundred hits is not going to work in your favor (of course, you can fake this by setting the starting number at some arbitrary number). Unless you want to track how many visitors your website is attracting, we suggest that you not use hit counters. FrontPage includes several styles of hit counters, and there are hundreds more available on the Internet.

Choosing a Domain Name and Host for Your Site

The first decisions you'll need to make when planning your site are what name to use for it, how you want people to find it, and where it will be hosted. With many hosting and naming services, you'll make these decisions as part of the same registration process.

The name you give your site is known in Internet-speak as its *domain name*. This name isn't important to the computers on the Internet; they identify each other by a number (for example, 207.46.195.2) known as an Internet Protocol (IP) address. However, your site name is important to people looking for your photography, because it's how they will find you. Most photographers, especially commercial photographers, will want to register a domain name for themselves or their business. Choosing your own name lends a professional feeling to your website and improves your "hits" in search engines. For example, our domain names are www.joncanfield.com and www.timgrey.com. (If your own name isn't recognizable, an alternative might be a short phrase describing your work, whether that's gothic fantasies, documenting local wildlife, or whatever. These short phrases, or *keywords,* are special text upon which search engines will perform a search.) No matter what name you choose for your site, it needs to be registered with the Domain Name System (DNS) before it can be used. Registration associates your name with a unique IP address. By registering a domain, you are leasing the name and the right to assign that name to a specific address, making it easy for visitors to find your website. Many companies provide this service, and frequently they will also host your site.

A website *host* is, ultimately, the server computer where the files that make up the site are stored and that your visitors' browser software connects to when they visit your site. Nearly all individuals and smaller businesses prefer to let someone else—an Internet Service Provider (ISP)—handle the details of hosting. Your host ISP may or may not also allow you to register your own domain name. If your ISP allows personal domain naming, this may be the most affordable approach, as service providers typically give their subscribers a set amount of storage space.

If you decide to go with the package provided by your ISP and they do not provide for personalized domain naming, you will likely have a less obvious path to your website, such as www.myprovider.com/~mywebsite. Unless you have no other option, we strongly recommend registering and using your own personalized domain name. You will project a much more professional image, and you will likely have more control over layout and features for your website. A multitude of services is available for both registering a domain and hosting your website. We recommend www.register.com and www.mydomain.com as two of the better services available.

What to Look for in a Hosting Service

Almost all hosting services provide the basic functionality you'll want for your website, especially as you start out. Just make sure the host you select offers services that will allow your site to expand. What should you look for?

Customer support Most large hosting services have 24/7 support available. We can't stress the need for support enough. When you need it, you need it now, not two to three days from now.

Connection speed Your hosting service should have fast connections to the Internet. T1, T3, and fiber optic support faster transfer speeds, which is very important for the visually rich websites that photographers have.

Web-based administration Administration tools that run on the Web are great for getting site statistics such as usage, most-used keywords, and, perhaps most importantly, information that helps you see where your visitors are coming from.

E-mail forwarding E-mail aliases help to give you a more professional look. Aliases are multiple e-mail accounts that are all forwarded to one address. For instance, Jon has e-mail aliases for orders@joncanfield.com and info@joncanfield.com. Mail sent to these addresses are forwarded to his main account, jon@joncanfield.com.

Private scripting folder Scripts are commonly used for form data such as order forms, feedback forms, etc. If your selected host doesn't provide for scripting, you may find that you can't take orders online. Perl, PHP, and ASP.NET are the most popular scripting options. Server programming is beyond the scope of this book. However, for those who are interested in learning more, two excellent sources for programming web applications are *Creating Interactive Websites with PHP and Web Services* by Eric Rosebrock (Sybex, 2004) and *Developing Killer Web Apps with Dreamweaver MX and C#* by Chuck White (Sybex, 2004).

Secure server support for shopping carts If you want to sell online directly from your website, Secure Sockets Layer (SSL) will allow your users to safely provide payment information. SSL works by encrypting the information sent. If you don't want to handle transactions yourself, services such as PayPal (www.paypal.com) are available for your buyers to use.

FrontPage server extensions These are important only if you plan to use Microsoft FrontPage automation features known as web components or *bots*. Bots are commonly used to help create navigation bars and photo albums, but they are not required when you run FrontPage. If you don't intend to use bots, the server extensions are not important.

Regular backups Any reputable hosting service will perform regular backups and have these backups available should you need to restore your website for some reason.

Your ISP may offer registration and hosting services; but if not, you can use Google (www.google.com) to look for a registrar and hosting service. With our checklist in hand, search on "domain registration" for a service that meets your needs and budget.

The Registration Process

Once you've chosen a domain name and a hosting service, you're ready to register your name. You may want to do this even before you design and build the site, so that no one else takes the name. While each registration service will have a different look to their registration forms, the overall steps are the same regardless of which registrar you select. We'll be using Register.com for our examples. In your browser, navigate to www.register.com. The first step is to search for the availability of the name you'd like to register.

Note: The number of available top-level domains, or *extensions*, has gone up tremendously in an effort to better organize and expand the number of domain names available. The most common extensions are .com, .net, and .org. In the early days of the Internet, .com was created to identify a for profit business. The .org top-level domain was created mainly for nonprofit organizations, and .net was used mainly by individuals. Today there is a bewildering array of extensions. While you can select any of the available options, you'll have better results in most search engines by staying with the .com, .net, or .org extension. To give your website the most professional appearance possible, try to use a .com extension.

Let's go through the steps to register your domain.

1. Enter the name, and choose the extension on which you want to search.
2. You may find that your initial choice of name is already taken. If so, you have a several options. You can modify your selected name, select one of the alternative names shown, or you can select your original name with an alternative extension if it is available.

Note: Be aware that visitors can be misdirected to the wrong website (sometimes with very unpleasant results) by mistyping an unusual spelling or a very similar name to yours. Search for similar names before you register your domain.

3. Your next step is to select the type of service you want. You can choose to only register the domain name, but then you will still need another service to do the hosting. For most users, having the registrar also host your website makes the most sense. Most registration services offer website hosting for an additional fee. These fees vary depending on the amount of disk space you need, and the amount of traffic (or bandwidth) you expect. As an example, at the time of this writing, MyDomain.com offers hosting packages starting with 5MB of storage space and 200MB per month of bandwidth with no e-mail account. At the high end, you can have 200MB of storage and 10GB of bandwidth, along with e-mail accounts, and support for PHP, a popular web programming extension. As the options go up, so do the costs.

    When you're just starting out, bandwidth isn't a huge concern. However, as the number of site visitors increases, and the content you have available grows, bandwidth quickly adds up. Check with your chosen ISP to make sure you can upgrade your package when the need arises.

4. After selecting your name and extension, you'll need to set up the administrative contact information. The administrative contact is typically yourself. If you want to have someone else act as the technical contact, you'll be able to add that information later. The technical contact or "organizational contact" will have the ability to make changes, such as the host server address and contact information, to your domain information. For most photographers getting started on the Web, the administrative contact and technical contact will be the same person.

5. After confirming your contact information, you'll need to select how long you want to reserve your domain. Most services charge a standard yearly fee with a two-year minimum registration, although some services will register your domain on a month-to-month basis and usually charge a premium to do so. Enter your payment information and confirm the request. You'll receive a confirmation e-mail at the address provided in the Administrative Contact form. This confirmation will include a summary of the information and, most importantly, the IP address that will uniquely identify your website on the Internet.

Note: The name and extension you select are actually just "friendly names" that allow users to find your website without typing in the IP address. Remembering www.photofinishbook.com is much easier than remembering 255.255.255.0.

Congratulations! You've just taken a major step toward showing and selling your photographs around the world.

Choosing Your Tools

Another important decision to make when planning your website is how you will build it. You need to decide which of the many web-authoring tools best meets your needs. Way back in the mid 1990s, web authors built pages and sites by specifying every aspect of their appearance and function in HyperText Markup Language (HTML). They used text editors such as Windows Notepad and Macintosh SimpleText. Even in its simplest form, HTML is cumbersome to read and write, and we don't recommend it—especially for first-time web authors. Today many programs are available to assist with creating a website, and this section covers some of our favorites. Besides web-authoring software, your toolkit will include programs for editing images, for managing and organizing image files, and for creating photo galleries. (The last two capabilities are available through image editors, but there are also programs that specialize in them.)

Website Design Applications

Just as no one camera system is right for every photographer, personal preferences will play a big part in the program you choose for web design. Many programs are on the market, but Dreamweaver MX 2004 and FrontPage 2003 have the largest user bases. If you're just starting out in web design, the ability to find templates, in-depth books, and an active support community online for these two applications will be a great asset to you.

Dreamweaver MX 2004

Macromedia Dreamweaver MX 2004 (www.macromedia.com/software/dreamweaver, about $500) is perhaps the most popular web-creation product available, and it works on both the Macintosh and Windows systems (except for Windows ME). We'll be using Dreamweaver MX 2004 for most of our examples throughout this part of the book. As you can see in Figure 7.1, Dreamweaver MX is a full-featured product with integrated graphics, page layout, link checking, source control, and file upload tools. The latest version has increased support for CSS and better browser-compatibility checking. Dreamweaver MX is from the developer of Flash, the standard application for animation development on the Web, and it offers excellent integration with Flash MX. Because of its cross-platform support and excellent selection of tools, this is the program we recommend and use.

FrontPage 2003

Microsoft FrontPage 2003 (www.microsoft.com/office/frontpage/howtobuy/default.mspx) is only available for Windows-based systems at about $200. It is a very popular and easy-to-use web-creation program. Some of the most useful features in FrontPage are its web *components*, programs that handle special features such as hit counters and navigation bars. Also known as bots, these components are helpers that handle more complex tasks for you. For example, the Photo Gallery web component handles the layout, page generation, and thumbnail creation with several built-in options. As you can see in Figure 7.2, creating a photo gallery with it is very easy, but you are limited to the features provided. Although using the Photo Gallery is an easy and effective way to implement complex features, it does limit the customization of your website. Some web components, such as the hit counter, require that your host provider have the FrontPage extensions running on their server. FrontPage is one of the easiest web-creation tools to learn, especially for the novice.

Figure 7.1 Macromedia Dreamweaver MX 2004 is a powerful and easy-to-use website creation tool.

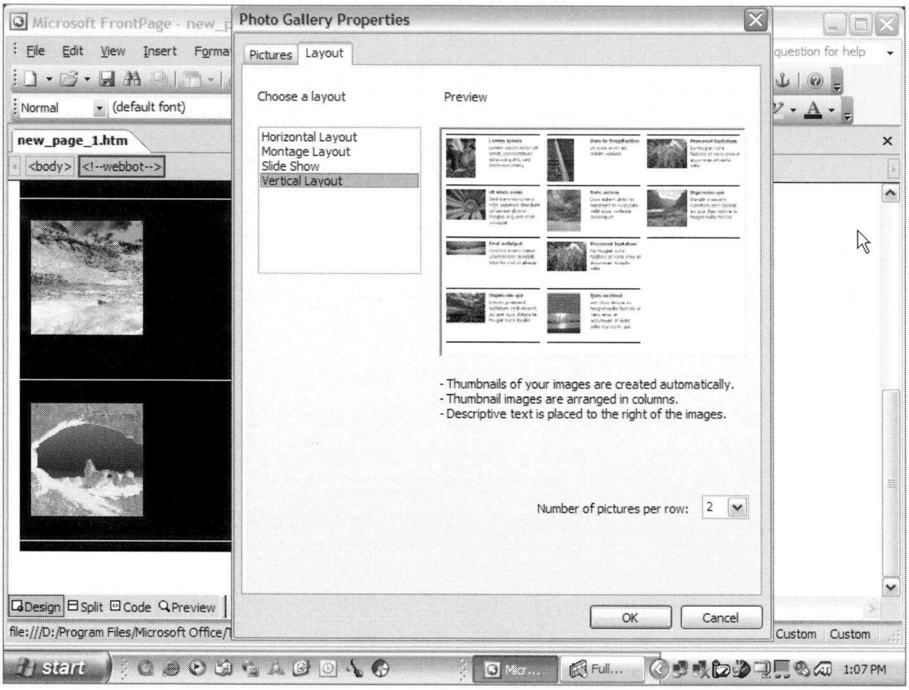

Figure 7.2 Microsoft FrontPage 2003 uses web components or *bots* to automate complex features, as shown in the Photo Gallery Wizard

A Brief HTML Primer

Hypertext Markup Language, or HTML, is the language of the Web. When you use a web-authoring tool like Dreamweaver, the software generates HTML code, just as if you had written it manually. So even if you never write HTML yourself, you may want to learn something about it.

The features and capabilities have grown immensely over the past few years; but at its heart, HTML is still just text that consists of tags, or commands, and content. The sample below shows the most basic page possible, the venerable Hello World! example.

```
<html>

<head>

<title>Hello World!</title>

</head>


<body>
```

Continues

```
<p>Hello World!</p>

</body>

</html>
```

To break this down into plain language, let's examine each element:

<   All HTML tags begin and end with these brackets. Everything between < and > is considered part of the command.

<html>   This tag tells the browser that everything that follows is HTML.

<head>   The head section of a page contains special information that will not be displayed on the page. Page title, keywords for searching, and style sheet information all go into the head.

<title> Hello World!</title>   This tag instructs the web browser to use Hello World! in the title bar of the browser. </title> ends the tag, and </head> ends all the header information.

</   This tells the browser that a command is ending. For example, </title> means the end of the title tag.

<body>   The content on your page is placed between the <body> and </body> tags. In our example, the content consists of a paragraph, <p>, and the text "Hello World!"

<p> and </p>   are paragraph start and end tags.

Our sample page ends with </body> and </html>.

Leaving out any of these closing tags will usually provide interesting, but unwanted formatting side effects.

If we save this file as hello.htm and open it in our browser, the words "Hello World!" will appear in the browser title bar. The browser also shows Hello World! in the content area. That was quite a bit of work for two very lonely words, and you can see why HTML editors and web-design tools have become so indispensable. Here's another example that simply creates a link to another website:

```
<a href="http://www.timgrey.com/">Tim Grey's Site</a> -Home page of
world famous author and speaker Tim Grey<br>
```

As you can see, while it's not difficult to understand, HTML requires quite a bit of formatting and special indicators to work properly. That's why even people who are fluent with HTML or programming often use one of the full-featured web-creation programs for at least some of their work.

If you decide to learn more about HTML, programs like Dreamweaver and Frontpage offer a feature, known as *code view*, that can help. Designed to let skilled programmers make changes quickly, code view also lets newcomers open a page and see what's happening in the background. This example shows both views of the same page.

Continues

A Brief HTML Primer *(Continued)*

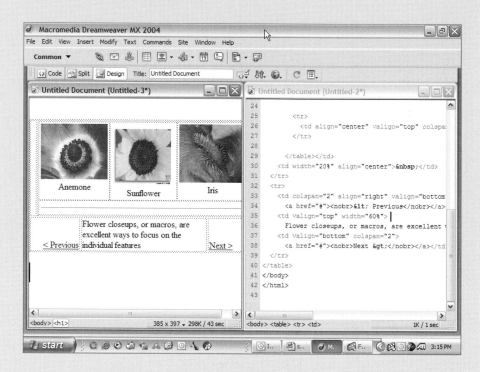

Of course, to learn HTML you should use code view only as a supplement to a good reference guide. Sybex publishes *Mastering HTML and XHTML* by Deborah S. Ray and Eric J. Ray (2002), as well as the compilation *HTML Complete* (Third edition, 2003). Another good choice is *HTML 4 for the World Wide Web: Visual QuickStart Guide* by Elizabeth Castro.

Here's a preview of some elements of HTML that we'll discuss in this chapter and the next:

Cascading Style Sheets (CSS)   A form of HTML coding designed to ensure consistent-looking pages throughout a website. A style sheet is a set of definitions for how different page elements will be handled, and *cascading* means that definitions created for one page can be inherited by other pages. By defining a style, or description, of a page element in one location, every page that uses that element will automatically use the same format. As with other HTML features, you don't need to write CSS code yourself; it can be generated by web-authoring tools such as Dreamweaver and FrontPage.

Frames   A feature of HTML that divides the screen into separate areas that function independently, allowing the web designer to present multiple documents in a single window. However, you'll see that frames have some significant disadvantages, and we don't recommend them for most sites.

Alt text   Text descriptions of graphics, originally conceived as an "alternative" for browsers that can't display them. For photography sites, the main advantage of Alt text is that using it with link buttons can improve your site's placement in search engines.

Image Editing and Web Graphics Applications

Image-editing tools aren't just for creating websites, of course, and you probably worked with at least one before you decided to display your photographs on the Web. Chapter 2 briefly discusses this type of software in the context of preparing your photographs for print. Here we'll take a quick look at their web capabilities.

You'll find programs to fit every budget and skill level, but the products from Adobe Systems have set the standard for quality output and features, and we highly recommended them.

Photoshop/ImageReady CS and Photoshop Elements 2

There may be no shortage of choices in this area, but the integration between Adobe Photoshop and ImageReady (www.adobe.com/products/photoshop, about $650) makes this combo the tool of choice for many photographers, including us. Many of the most popular photography websites used this combination to design their pages, as shown in Figure 7.3. We can use Photoshop's tools to create graphic elements such as logos, navigation bars, and buttons, and then we can import them into ImageReady to convert them into webpage elements such as buttons with roll-over effects. After you prepare your images in Photoshop, ImageReady will also break your image files into smaller pieces, or "slices," that load quickly (and are more difficult for viewers to copy without your consent). Perhaps the most important features of Photoshop for web use are the image optimization features. Setting screen resolution, file size, and color space are all major parts of the work involved with a photography-oriented website.

Photoshop is the standard to which every other image editing program is compared. The program is extremely powerful and yet can be used by novices with a bit of instruction. Photoshop has a number of plug-ins, or extensions, that increase its usability and feature set. Some of these plug-ins are designed specifically with photographers in mind. You'll find links to some of our favorites on the companion website, www.photofinishbook.com. Photoshop CS is available for Windows and Macintosh.

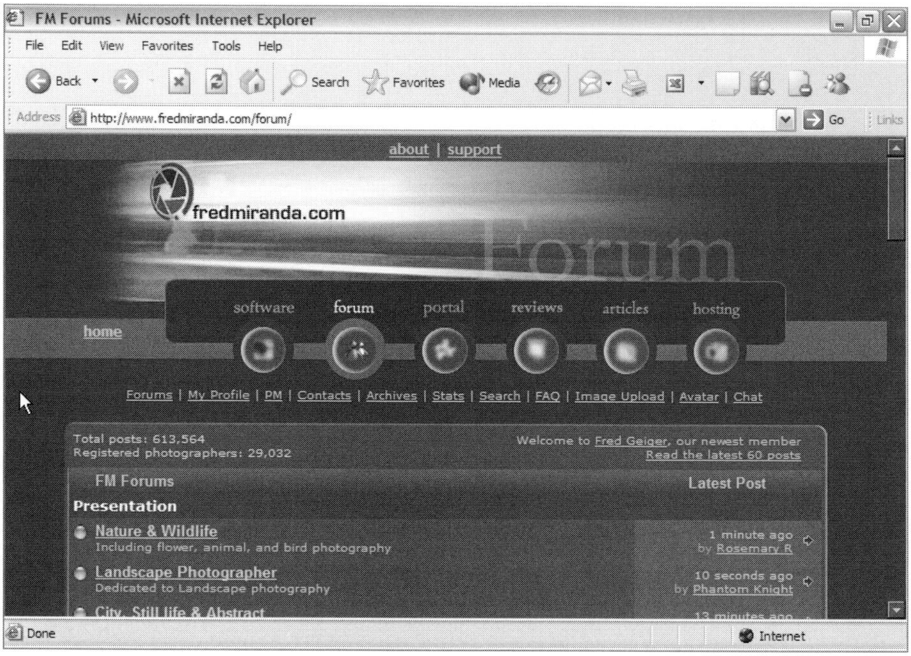

Figure 7.3 Photoshop can be used to create a graphically rich web page design, which can then be converted in ImageReady for web use. The home page for photographer Fred Miranda (www.fredmiranda.com) shows what you can achieve.

Photoshop Elements 2 (www.adobe.com/products/photoshopel, about $100) is a good alternative for those on a budget, or those just starting out with image editing. It has most of the features of Photoshop, while presenting them in a more user friendly way. Like Photoshop, Elements is available for both Windows and Macintosh systems.

Paint Shop Pro 8

Paint Shop Pro 8 (www.jasc.com/products/paintshoppro, about $100) is perhaps the second most popular image-editing program. Originally designed to be an easy-to-use graphics application at an affordable price, Paint Shop Pro has grown into a very powerful application that competes with Photoshop in many areas. Paint Shop Pro is easier to learn than Photoshop, and most Photoshop plug-ins work with it. The biggest drawback to Paint Shop Pro, and the one that keeps us from recommending it, is its weak support for color management. Still, if you are on a budget, or Paint Shop Pro was bundled with your new computer, this is a worthwhile alternative to the Adobe product.

Image Browser and Web Gallery Programs

Two more essential features for the digital photographer going online are an image browser and organizer and the ability to easily create a gallery display of your images. As your collection of images grows into the hundreds and thousands, you'll need some sort of organizational tool to organize and find them. Photoshop CS and Photoshop Elements 2 both have a built-in image browser that may be perfect for your needs, and most authoring and editing programs include built-in HTML photo gallery tools.

If you need more options or control over your images, the following programs will do an excellent job.

ACDSee

ACDSee 6.0.3 (www.acdsystems.com/english/products/acdsee/index, about $50) has a very strong organizational component, and a very well designed user interface. (A less robust version, ACDSee 1.6 for Mac, is available for Mac OS X users for around $40) With ACDSee, you can create categories for your images, perform basic photo editing and resizing, and create presentations in several forms—including slideshows and web photo galleries. Figure 7.4 shows the HTML Album Generator Wizard.

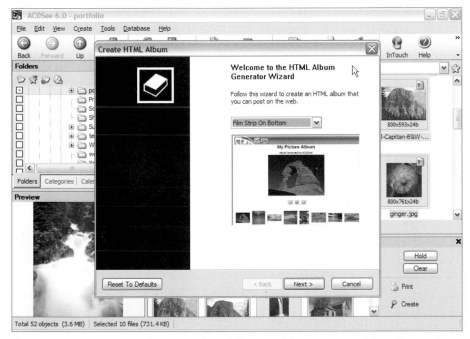

Figure 7.4 ACDSee is a full-featured application that includes image editing, organizing, and photo album creation.

BreezeBrowser

BreezeBrowser (www.breezebrowser.com, about $50), a Windows-only product from Breeze Systems, is a very popular application for managing digital photographs, especially with Canon photographers because of its support for the RAW files produced by Canon digital cameras. It uses Canon's own raw conversion process for the highest possible image quality. The image management features are powerful, making it easy to use for selecting images to keep or delete, as well as quickly making slideshows. You can also use it to create web galleries with thumbnails and photo pages as seen in Figure 7.5. A number of readily customizable templates, including templates for PayPal shopping cart links, are included with the program.

JAlbum

JAlbum (www.datadosen.se/jalbum, free) does one thing, and it does it very well. It creates photo galleries. For this reason and because its free, it is one of the most popular photo gallery tools available. You can quickly generate high-quality thumbnails and gallery pages using the supplied templates, or *skins,* as shown in Figure 7.6. Many other skins and excellent instructions for those interested in creating customized skins are available online.

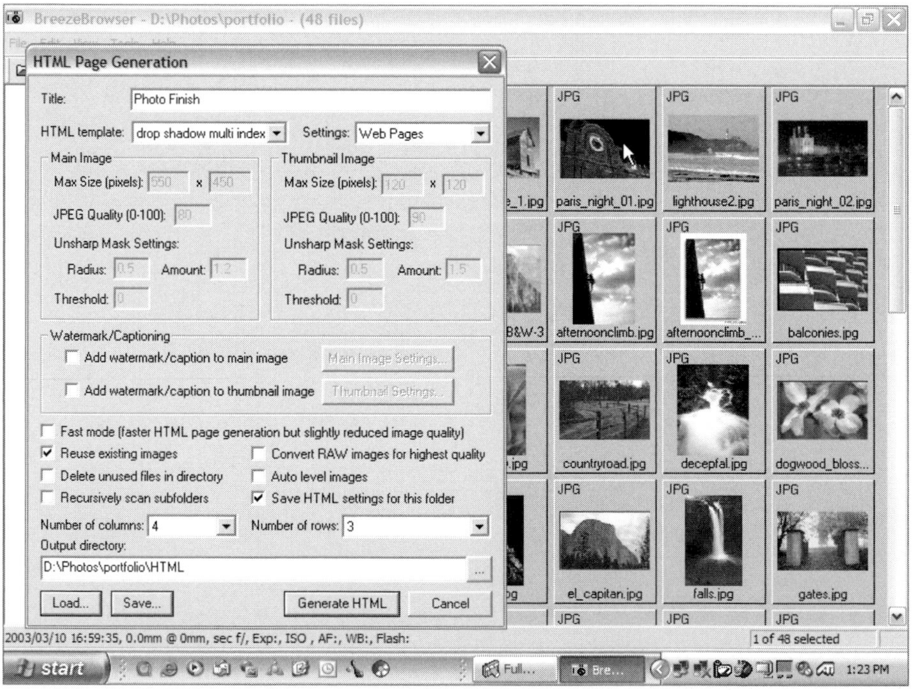

Figure 7.5 BreezeBrowser is a popular tool for editing and organizing images, and it has a very good thumbnail and photo gallery creation tool that can be customized.

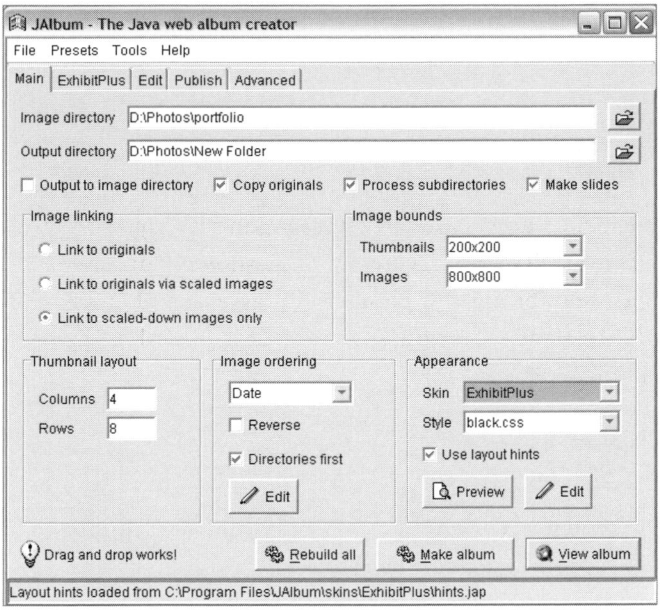

Figure 7.6 JAlbum is one of the best photo gallery creation tools available. It works on Macintosh and Windows, and it's free!

iView Media Pro

iView Media Pro (`www.iview-multimedia.com`, about $160) is available for both Macintosh and Windows. Although more expensive than many of the other options in this category, iView Media Pro has an impressive feature set including slideshow creation, image editing, full color management support, and full scripting support. Like ACDSee and BreezeBrowser, iView organizes your images and supports a very robust web photo gallery option. One feature of iView Media Pro that we find particularly nice is its ability to automatically update your website periodically through AppleScript.

Although iView Media 1.3 is significantly less expensive, we feel that the added functionality in the iView Media Pro, larger catalogs, support for digital camera RAW format files, scripting, customizable HTML output, and basic editing features, makes it the better choice. Figure 7.7 shows the Web Photo Gallery Creation Wizard.

Lightbox

Lightbox (`www.lightboxsoftware.com`, about $25) is another alternative for Macintosh users. Lightbox offers strong image management features along with basic HTML gallery creation, slideshows, and file conversion. Lightbox also features excellent integration with Apple's iLife suite of applications.

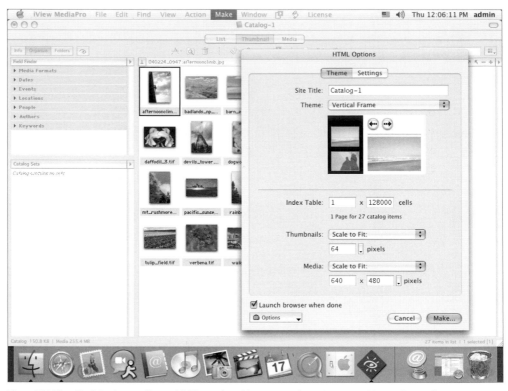

Figure 7.7 iView MediaPro has excellent publishing tools and is a very popular option among Macintosh users for image management and photo gallery creation. (Screenshots of iView Media and iView MediaPro are provided courtesy of iView Multimedia Ltd. London, UK. www.iview-multimedia.com)

Planning Site Organization and Design

Before dragging that first photograph into your website, you need to spend time thinking about what you want to tell the world. At the beginning of this chapter, we noted that the first step in planning your website is to determine the purpose of your site—is it to sell stock, sell prints, attract people for tours, give information, or simply show off your work? Knowing what you want the site to accomplish will enable you to design how the site will function and how it will look. Both aspects of planning are equally important. Think of your website as a visual resume. You want to encourage people to explore your pages and give them a reason to come back again. That means you need to offer content that visitors want, you need to present that content attractively and appropriately, and you also need to make it easy for visitors to get around your site. That last point is easy to lose sight of; however, the biggest problem most people have with their website is poor planning and construction. By thinking through design and navigation before you create your pages, you'll have a website that reflects your true message. Time spent planning your website up front will turn into time and frustration saved later.

The first step in planning the look of your website is to determine your message. What is it you're trying to convey to visitors to your site? Are you a portrait or commercial photographer? If so, you want to use a more formal and professional presentation that showcases past work and that illustrates what makes you unique in your field. On the other hand, a nature photographer will probably want to take on a less formal appearance with a website that conveys their special interest, such as landscape, architecture, birds, or flowers. Your choices of fonts, background colors, imagery, and other design elements will all contribute to the "look and feel" of your site. The color section includes examples of both formal and informal approaches.

Planning the Organization

Before designing the look of your site, you need to plan its organization—what the individual pages will be and how they will connect to each other (the site *navigation*). Because your site will consist of files stored on a server, you also need to plan the folder structure for those files.

Most websites contain similar elements. All websites contain a home page. The home page is the starting point for all websites, and it is the first page viewers see when they visit your website. Most photographers will also have several galleries of images, organized by subject, location, or style. Beyond that, you may want to include a page about yourself, perhaps a contact page for e-mail comments and ordering information, and a links page for other websites you want to share with visitors.

Perhaps the best place to start is with an old-fashioned but reliable method— paper and pencil. Sketching your planned website on paper can really help you see potential problems, such as image pages that are unreachable or a gallery thumbnail page with no link back to the home page, before you spend too much time creating and changing the actual site. Figure 7.8 shows an example.

The Navigation Map

As you sketch your website, using an outline or flow chart to visualize your website navigation may help you plan how the pages of your site will link to each other. Some pages might connect only to the home page; others will lead forward from general categories to specific items and back. You might also want "sideways" connections between, for example, a Weddings gallery and a Senior portraits gallery.

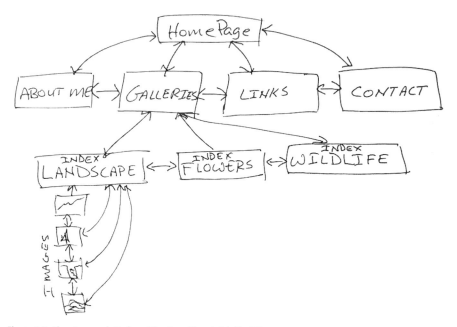

Figure 7.8 Planning a website layout begins with a sketch like this.

Planning where the connections will go is only part of setting up site navigation; you also need to design and implement the links that site visitors will use to make the connections. The "Ease of Navigation" section later in this chapter looks at that aspect.

The Folder Structure

The structure of folders and files that make up your site will be very similar to the navigation layout you sketched earlier. At the top, or root, level of your website, will be your home page (typically, this is named `default.htm` or `index.html`) and an images folder that should contain all of the graphics used throughout the website, such as logos, navigation bar graphics, and buttons. If your site includes features that require scripting, you may have a cgi-bin folder or scripts folder at the root level as well (depending on your host provider). One difference between the folder structure and navigational layout is that additional folders for our main areas, which in navigation follow from the home page, would also begin at the root level. Figure 7.9 shows an example using Jon's website.

As you can see, all of the main pages are at the root level of the website. The Galleries folder contains a subfolder for each gallery of photographs, and each of those subfolders contains the index page for that gallery along with a thumbnail folder and the actual images.

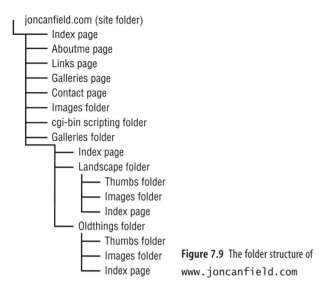

```
joncanfield.com (site folder)
    ├── Index page
    ├── Aboutme page
    ├── Links page
    ├── Galleries page
    ├── Contact page
    ├── Images folder
    ├── cgi-bin scripting folder
    └── Galleries folder
            ├── Index page
            ├── Landscape folder
            │       ├── Thumbs folder
            │       ├── Images folder
            │       └── Index page
            └── Oldthings folder
                    ├── Thumbs folder
                    ├── Images folder
                    └── Index page
```

Figure 7.9 The folder structure of
`www.joncanfield.com`

Note: Always include an `index.htm` or `default.htm` page in each of your gallery folders. Why? If someone types the gallery name (for example `http://www.joncanfield.com/galleries/landscape`), it will automatically load if you've included an `index.htm` page. Without this, viewers will see a "You are not authorized to view this page" error message.

You'll find that maintaining your website will be much easier if you keep your images separate from their thumbnails. If you use any sort of photo gallery creation software, this is usually done automatically. If you're creating your gallery manually with tables, selecting the thumbnail for the index page is easier when they are stored in their own directory.

Planning the Design

The old adage about first impressions is doubly important on the Web: you may get only one chance to impress a visitor to your website. Again, the design of your site includes both its appearance and its functionality. Simple layout, logical consistent placement of navigation controls, and a common color scheme are all critical elements to a successful website. The catch is that visitors won't notice these things if you're successful; only if you're not. The focus of your site should be your photography, not your web-authoring skills. However, if your site is hard to navigate, or your choice of fonts is jarringly inappropriate, visitors may never even see your photographs.

Some common pitfalls to avoid are listed here:

Slow-loading pages   Large pictures are the main culprit in slow-loading pages. We'll show you how to optimize your photographs for both size and quality in Chapter 9.

Hard-to-read text   Ideally, a page should use only two fonts. A sans serif font for headlines and a serif font for body text. (The companion website www.photofinishbook .com follows this guideline.) Avoid using too many sizes of type and excessively stylized fonts.

Bad color selections   Dark blue text on a black background is hard to read, but a surprising number of websites use that, or similar, combination of background color and text color.

Confusing navigation   Links are meant to be seen and clicked. A common style and location will keep visitors focused on your content, not on how to get away. Using more than one navigation style is fine and, in fact, we recommend using multiple styles. A common use of multiple navigation styles is shown later in this chapter when we create a template page. The important thing is to stay consistent in similar areas.

If you've followed our advice about sketching your website before you start building it, you're already well on your way to a professional and functional website.

Frames or No Frames?

One of the major design choices we need to make is whether or not to use *frames*, a feature of HTML that divides the screen into separate areas that function independently, allowing the web designer to present multiple documents in a single window. In theory, frames are a good organizational tool and help tie related pages together. Many photo galleries are designed with frames, keeping the thumbnail images in one frame and showing the full size image in the adjoining frame. The advantage to this method is that navigation controls and links are not required for the photo page, because all photograph thumbnails are visible regardless of which image is being viewed full size. This method also makes it easy for the viewer to select which image(s) to view larger. Figures 7.10 and 7.11 show examples of photo galleries designed both ways.

Figure 7.10: Here is an example of a photo gallery that uses frames. When a visitor clicks a thumbnail on the left, the full size image is displayed in the right-hand frame.

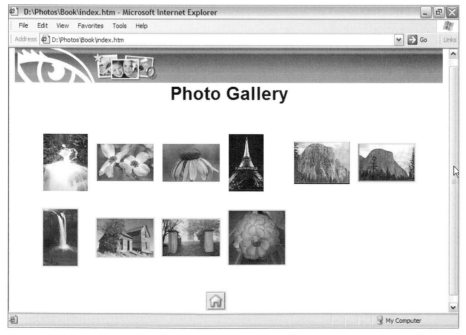

Figure 7.11 A photo gallery that doesn't use frames can be just as compelling and easy to navigate.

Frames are created as *framesets*. A frameset is a master page that contains other pages. For example, in a photo gallery, a frameset would have one frame that showed the thumbnail index page. The other frame would show individual photos by loading a page with the full-size image when you clicked the thumbnail.

Frame-based websites do have their problems, though. Because of the way framesets work, linking to a page is more difficult when it is displayed in a frame. This is a problem because some search engines might not find your page, and it may be harder for other people to link to you.

Note: Keywords and links to your site are the secrets to improving your placement in search engines. We'll cover keyword strategies in Chapter 9.

Another problem with framesets is that not all browsers handle them the same way. Users with older browsers may not see any content in a frame-based page. This is less of a problem than in the past, but it is something to consider. Finally, frame-based pages are more difficult to maintain. It's very easy to have a page show up in the wrong frame or in a completely different window, which ruins your careful layout. For the new web author, we advise against using frames when you first start out because of the difficulty in managing them. As your experience level grows, switching to a frame-based layout can be done fairly easily in Dreamweaver or FrontPage.

If you decide to use frames, the major web-authoring programs have tools for creating them. In FrontPage, for example, you can choose between various frame-page templates.

Effective Photo Galleries

Galleries are the most important content on a photography site. The most effective photo galleries are those that contain a limited number of related images. By keeping the number of images per gallery to no more than 20, you accomplish two things. First, your thumbnail page will load faster, which is especially important for visitors with slower connections. Most people won't wait for a slow page to load. Second, too many images on a page detract from the quality of all the images. A gallery with 20 outstanding images will have more impact than one with 40 images of the same quality. Some photographers feel the need to display every image in their collection, but many visitors will tire of page after page of image thumbnails. We've found that by keeping the number of photographs in a gallery at 20 or less, each photo tends to be viewed, and updates to the gallery are more apparent to returning visitors. Rotating your photographs in and out of your online gallery keeps your website fresh and interesting.

> **Note:** By restricting the number of photographs in each gallery, you force yourself to give each image a critical evaluation. Does the photograph truly represent your finest work? Does it fit well with the other photographs in the gallery?

There are times when a large number of images are required. For instance, a website featuring event photography might have several hundred images. Keeping them down to a manageable size is still important to enable visitors to find the images they want without having to wade through countless others first. Breaking the images down to galleries by name, subject, or sports team is an effective way to present large numbers of photographs while maintaining an easy to browse website.

The first page a visitor should see in each gallery is the index, or thumbnails of all the images in the gallery. A common method of displaying thumbnails is through the use of tables. HTML tables are similar to cells in a spreadsheet. They allow you to quickly create a uniform layout for your content and give you a great deal of control over spacing, background color, and borders. Tables have been used since the early days of HTML to position elements on a page, and almost all the HTML gallery tools listed earlier use the table for their pages.

Ease of Navigation

Ease of navigation is important for your visitors. Few things are more frustrating than trying to find your way around a poorly designed website. At a minimum, you should have a navigation bar on all your main pages that includes a link back to your home page. Here are some guidelines that will help you design an effective navigation scheme:

Fonts   Regardless of the link style, use a basic, easy-to-read font for your links. A sans serif font is usually the best choice.

White space   No, you don't need to use the color white. We're talking about the open space between links and other elements on the page such as text and graphics. Giving your navigation links some white space makes them stand out more, and it makes them easier to click.

Consistent placement   Your navigation links should be consistent in appearance and location on all pages. Continuity helps the user navigate more easily and keeps attention on page content. Depending on your design, navigation can be as simple as page names with hyperlinks or as complex as popup or dropdown menus, as shown in Figures 7.12 and 7.13.

Ease of movement   Unless your design uses popup windows, all image pages should link to the previous and next image, along with the index page for all galleries to allow your visitors to easily move from one gallery to another.

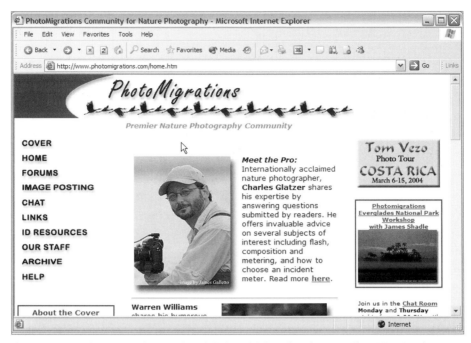

Figure 7.12 A simple navigation bar using hyperlinked text labels, such as this one on Photo Migrations (www
.photomigrations.com), provides a clean look and may be just right for your website.

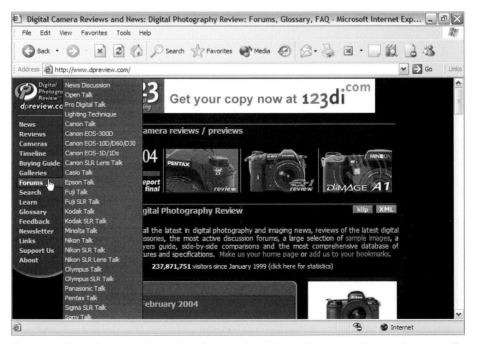

Figure 7.13 Menu style navigation bars, such as the one used on DPReview (www.dpreview.com), are an excellent
choice when you have many options or screen space is at a premium.

Alternative Text and Navigation Links

Navigation buttons can play a role in improving your site's placement in search engines, a topic you'll learn more about in Chapter 9. That's because these buttons link to page URLs, and the more links to a URL a search engine finds, the higher it will place the site in a results list. However, most search engines do not index the text in a button because it's stored as part of a graphic. Fortunately, HTML provides the `alt` element to include a text description for any graphic, and you can use this feature to ensure that search engines find your buttons and other graphics.

The `alt` element was originally included in HTML because not all browsers supported graphics. Additionally, many people with slower dial-up connections turn off graphics display to speed up page loading times. While browsers still support turning off graphics, for a photographic website, we shouldn't worry about this for obvious reasons. Web editors, such as Dreamweaver MX, make it easy to include `alt` text when you create links from buttons, and you'll do that in Chapter 9.

Navigating within Galleries

Within a photo gallery, providing links to all of the main pages of the site is not important. Depending on the style of gallery you choose, navigation may be as simple as Previous Image and Next Image buttons or text links. You want people to explore and enjoy your photographs, so make it easy for them to view individual images and return to the gallery index.

Figures 7.14 and 7.15 show examples of effective gallery navigation. Note the difference between gallery navigation and the examples shown in Figures 7.12 and 7.13.

Establishing the "Look"

Along with your unique vision as a photographer, the look of your website will help you stand out from the crowd. Your website should be a reflection of both you and your photography.

Ready-Made Templates

If you're a great photographer but not much of a graphic artist or designer, you'll immediately recognize the value of templates. Like other kinds of templates, web templates are essentially patterns for molding content into a given form. Like document templates, they may also provide some of the content. Web templates typically set background colors or patterns, navigation bars, buttons, text styles and colors, etc. A template gives all the pages of a site a uniform look, and it allows you to add new pages without designing them from scratch. We've included several template designs on the companion website (www.photofinishbook.com) along with links to collections of templates. Both Dreamweaver MX and FrontPage come with a selection of templates, and thousands more are available online.

Figure 7.14 Navigation in a photo gallery can be as simple as using Previous and Next links along with a link to the gallery index.

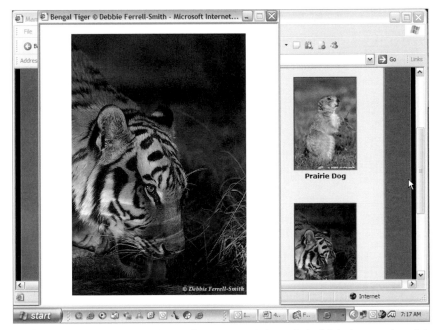

Figure 7.15 Nature photographer Debbie Ferrell uses a popup window to display full size images on her website (`http://www.dfsphoto.com`). By showing each photograph in a new window, a Close button or simple mouse click is all that is needed for navigation. Using Popup windows such as this is also a good way to make it difficult for viewers to copy your images.

Templates can be great timesavers and typically provide a complete website skeleton that you will modify with your personal information. Some templates are completely customizable, and others limit the extent of change you can make. When shopping around for a template, be sure to look into the restrictions on use. For example, we've seen some very nicely done photo gallery templates that limit you to a total of 20 photographs. If you want to expand beyond that, you need to contact the developer and pay an additional fee for adding more gallery pages. Given the number of templates available for Dreamweaver and FrontPage, we see no reason to lock yourself into a design that is so restricted in use.

Although FrontPage and Dreamweaver both come with templates, many of them—particularly those with FrontPage—are not suitable for photographers (or most professionals for that matter). When you want to go beyond the basics, it's time to point your browser to some of the template collection sites. Of the many available, we've found that TemplateMonster (`www.templatemonster.com`) and The Template Store (`www.thetemplate-store.com`) are among the most comprehensive sites around. For Dreamweaver users, a stop at `www.dreamweaver-templates.org` will provide you with links to many other template sites. FrontPage users should be sure to visit both `www.frontpageworld.com` and `www.frontpage-templates-themes.com`. You'll find these links and more available on our companion website.

Using a Ready-Made Template

If you just want a quick way to share your photographs with others and aren't concerned with selling yourself or promoting your photography business, the somewhat generic look of a ready-made template may be perfectly acceptable. If that's the case, creating a page or a whole site from a built-in template in FrontPage or Dreamweaver is extremely easy; many of the templates include wizards that walk you through the information you need to provide.

Creating Your Own Template Pages

The biggest problem with ready-made templates is just that—they're already made and readily available. Others are using "your" design too. Again, this may be acceptable for a nonprofessional site. But if your site is a business venture, you'll want to give it a unique look.

Fortunately, you can create your own unique template pages quite easily. Although they take more thought and effort, you'll have all the benefit of template-based pages with your own unique look. If you look at a variety of websites, you'll see that many of the most effective and intuitive sites use a similar layout. Typically, this consists of a logo in the upper left of the page, navigation controls down the left side, content to the right of the navigation bar, and locator links at the bottom of the page. This is a design that flows well for viewers and allows them to focus on the content by always keeping common elements in the same location.

By creating and using a template page, you give your website a consistent look for visitors, and cut down on the work required to add pages as your website grows. Let's go through the process of creating a template page using Dreamweaver MX 2004:

1. If you haven't already created a site in Dreamweaver, you will need to follow the prompt on the initial screen to do so. Click Create New – Dreamweaver Site and follow the prompts. This will create a local site. We'll add the information for our remote, or published website, in Chapter 9. Give the site folder the same name as the website (for example, the site folder for www.photofinishbook.com would be named **photofinishbook**) to make it easier to maintain multiple websites in the future.

2. Create a new blank HTML page by selecting File > New. In the New Document dialog, select Basic Page under Category, select HTML Template, and click Create.

3. Select Insert > Table (Ctrl+Alt+T Windows; Cmd+Opt+T Macintosh). In the Table dialog, leave Rows set to the default of 3, and change Columns to 2. Set the Table width to **100**, and select **percent** from the dropdown list and click OK.

4. Click on the vertical separator bar between the left and right cells in the middle of the table and drag to the left until you see 120 below the left column. This sets the width of this column, which will be used for our logo and navigation buttons. Because most of our content will be in the center row, we'll resize it the same way. Click on the horizontal separator bar between Rows 2 and 3, and drag the mouse down until the middle row is about ¾ of the page in height.

5. Click in the upper-left cell to select it.

6. Select Insert > Template Objects > Editable Region (or Ctrl+Alt+V Windows; Cmd+Opt+V Macintosh). Name this region **Logo**. Click OK. In the Properties panel, set the Vertical alignment to Top by selecting it from the Vert dropdown list.

> **Note:** In Dreamweaver, *panels* are the small windows typically displayed at the bottom of the screen (as shown in Figure 7.16) or displayed to the side. The information in a panel changes depending on the current selection on your page.

7. Select the next cell in the first row and repeat Step 6. Name this region **PageTitle**.

8. Repeat steps 6 and 7 for the second row. Name your regions **Navigation** and **Content**. Set the Vertical alignment for both cells to Top by selecting Top from the Vert dropdown list in the Properties panel.

9. Click the right-hand cell in Row 3, and add another editable region named **Footer**.

10. Select the top cell in the right-hand column by clicking the mouse in the cell. Set the alignment for the column to Centered in the Properties panel. Repeat this for the bottom cell in the right-hand column.

Your template page should look very similar to Figure 7.16.

If we were to leave this page as is, every region on the page would be editable. This might be appropriate, especially while designing the website when things tend to change. However, the true value of templates comes into play when you have static items you want to include on every page. In Chapter 9, we'll show you how to customize this template to be used in different areas of the website.

Figure 7.17 shows a template with the elements inserted.

The final step is to save your page. Select File > Save, and save the file as a template. Templates in Dreamweaver use a .dwt extension, and like templates in Microsoft Word, they open as an untitled file to prevent accidental overwriting.

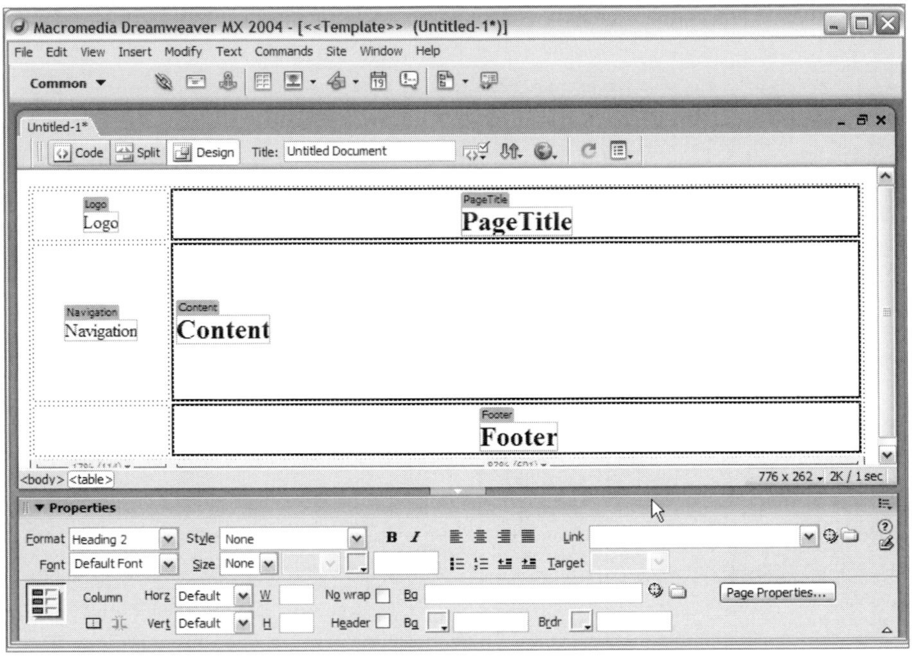

Figure 7.16 The template page in Dreamweaver MX 2004 after creating the table and naming each of the regions

Figure 7.17 Our completed template page

Themes

A *theme* is nothing more than a common look and feel that is used throughout your website. Both Dreamweaver MX and FrontPage offer support for themes, and they can be an effective way for you to have a professional and consistent design throughout your website. Typically, themes use Cascading Style Sheets (CSS) for formatting text, links, and colors. They also include the consistent use of graphic elements to enhance the look of the page.

Color Scheme

The color scheme you select should be based on the style of photography you are presenting and the formality of your website. The background and text color you select will have a major impact on the way your photographs are viewed, so careful consideration should be given to select complementary colors.

Many photography sites use dark backgrounds with great success. Dark colors recede, both in nature and on the screen. Selecting black or dark gray will allow your photography to stand out from the page and give it a stronger feel. This design is well suited for portrait and nature photography, and it goes well with a formal presentation.

Light backgrounds, such as white, make text more readable, but they can compete with the photograph for the viewer's eye. White is an excellent choice for the presentation of black-and-white photographs because the gray tones appear more pronounced, and the blacks that are crucial to a strong image do not blend into the background.

Unless your photo galleries are primarily composed of children or candid work, avoid using bright colors, such as yellow and red for the background.

Color schemes are more than just background colors, but the background will have the largest impact on the rest of your color choices. Text color is the next area upon which to focus. Here again, you want to keep the color consistent and have an easy-to-view contrast from your background. Dark background colors should usually use white or other similar color text, while black or dark blue is a good choice for light backgrounds.

Note: Many people suffer from some degree of red or green color-blindness. Avoid using these colors for important elements of your website.

Using CSS for Consistency

We've mentioned that CSS is a tool for ensuring consistency throughout a site. For example, we can set the style for body text font to be 14-point bold Arial (or Helvetica, or simply sans serif), and all paragraph text on every page that uses the style will use that font. If we later decide to change from Arial to Times New Roman, we only need to change the style description in one place and all of our pages will be updated. Another advantage to CSS is the improved control over the layout of elements on your page. Prior to style sheets, almost all positioning of elements on a page was accomplished by using tables. This is still the most common approach; however, with the advent of CSS, the web designer now has more control over placement through the use of positioning tags.

Both Dreamweaver MX and FrontPage 2003, along with other web authoring tools, provide interactive tools for creating and applying CSS styles in your web pages, so you don't need to write your own HTML. Figure 7.18 shows Dreamweaver's CSS Style Definition dialog box for our Arial example.

CSS can be a great timesaver when used properly. As a general rule, if you want to change the appearance of a page or text on a site-wide basis, CSS is the best way to do so. Changes to an individual paragraph on a single page can be easily done through the formatting commands in the Properties panel.

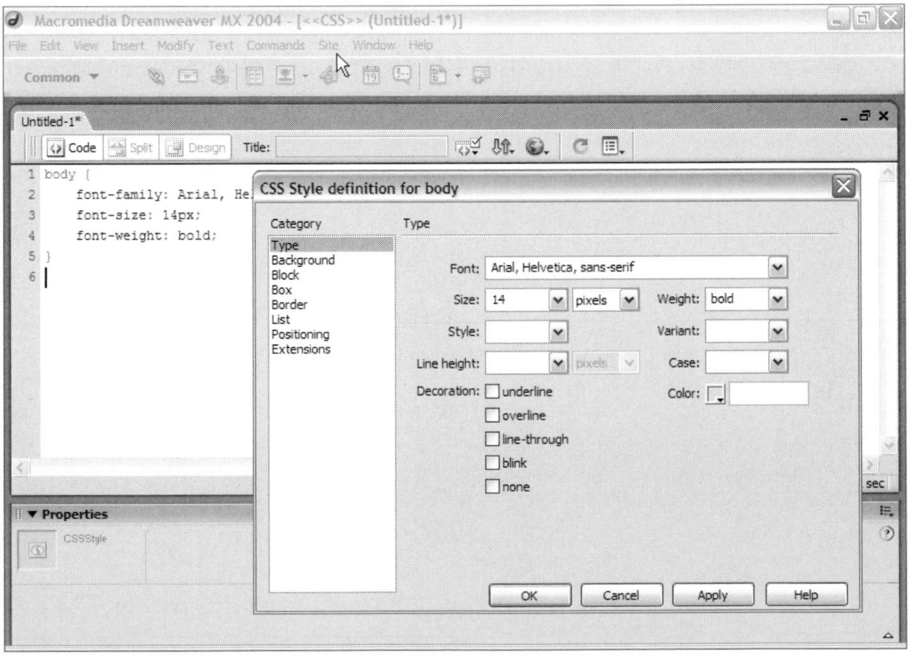

Figure 7.18 Using the CSS style definition dialog in Dreamweaver MX greatly simplifies creating and assigning styles.

CSS behind the Scenes: The HTML

Here's what the HTML generated by Dreamweaver for the settings shown in Figure 7.18 would look like:

```
<style type="text/css">
<!--
body {
    font-family: Arial, Helvetica, sans-serif;
    font-size: 14px;
    font-weight: bold;
}
-->
</style>
```

Let's go through this style line by line to set the default font for our pages:

`<style type="text/css">`   This code tells the browser that everything that follows until the `</style>` end tag is reached should be treated as CSS formatting commands.

`<!--`   This is a comment indicator. Older browsers that don't understand CSS will display all of our formatting commands as plaintext when the page is viewed. By placing a comment tag around the formatting commands, the browser will ignore everything between `<!--` and the closing `-->` tag.

`body {`   This code tells the browser that the following command will affect all normal text on the page.

`font-family: Arial, Helvetica, sans-serif;`   Here, we tell the browser that all default text will be in Arial (Windows), Helvetica (Macintosh), or sans-serif if neither of these fonts is available.

`font-size: 14px;`   This code tells the browser to display all default text in 14 point. (Although HTML uses pixels, most users are familiar with points when talking about font sizes.)

`font-weight: bold;`   This code sets the font to be bold.

The above example changes the body text in every page that uses this stylesheet. In CSS, the attribute is always listed first, followed by the colon (:) and finally the formatting change. We can also change multiple attributes for a tag in one command by separating them with semicolons. When multiple attributes are changed in a single style command, each attribute is separated by a semicolon, and all attributes are contained within curly braces ({}).

CSS does add complexity to the learning curve, and not all browsers fully support CSS. If you're interested in learning more about CSS, both Dreamweaver MX and FrontPage have excellent help files and examples. We also recommend *Cascading Style Sheets: The Designers Edge* by Molly E. Holzschlag (Sybex, 2003).

Using a Consultant

Now that you've seen what goes into creating a website, you may decide that your business needs a more ambitious site design than you have the time to create. If that's the case, as a final option you might want to consider using a design consultant. A consultant will create the complete website. Depending on the features you need implemented, this can run from several hundred dollars to well into the thousands. Another alternative is to consider a service such as Bludomain Multimedia (www.bludomain.com); we've found that Bludomain has some good designs for photographic websites, and their pricing starts at $600. This will buy a predesigned template customized to your needs with logos, contacts, buttons, and photo galleries. Once the design is done, they will upload it to your hosting service for you.

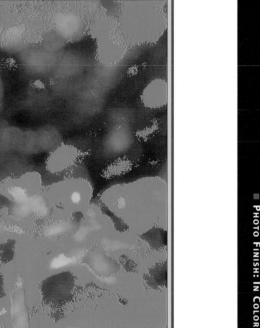

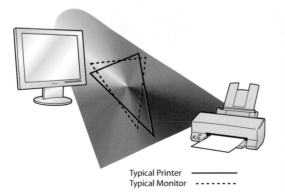

Typical Printer ——————
Typical Monitor - - - - - - - -

TOP: Photoshop's Gamut Warning feature allows you to see which colors in an image can't be reproduced on a particular printer using a specific ink and paper combination, based on a profile for that combination. As a result, you can fine-tune the image to produce the best results within the limitations of your output conditions.

BOTTOM: The color space, or gamut, for a display device such as a projector or monitor is different from that of a printer, making it important to optimize your images for the intended use.

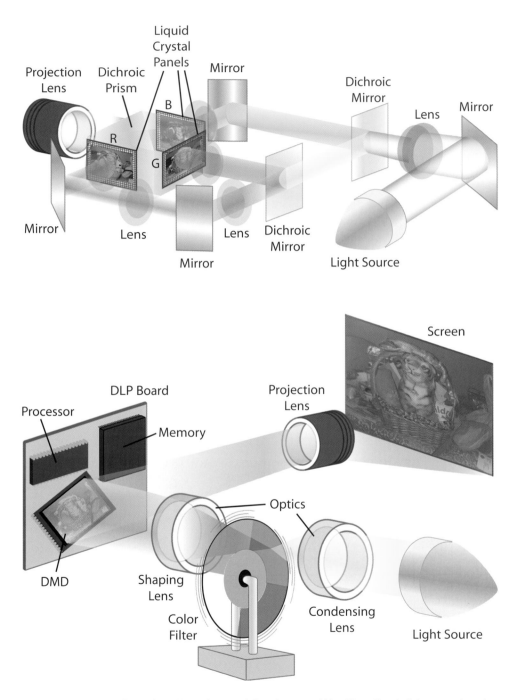

TOP: LCD projectors typically use three LCD panels, one each for red, green, and blue. Filters allow the light to pass through or reflect into each panel depending on their color value. **BOTTOM:** DLP projectors use fewer components than LCDs, making them smaller and lighter. (Images courtesy TI Corporation.)

Creative border treatments are an excellent way to add a unique touch to your images. If the texture and shape of the treatment complements the image, the result is a border that adds to the image rather than competes with it.

TOP: When many images are placed in a frame, they lack the vibrancy many photographers are accustomed to seeing in slides or on monitor displays. **BOTTOM:** An illuminated frame, such as this one from PhotoGlow (www.photoglow.com), brings the image to life.

Selecting the correct compression options for your images can greatly reduce the file size and load times for your visitors. **TOP:** In this version of this image, the file is saved at JPEG quality level 12 and has a file size of 398KB. **BOTTOM:** The same image saved at JPEG quality level 7. The file size is reduced to 113KB, resulting in a image that downloads over three times as fast. Both images are available for comparison on the companion website at www.photofinishbook.com.

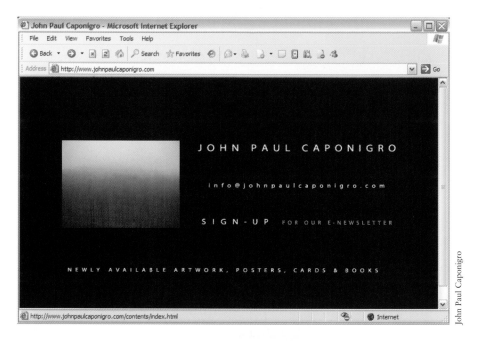

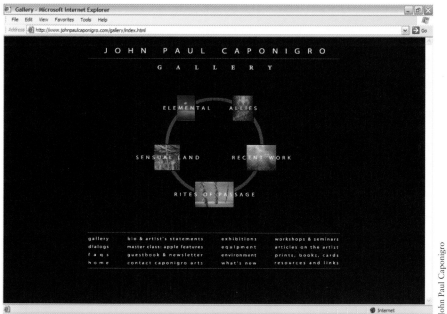

John Paul Caponigro

John Paul Caponigro

Photography websites vary from elegant formal looks to casual inviting designs. **TOP:** The Home page for award winning photographer and instructor John Paul Caponigro's website (www.johnpaulcaponigro.com) is an example of a more formal design. **BOTTOM:** Clicking the Gallery link takes you to a selection of galleries with a unique layout.

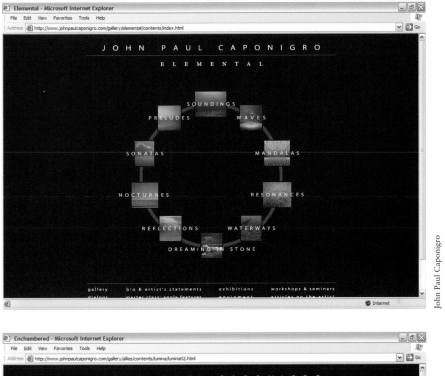

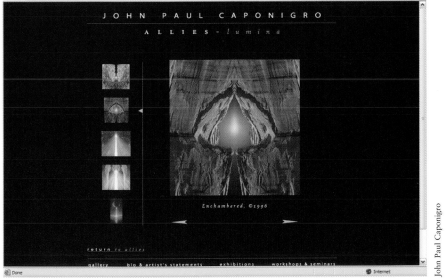

Continuing into the individual galleries on John Paul Caponigro's site, the main theme is repeated for consistency. **TOP:** The index page of the Elementals gallery. **BOTTOM:** Individual images in each gallery are shown, with a scrolling list of thumbnails.

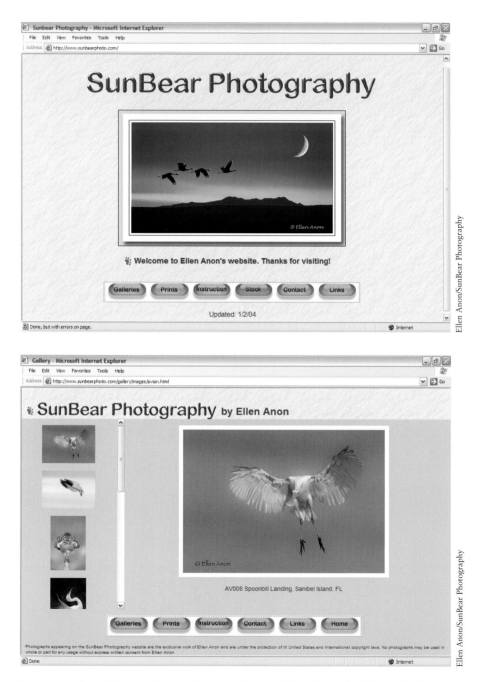

Nature photographer and Photoshop instructor Ellen Anon takes a more informal approach with her website (www.sunbearphoto.com). **TOP:** Using simple clearly visible buttons from the Home page, visitors have clear navigation choices. **BOTTOM:** SunBear Photography uses frames to present thumbnails on the left with the full size image displayed on the right.

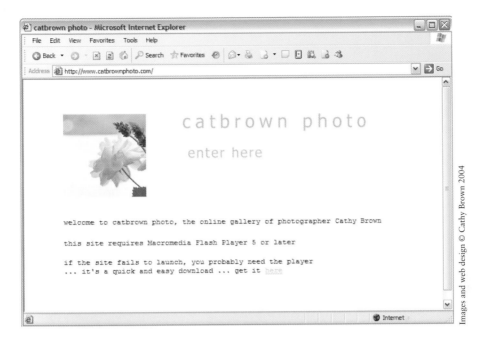

Flash based websites can be effective when they emphasize the photography, not the coding skills of the site designer. **TOP:** Cathy Brown (www.catbrownphoto.com) uses a simple Home page that contains a link to the Flash player if visitors need to install it. **BOTTOM:** The Flash design used by Cathy Brown shows small thumbnails for navigation, or the visitor can click the slideshow button for a full tour of each gallery. Flash provides dropdown menus at the top of the page for easy navigation.

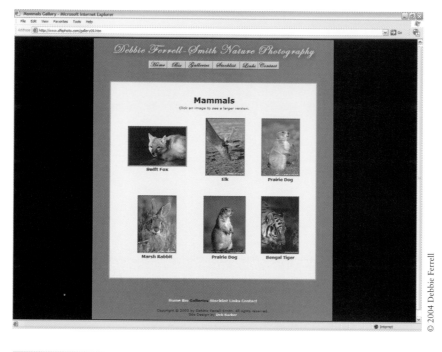

Nature photographer Debbie Ferrell's website (www.dfsphoto.com) uses a clean table layout for her galleries. **TOP:** The index page uses large thumbnails with clear labels. **BOTTOM:** Selecting one of the thumbnails displays the full size image in a popup window, which closes on mouse click.

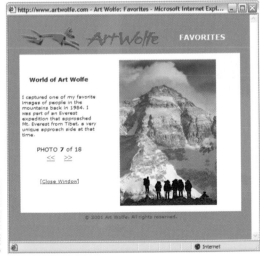

Award winning nature photographer Art Wolfe (www.artwolfe.com) uses a custom shopping cart to allow visitors to purchase images. **TOP LEFT:** The Search page allows visitors to select what type of images to view. Clicking a thumbnail takes the visitor to the order page. **TOP RIGHT:** Individual images are shown with information on the image, size, frame, and price options. **BOTTOM:** Wolfe features a slideshow option in a separate popup window.

Mahesh Thapa's website (www.starvingphotographer.com) uses a version of the PayPal shopping cart system we discuss in Chapter 8 to showcase his stunning photography. **TOP:** The index page serves a dual purpose: clicking the thumbnail shows the full size image, while selecting an image size from the dropdown list and clicking Add to Cart generates an order request. **BOTTOM:** Individual images are shown with mat and frame.

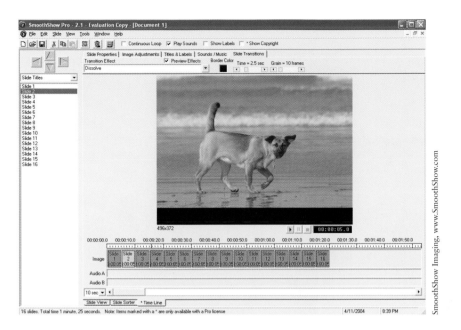

TOP: SmoothShow is a multimedia slide show program that offers unlimited display resolutions, audio coordination, and the ability to easily create CD or HTML shows. It uses an intuitive interface with a large preview area to make building slideshows easy. **BOTTOM:** ProShow Gold supports every type of output you might want, from screen saver to high quality DVD.

LEFT: This image uses a complimentary mat color. The mat has a blue suede finish that sets the silhouette and clouds off from the frame while not competing with either element. **RIGHT:** The mat choices for this image were particularly difficult because of the difference in colors between the two images. Selecting two earth tone shades compliments both photographs.

Using a double mat can create more depth to your photograph. In this colorized black and white example, we've used a color from the bride's bouquet for the inner mat with a plain white outer mat. A simple wood frame finishes off the piece.

The same image can show dramatic differences with a change in mat color. **TOP LEFT:** A dark green mat brings the subject forward. **TOP RIGHT:** Using a white mat gives more prominence to the background. **BOTTOM LEFT:** Here we've used a blue mat which pulls color from the flag forward. **BOTTOM RIGHT:** Finally, a red mat blends all the elements together but lacks focus on the subject.

Going Live

Now that we have finished planning and designing our ideas, it's time to put everything together and actually fill the new site with pages and content. In this chapter, we'll focus on creating pages, building photo galleries, and publishing them to the website we designed in Chapter 7, "Planning Your Site." We'll also cover using keywords and search engines, promoting your website, and setting up for online sales of photographs.

Throughout this chapter, keep in mind that a website is really nothing more than pages. What makes a website unique is the content on those pages and the way it is presented. Our goal is to create pages that have visual impact and present your photographs in their best light.

Chapter Contents

Creating the Navigation Bar

Once you've decided on the structure of your website, you can create the navigation controls. Navigation bars should contain links to each of the major sections of your website. Typically, the major sections consist of the home page and all pages one level below. In our example site, we would have links to Home, Galleries, About, Contact, and Links. The Gallery index page will contain additional navigation controls for each of the separate photo galleries.

Dreamweaver MX 2004

In the previous chapter, you created a template page in Dreamweaver MX and then saw a preview of how it would look with the spaces (editable regions) for navigation, title, and other fixed elements replaced with actual content. The buttons in our example were included with Dreamweaver; they just had to be customized for our needs. Now, you'll see how to add those buttons. Just follow these steps:

1. Click your mouse in the Navigation region, and then select Insert > Media > Flash Button.

2. As shown in Figure 8.1, the Insert Flash Button dialog box allows you to select from several styles of ready-made buttons. In our example, we used the Beveled Rect-Grey style.

3. Set the properties for this button, including the text the user will see and where the button will send the user when clicked. If you want to open a new window, you can specify this by selecting _blank from the Target list. If the background color of your page is different than the default, you need to set this by clicking on the Bg color popup Color Picker.

Note: Flash buttons do not use the `<img>` tag, which means that Alt text is not supported.

A very similar option is available if you want to use regular text style links. Insert > Media > Flash Text creates a text label that performs just like a Flash button. Select the font, size, and color, but here you also need to set a *rollover color*. This is the color the text will change to when a visitor moves their mouse pointer over the text, and it is a good visual indicator that something will happen when clicked.

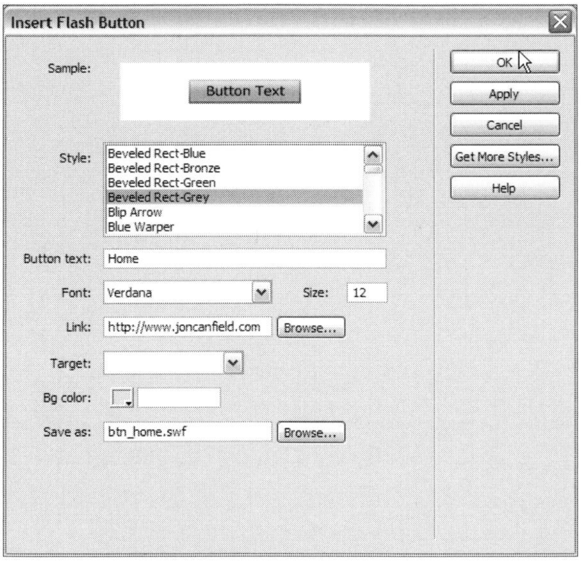

Figure 8.1 Dreamweaver makes it easy for you to include Flash Button objects on your web page with the included objects.

> **Note:** When using the Color Picker controls in Dreamweaver, you can click the color you want to match on your page any time you have an eyedropper cursor. This is much easier than clicking the correct color patch or typing in a color number.

As with the Flash buttons, you also need to set the link property. In Figure 8.2, the link is set to the default home page. For other pages, setting the link to specific pages is important. For example, if you want this button to open the Contact page when clicked, enter the Contact page's URL. In this example, we entered `http://www.joncanfield.com/contact.htm`. Finally, save your Flash buttons or Flash text with descriptive names. Dreamweaver saves these files with a `.swf` extension (by default, these files are saved to the root directory of your website). The name should include a reference to the button's label—in this case, `fltxt_home.swf` indicates that your file is a Flash Text object labeled `Home`.

> **Note:** Dreamweaver includes a good selection of Flash buttons. However, if you don't see anything that fits your design ideas, many more Flash buttons are available on the Internet. A search on "flash buttons" will return many possible sites. We suggest `www.flashbuttons.com` as a good starting point.

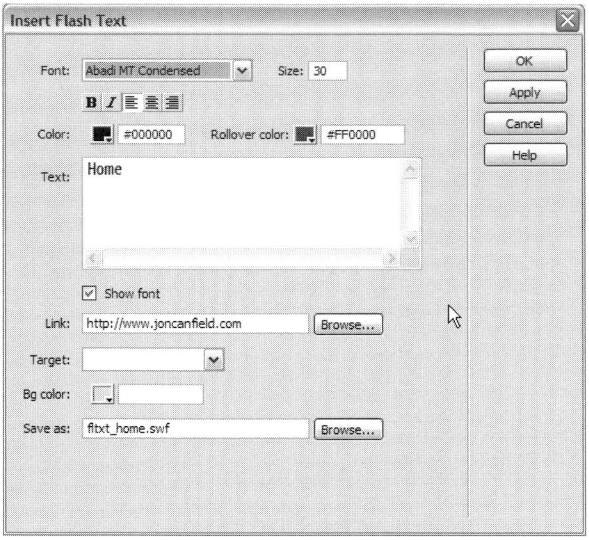

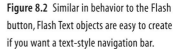

Figure 8.2 Similar in behavior to the Flash button, Flash Text objects are easy to create if you want a text-style navigation bar.

Using the Dreamweaver Insert Navigation Bar Feature

There is a third built-in way to create a navigation bar in Dreamweaver. The Navigation Bar object uses multiple graphic files to create buttons. The end result is very similar to the Flash button, but you have full control over the images used, and there is no need for the Flash player on a visitor's system. The buttons are created in a table and Dreamweaver creates JavaScript code that is inserted into the <head> section of the page. You'll need to create the graphics files used for this method prior to starting. At a minimum, you'll need to have an "up" image that will be used as your default navigation button. If you want the user to have feedback when using the button, you'll need "over" and "down" images as well.

Let's go through the steps to create the Home button:

1. Insert > Image Objects > Navigation Bar.

2. Type **Home** in the element name field.

3. In the Up Image field, enter the name of the graphic file you'll use as the default, or click the Browse button and select the file. You'll find sample images for buttons on the companion website, www.photofinishbook.com, in the Resources section.

4. Optionally, provide the information for the Over, Down, and Over While Down graphics. If you leave these blank, the button will give no visual indication that it is a link or that it has been selected. The Over image will show when the mouse pointer touches the graphic. The Down image will display when the button is actually clicked, and the Over While Down image will display when the button is clicked and the mouse is moved.

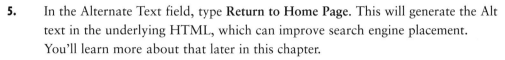

5. In the Alternate Text field, type **Return to Home Page**. This will generate the Alt text in the underlying HTML, which can improve search engine placement. You'll learn more about that later in this chapter.

6. Type the URL of the page you want to go to when this button is clicked.

7. Repeat Steps 2 through 6 for each button you want to include in the navigation bar, first clicking the plus sign (+) above the element list.

8. Click to select the checkbox for Preload Images. By preloading the images, the browser doesn't need to ask the web server for the next image. This helps to improve the responsiveness of the button when graphics change.

9. Select Vertically in the Insert dropdown list.

10. Click to select the checkbox for Use Tables.
    The dialog box should look similar to the one in Figure 8.3.

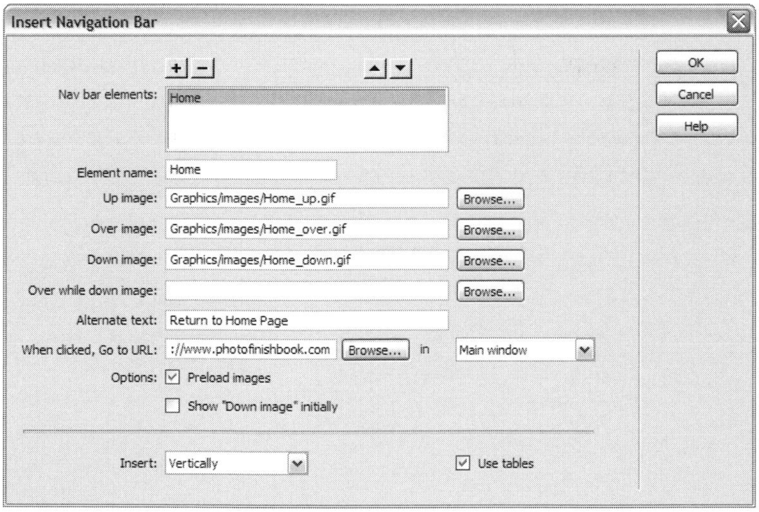

Figure 8.3 You can create custom navigation buttons in Dreamweaver by using the Insert Navigation Bar feature. Very similar to using Flash buttons, this method inserts JavaScript code into your web page and does not require the use of Flash.

As we previously mentioned, one advantage to this method is that Flash is not required on a visitor's browser. The disadvantage is that there is more work on your part to create the navigation bar. A second possible issue with this method is in the script itself. Not all browsers have scripting enabled. This is usually more of a problem for viewers at work, because their network support groups tend to be more careful (or paranoid, depending on your point of view) about downloading code.

Photoshop CS and ImageReady CS

If you choose not to use the features built into Dreamweaver MX or FrontPage, but you still want to have a graphical look, you can create your own navigation bars using Photoshop/ImageReady or Flash.

Using Photoshop is second nature for many photographers because we do most of our image editing with it. ImageReady, which is included with Photoshop, takes the graphic capabilities of Photoshop and adds features to quickly create buttons and rollover effects from your graphics. With Photoshop CS, ImageReady has made even more improvements to the process and allows you to quickly create and test your navigation bars. Let's go through the process of creating a simple navigation bar in ImageReady, using Figure 8.4 as a guide. For this example, we are designing the navigation bar to fit a window size of 800×600 pixels. Just follow these steps:

1. In ImageReady, select File > New.
2. Create a new document 700 pixels wide and 60 pixels high. Set the background to transparent so that any background area shows through. This is especially important if you're using rounded edges for your graphics. Give the document a descriptive name, such as **navbar**.
3. From the toolbar, click on the TabRectangle tool or press **R**.
4. In the document window, drag out a rectangle large enough to contain a text label.

> **Note:** ImageReady will use the current foreground color to fill the rectangle. If you want to use a different color to fill the tab, select the color first by clicking on the foreground color in the toolbar and then choosing your new color in the Color Picker dialog box.

5. Duplicate this layer by holding the Alt key and right-clicking (Opt+Cmd key, Macintosh) and dragging the new rectangle to the right of the first tab. Repeat this step four times to create a total of five equal-sized tabs.

6. Name each layer by double-clicking the label in the Layers palette. Name your layers **Home**, **Galleries**, **About**, **Contact**, and **Links**.

7. Click the Text tool **T** , or press **T**.

8. Set the foreground color to White and select a font. We used 14-point Arial for this example. In each tab, enter the appropriate label (for example, **Home, Galleries, About, Contact,** or **Links**).

9. Click the Slice Selection tool , or press **O** and drag a selection rectangle the size of the first tab.

10. In the Slice palette, enter the name of the slice and the URL to which you want to attach this tab. For example, the Contact tab for our website would be `http://www.photofinish.com/contact.htm`. Enter Alt text that describes the tab.

11. Finally, Select File > Save Optimized. Save the file as `navbar.html`.

You can test this navigation bar by opening it in your browser using the Browser button , and clicking each text label. You'll be taken to the web page you associated with the tab in the Slice palette.

Like the Navigation bar feature in Dreamweaver, ImageReady works its magic by creating JavaScript for our buttons.

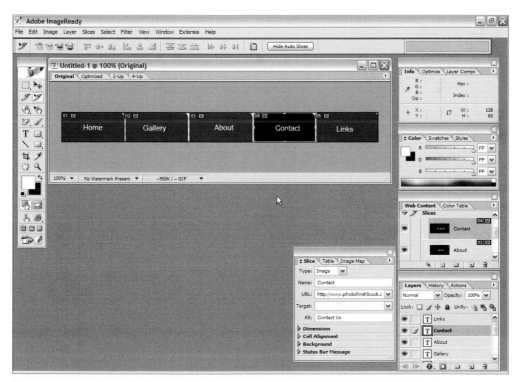

Figure 8.4 ImageReady CS makes creating a tabular navigation bar complete with rollover effects very easy.

GIF or JPG?

When should you use the GIF format and when should you use the JPG format? GIF is an excellent choice for buttons and navigation bar graphics. It has a smaller color palette than JPG and tends to have smaller file sizes. However, the most important benefit to GIF is its support of transparency. If you're designing a button or other graphic that has rounded corners or irregular shapes, transparency will allow your background to show through.

JPG is typically a better choice for photographs. The color palette is not limited, and the ability to set the level of compression is helpful with larger files. See "Preparing the Images" later in this chapter.

Flash

Flash MX (www.macromedia.com/software/flash/, about $500) is another popular means of creating animations and graphic effects. Flash is frequently used to animate buttons and give the designer a great deal of control. While Flash programming is beyond the scope of this book, a multitude of books are devoted to programming ActionScript, the language used by Flash, including *Flash MX ActionScript: the Designer's Edge* by J. Scott Hamlin and Jennifer S. Hall (Sybex, 2003).

Some websites, particularly those designed by professionals for sale, use Flash. Aside from the added glitz possible with this approach, using Flash enables web masters to protect their web photos from being copied. A Flash-designed template typically comes without the source code needed to make modifications.

Note: If you're interested in learning Flash but you are put off by the cost, you should look into SWiSH (www.swishzone.com), which is Flash compatible but much easier to learn.

Creating the Home Page

In Chapter 7, "Planning Your Site," we talked about keeping your home page simple, clean, and quick to load. Some photographers use a Welcome or "splash" page as the entry point to their websites, as nature photographer John Shaw (www.johnshawphoto.com) does in Figure 8.5. The advantage to using a text link to enter the site is that it loads almost instantly. Another approach is to use a large image as a splash page, such as the PhotoMigrations website (www.photomigrations.com) used in Figure 8.6. The image changes on a monthly basis. (We'll show you how to create a page with rotating images in Chapter 9, "Publishing and Maintaining Your Site.") With both styles of Welcome pages, your visitors must click a link to access the rest of your site.

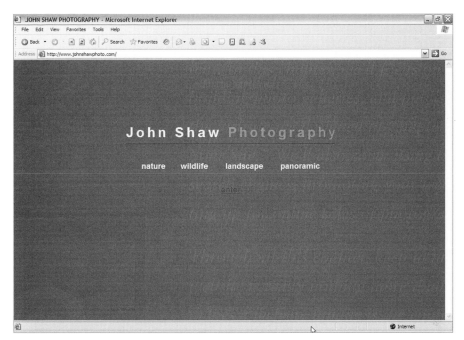

Introductory Page

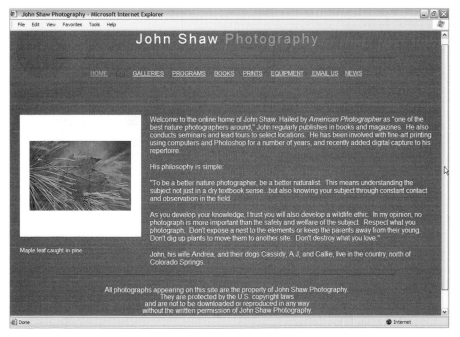

Home Page

Figure 8.5 Nature photographer John Shaw uses a simple but effective Welcome screen as the introductory page to his website (www.johnshawphoto.com), which takes the user to the actual home page.

170

Figure 8.6 The PhotoMigrations website (`www.photomigrations.com`) uses a larger image as a Welcome page. Clicking the image takes the user to the actual home page.

Note: A Welcome or splash page is a good place to display your copyright statement or content warnings so that they will be seen. If your galleries contain nudes, or other content that is not appropriate for all ages, a warning up front will be appreciated by visitors (and parents). Adding the text "By entering this site, you agree to these terms" may give some measure of recourse in the event of copyright violations.

Of course, having a Welcome page isn't a requirement. The majority of photography sites go directly to a home page that often has a welcome statement and all navigation links.

Your home page sets the tone for the entire site, and it often determines whether a visitor stays to browse or leaves without going further. Because of this, it's important to present what your site is about, and entice visitors to look around. Because search engines often index sites based on the home page, you'll want to be sure and use the `title` and `description` META tags, which we'll cover later in this chapter.

To build your home page in Dreamweaver, start off by creating a new page at the root level of your site. Just follow these steps:

1. If you've created a page template, as we did in Chapter 7, select File > New. In the New Document dialog box, click the Templates tab, and then select the template from the list (see Figure 8.7). If you're starting from a blank page, select Basic Page > HTML on the General tab of the same dialog box.

> **Note:** Browsers look for files named `default` and `index`. By using `default.htm` or `index.htm` as the filename, the page will load automatically when a visitor types the URL. If you decide to use a Welcome page, it will use this name. You'll need to rename your home page, and logically enough, `home.htm` is a good choice.

2. In the Document pane at the top of the page, select Untitled Document and give your site a descriptive name. In our companion website (`www.photofinishbook.com`), we use "Welcome to the Photo Finish Companion Site." The title for your site should be closely related to the content. For example, Jon's site title is "Landscape and Nature Photography by Jon Canfield." The page title is the highest ranking criteria for search engines. By stating what your site is about, you increase your chances of being found on the Internet.

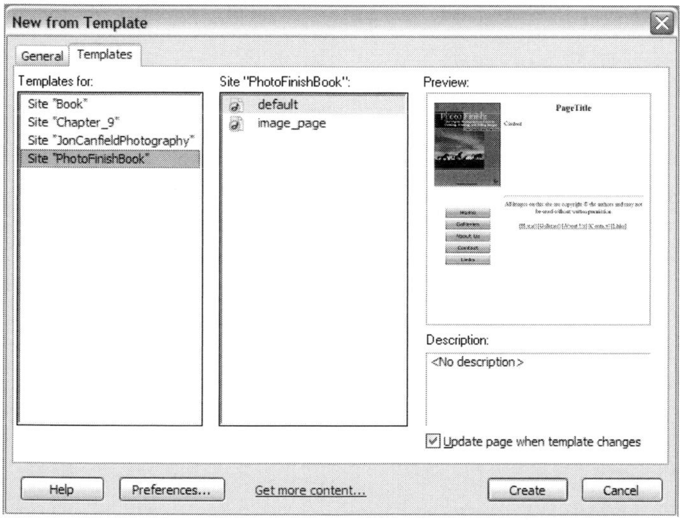

Figure 8.7 To create a home page from a template in Dreamweaver, select the template from the Templates tab of the New Document dialog box.

3. Save the new page by selecting File > Save. If visitors will be coming directly to this page, name it `default.htm` or `index.htm`. If you plan to use a Welcome screen, name the page `home.htm`.

4. Add your introductory content. This might be information about your business, a greeting to visitors explaining what motivates your photography and why you want to share it with others. Remember, keep it simple and clean.

5. If you started from a blank HTML page, you'll need to add navigation links for other pages in the site. Refer back to Chapter 7 for help on building navigation bars and links.

6. Select Insert > HTML > Head Tags > Description. The `description` tag is used to help search engines determine the relevancy of a website. This should be a paragraph or less of information that defines what the site is about in more detail than a page title will allow (see Figure 8.8).

7. Once you've finished adding content to your home page, select File > Save (Ctrl+S Windows; Cmd+S Macintosh) to save the page.

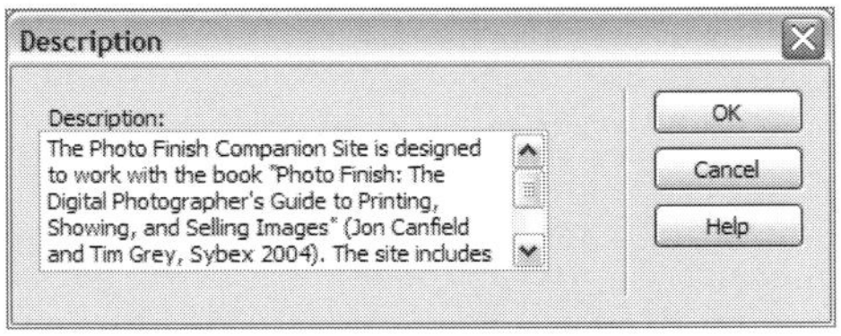

Figure 8.8 The Description for your website helps search engines determine how relevant a site is when a search query is done. This should be a brief summary of what your site is about.

Selecting and Organizing Your Images

Once you determine what the focus of your photo galleries will be, start reviewing potential images for inclusion. As we pointed out earlier, your photographs are your online resume and portfolio. The same care given to preparing a conventional print portfolio should be taken when selecting images for your website.

Making the Selection

Regardless of the number of incredible images you have to share with the world, keeping the number of images in each individual gallery to a select set—no more than 20 or so—allows you to change the images on a regular basis, and keeps customers coming back to view your new work. Keeping the number small also allows your customers to focus on individual images better.

We find that it works best to create a folder for each gallery and then copy potential images to the appropriate folder. At this point, you are selecting the "semi-finalists" and shouldn't be too concerned with picking only those images that will be included.

Creating a Welcome Page

If you'll be using a Welcome page, you'll start off with a blank page. (You don't want a navigation bar on this page because you only want your visitors to click one link to access your home page.)

1. Create a new empty page by selecting File > New. In the New Document dialog box, select Basic Page, HTML and click Create.

2. For a simple Welcome page with a copyright statement, name, and logo, create a table by selecting Insert > Table. In the Table dialog box, set Rows and Columns to **2** and width to **100** percent.

3. In the upper-left table cell, insert your logo graphic by clicking the cell, selecting Insert > Image, and navigating to the location of the image. If the graphic isn't already in your site, you'll be prompted to add it to the site.

4. In the upper-right table cell, enter the title of your website. For this example, we set the alignment to Centered ▤ ▤ ▤ ▤ and the Format to Heading 2. We added a horizontal rule by selecting Insert > HTML > Horizontal Rule to separate the title from the copyright statement.

5. In the bottom-right table cell, enter your copyright statement. Again, we set the alignment to Centered.

6. Create the link by selecting Insert > Hyperlink. Type **Enter** in the Text field, the full URL of the home page in the Link field, and in the Title field optionally enter the text you want to display as a tooltip when the visitor pauses a cursor over the hyperlink.

7. Add the Title and Description using Steps 2 and 6 from the home page creation steps.

Once you've gathered the images you're considering, it's time to review and select the best of your work. One of the most difficult tasks for a photographer when reviewing their own work is to be objective. Everyone takes images that they are emotionally attached to, but these are not necessarily the best images in a collection. Your goal here is to select the images that are technically and aesthetically the strongest. Remember that your visitors and customers typically will not have the same emotional tie with your photos, unless they just happen to have a sentimental connection.

Grouping Strategies

Some groups are obvious. Flower images can all be grouped into a common gallery, for instance. What about the photographer who specializes in portraits or only flowers, and what about the portrait or studio photographer? Unless you are planning to have 20 or fewer images total on display, these images will need to be broken down into subgroups. The color section of this book has examples from several websites that we consider excellent examples of these grouping strategies.

Subject Matter

A common grouping strategy is to separate your photographs by subject. The portrait photographer would likely want to create galleries for Family, Formal, Children, Corporate, Glamour, etc. A website devoted to flower photography might be broken down into seasons—Spring Flowers, Summer Flowers, Winter Flowers,—or perhaps by species. A good example of this would be creating a gallery of Tulip photos, another of Iris, and so on. Jon breaks down his landscape galleries by region—Western US, Midwestern US, Europe, and so on.

One grouping we have found to be particularly useful is to keep panoramic photographs in their own gallery. Most people are drawn to the panoramic image, and by grouping them together and separating them from the normal format, you'll increase their visibility and make the thumbnail page layout more attractive.

 Note: Try to keep similar format images together. Mixing portrait and landscape orientation images on the same thumbnail page is less visually appealing. If you have both formats in the same gallery, try to group them together on the thumbnail page if possible.

The key to a successful presentation is to make your groupings as logical as possible while keeping the number of different groups to a minimum. As a guideline, try to keep subgroupings to five or less. Again, you want to focus on the quality and not overwhelm the visitor and potential customer with numbers.

Color Continuity

Another popular and effective way to group images is by color continuity. Consider grouping your black-and-white photographs separately from your color photographs, even if the subject matter is similar. As an example, you may have a Landscape group that is split into black-and-white and color galleries. Black-and-white images tend to have more visual impact when viewed separately from color.

Naming Your Images and Galleries

By following a few simple guidelines, your images and galleries will be easy to navigate and, more importantly, easy to maintain and update.

Because images are the focus of a photographer's website, using a standard naming convention helps to identify what the image is and whether it's the main image or the thumbnail version. We suggest using a common name for both versions of the image with `thm_` as the prefix to all thumbnail files. Finally, by including gallery location information, you can quickly tell where the files are located on your site. For example, an image named `fl_tulip_detail001.jpg` would be located in the Flowers gallery, and it would have an associated thumbnail named `thm_fl_tulip_detail001.jpg`.

Note: As shown in the example filenames, using an underscore as a separator helps make the filename more readable. Avoid using spaces in filenames, as not all web servers support spaces. In HTML, a space is translated to %20, which is not very readable and is hard to type in the address bar.

File Naming

There are several basic guidelines that will make file naming and management easier for visitors and for web designer.

- Do not use spaces in filenames. Although Windows and Macintosh systems handle files with spaces, the web server needs to process them differently. When you type a URL in your web browser, the space is seen as the end of an address. HTML translates the space character into %20, so a file named `red tulip field` would be interpreted as `red%20tulip%20field001.jpg` in the browser. We suggest using an underscore character to separate words. In this example you would see `red_tulip_field001.jpg`, which is much more readable.

- Use descriptive names for each image and page so you can easily identify specific images. Active websites quickly grow from a handful of files to hundreds.

- Consider using a coding system for related files. For example, use a two-letter code for each category of photograph, such as `la_` for landscape, `fl_` for flowers, and `na_` for nature.

- Decide on a naming convention for your website. One method is to use the same filename for both image and thumbnail file and preface the thumbnail with `thm_`. Most of the thumbnail and photo gallery programs available use this or a similar method to identify files.

- End the filename with a three digit number. This will allow you to have up to 1,000 similarly named files.

Preparing the Images

Now that you've selected the photographs for your galleries, it's time to get them ready for the Web. Typically, this means resizing and saving as them as JPEG files.

Note: Always work on a copy of your photograph. Saving images for the Web almost always involves reducing image quality from the original.

Before doing anything else, make certain that you are using a copy of the original file. Choose Image > Duplicate. This will prompt you for a filename and then create a copy of your original image in a new window. The advantage to this method is that you still have the original file open to use as a reference for any edits made. Alternatively, you can save a copy by selecting File > Save As (Shift+Ctrl+S Windows; Shift+Cmd+S Macintosh) and providing a new filename. It's easy to select Save by mistake though, so duplicate is the best choice.

Screen Resolution

Photographers tend to invest in high-resolution displays and powerful computers. Depending on the audience you are trying to attract for your website, screen resolution may or may not be an issue to consider. On average, designing web pages for a display size of 800×600 is a safe and reasonable compromise between image size and visitor satisfaction. If you are focusing on corporate or higher-end users, then 1024×768 is a good choice. Jon's website, like those of many other photographers, is designed for users with this higher resolution.

Why is optimum resolution important? A web page is more readable and predictable when users do not need to use scroll bars to see all the contents. Usability studies have shown that users are less likely to view content, especially graphical content, and will spend less time on a particular page if scrolling is required. Horizontal scrollbars give visitors an even worse experience than vertical, so they should be avoided if at all possible.

Note: If you optimize your web pages for a particular resolution, consider putting that information on your home page. Jon's website, for instance, includes the text "This site is best viewed at 1024×768 or higher" on his home page.

JPEG Compression

The Photoshop Save For Web File > Save For Web (Alt+Shift+Ctrl+S Windows; Opt+Shift+Cmd+S Macintosh) feature can be very useful in helping you select the compression level. The ability to compare side-by-side the quality of the original and the compressed version using the 2-Up display can a great aid when you want to experiment with different compression settings, as shown in Figure 8.9.

> **Note:** Photoshop's Save For Web feature does have drawbacks. Perhaps the largest of these is that by default, Save For Web strips the color profile from your image. This means that a photograph edited in sRGB will have no associated color profile and might not appear as desired in a browser. To preserve the color profile, you must check the ICC Profile box in the Save For Web dialog box.

File Size Guidelines

Many users are still on dial-up connections with speeds of 56Kbps or less. Books on web design typically stress keeping graphics to a minimum so that pages load quickly for users on these slow connections. As photographers, we obviously aren't going to follow the minimum graphics plan, so we need to optimize our image sizes to keep the quality as high as possible with the shortest possible load times.

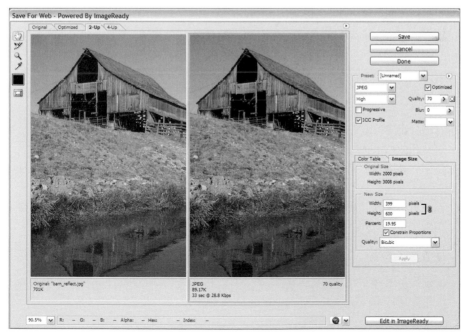

Figure 8.9 The Save For Web dialog box in Photoshop CS lets you see the effect different compression settings will have on a file.

Preventing Image Theft

The only sure way to avoid having your work stolen or misused is to keep it off the Internet. Similar to abstinence preventing pregnancy, it may be effective, but it sure isn't as fun.

The obvious way to deal with this is to post low-resolution images on your website. This helps reduce the risk that someone will download your image for print purposes; however, as a photographer, we need to walk a fine line with image quality. If you image quality is too low, visitors may not feel that your work is worthwhile.

Here are a few simple methods that will stop most casual users from misusing your work. Remember that none of these is foolproof though, and the determined person will almost always find a way.

- Disable right-click. To see why this is advisable, On any web page right-click the mouse on an image. If you see a popup menu, one of the choices will be Save Image As or Save Picture As. You can insert the following JavaScript code into the <HEAD> section of your web pages to disable this option:

```
<SCRIPT>

function disableRightClick() {

if (event.button==2) {

    alert('Right click disabled on this page.')

}

}

document.onmousedown=disableRightClick

</SCRIPT>
```

This works best when it is used with a template or style sheet to ensure that it is available on all pages.

- Turn off the image toolbar in Internet Explorer. By placing the following META tag in the <HEAD> section of your pages, the toolbar that shows when a mouse is over an image will be disabled: <META HTTP-EQUIV="imagetoolbar" CONTENT"="no">. As with disabling the right-click, this works best when it is used with a template or style sheet that is used on all pages.

- Use popup windows that close on a mouse click. An excellent extension for Dreamweaver, JustSo Picture Window3 from Valley Web Designs (www.valleywebdesigns.com/vwd_jspw3.asp) does two great things for those who decide to display full-size images in a popup window. First, it auto-sizes the window to fit the image. Second, it can be set to close the window on any mouse click.

Continues

Preventing Image Theft *(Continued)*

- Embed a copyright on the image, like the one shown here. In Photoshop, create a text layer for your image. Then, on Windows, hold down the Control key and type **0169** on the numeric keypad. (This only works with the keypad numbers. If you're on a laptop, you will most likely need to enable the keypad keys). On the Macintosh, you can press **Opt+G**. This will give you the © symbol. You can change the size, location, and transparency of the text before flattening the image and saving as it as a JPG file.

- Use slices to break the image into multiple pieces. Using Photoshop/ImageReady, you can slice an image into multiple pieces. The drawback to this method is the image loads in chunks on the browser. The advantage is that only one slice at a time can be downloaded, so the image will be in multiple files, which will need to be stitched together.

There is very little apparent difference in quality between an image saved at quality level 12 and one saved at quality level 70, as you can see in the color section and on the companion website. More importantly though, it takes one and a half minutes to download the image saved at level 12, compared to 32 seconds for the image saved at level 70 (at 56Kbps connection speed). In our experience, using a JPEG quality level setting of 70 in Photoshop provides a good balance between file size and image quality. As a goal, try to keep file sizes under 100KB each, unless you are optimizing for high-speed connections.

Color Management Considerations

As photographers, we spend a great deal of time and energy on ensuring that our photographs are accurate representations of what we see. Color management is all about control and consistent results. Sadly, web browsers are among the least color-aware photo viewers around. The color space of choice (or necessity depending on your point of view) for web display is sRGB.

The sRGB color space is optimized for screen display and tends to render colors with a bit more saturation than many of the color spaces designed for print. sRGB also has a smaller color gamut, or spectrum, than other color spaces, such as Adobe RGB.

To further complicate matters, the average visitor to your site will not be using a calibrated monitor. Depending on their particular display, your photograph may appear dark with little detail in the shadow areas, or overly bright with no detail visible in the highlights. One method of helping the user identify display problems is to include a black-to-white graded chart, as seen in Figure 8.10 and available on the companion website. A short description explaining that users should be able to see all the shades on their monitor will let them know that any display issues are on their monitor and not your website.

We go into more detail on calibrating your system in Chapter 2, "Preparing the Image." If you're interested in learning more about color management in general, we recommend Tim's book *Color Confidence*, which is also published by Sybex.

Creating the Galleries

There are several ways you can create the galleries once you've selected and optimized your images. You can use tools that automate at least part of the process, or you can build them "from scratch" if you want more control over the design. First, we'll try it the easy way.

Note: Unless you want to create placeholder pages, you should select your images and create thumbnails before building your photo gallery.

Figure 8.10 Including a grayscale chart on your website can help users identify display issues. This chart can be downloaded from the companion website (www.photofinishbook.com) for use on your site.

Quick Galleries

A photo gallery can be quickly and effectively created with little effort on your part. Photoshop, along with most other image browser applications, has a built-in Web Gallery feature that will create thumbnails, index pages, and full-size image pages for you. If you're in a hurry to get something online, this is a great way to start and gives you time to plan the final design.

Photoshop CS

Photoshop CS includes a Web Photo Gallery option that will generate web pages, thumbnails, and index page for our photographs. Just follow these steps:

1. In Photoshop CS, select File > Automate > Web Photo Gallery.

2. The Styles dropdown list has 11 choices available. Clicking each one will give you a small preview of the layout. For this example, we selected Simple from the Styles list (see Figure 8.11).

3. If you want to have e-mail information on your pages, enter your e-mail address in the provided space. It's worth noting that including your e-mail address on these pages increases the likelihood of receiving unwanted e-mail (affectionately referred to as *spam*.) We suggest confining your e-mail address to a Contacts page or an About page.

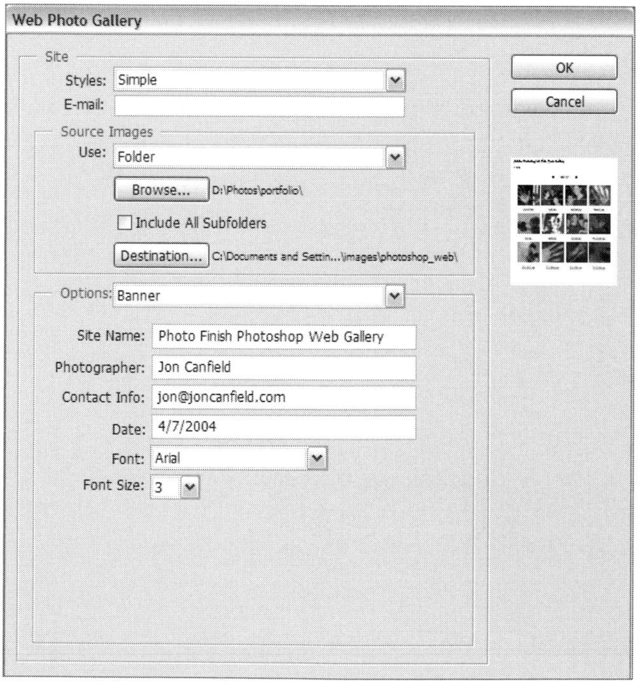

Figure 8.11 The Web Photo Gallery option in Photoshop is a quick way to get your photographs online with full navigation controls.

4. Next, select the source for the images. You have two options: selecting a folder of images or using all of the images displayed in the Photoshop Browser. We recommend using the folder approach, as it is more manageable. If you have subfolders you want to include, be sure to select the Include All Subfolders checkbox.

5. Click the Destination button and navigate to the location where you want to store your gallery files. Do not store them in the same directory that the original images are in, as you'll have additional files that are not needed for your web pages. We suggest you create a new folder for the destination option. Because these files will need to be copied into your site, we suggest creating this folder within your site's Images folder.

6. The Options dropdown list contains features that allow you to customize your gallery page:

   • General allows you to set the extension and the amount of data stored with the images.

   • Banner allows you to set the gallery name, photographer, contact information, and date information. Depending on the template you select, this option may not be available.

   • Large Images controls the size, quality, and display of attributes for your full-size photograph. If you followed our advice earlier in the chapter, your images should already be sized for your website. Uncheck the Resize Images box to leave them as they are. If you want Photoshop to automatically resize them, we suggest using Large, Constrain Both, and JPEG Quality of 7. The disadvantage to this method is that you give up control of sharpening the images for the final size, which is something that we advise doing as the final processing step.

   • Thumbnails control the size of the thumbnail used for the index page. Depending on the number of images on the index page, we suggest using Large and the default size of 100 pixels.

   • Custom Colors lets you set the colors for various page elements such as text, backgrounds, and links.

   • Security allows you to set attributes that will be displayed on the actual image itself. While useful for giving you some protection against unauthorized use, the text on your image is distracting at best.

7. Click OK, and you'll soon see your photo gallery displayed in your default browser (see Figure 8.12).

If you followed our advice to create a new folder for your content in Step 5, you now have a folder that contains all the files needed for your gallery to be used on the Web. The new folder will contain the index page(s) and subfolders for thumbnails, images, and pages for that web gallery. The final step is to add a link from your Galleries page to the new `index.htm` file created in the folder. We'll show you how to do that later in the chapter.

ACDSee

ACDSee (`www.acdsysytems.com/English/Products/ACDSee/index.htm`) calls their galleries HTML Albums. Like the equivalent Photoshop tool, the HTML Album Wizard will create all needed pages, thumbnails and index pages for us. Just follow these steps:

1. Select the images in the ACDSee browser window.

2. Select Create > Create HTML Album.

3. In the Wizard dialog box, select the style you want to use. Basic uses a regular thumbnail page, and the filmstrip styles both use frames. Click Next.

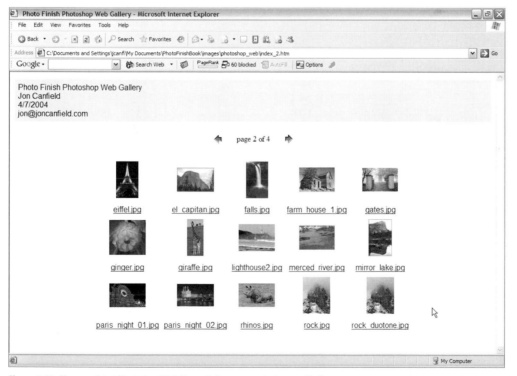

Figure 8.12 The completed Photoshop Web Photo Gallery as seen in Internet Explorer.

4. You are now prompted for a Photo Album name. This shows up on the index page as the title of the album. You also set the URL for your home page in here, as well as make changes to fonts and page color. If you want to change them, select the Page and Font Color tab. Click Next.

5. Next, you set the thumbnail size and layout. If you've selected a filmstrip style, the Columns and Rows fields will be disabled. For Basic, we usually use a setting of 5 columns and 4 rows with a thumbnail size of 100. Click Next when you've finished making your choices.

6. Now select the font and label information for both the thumbnails and the images. If you don't want any labels to display, leave all the checkboxes blank.

7. Next, you set the quality level of the thumbnails, and the maximum size of the image. (ACDSee will not enlarge photos to this size, it will only reduce them if needed). We suggest using a Image quality setting of 70.

8. Lastly, select the location for the album. When you click Next, your web gallery will be created and ready to use, as shown in Figure 8.13.

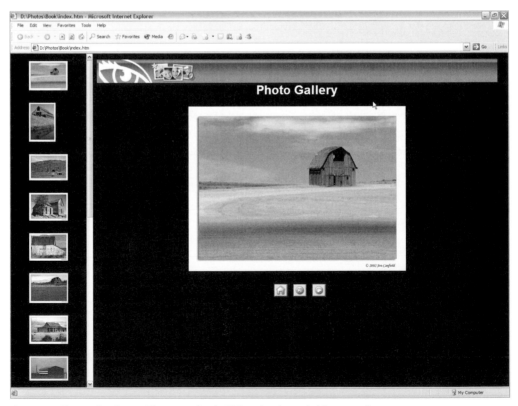

Figure 8.13 The completed HTML Album created with ACDSee using the vertical frame template

iViewMedia Pro

A photo gallery in iView MediaPro is referred to as an HTML Gallery. iView has some of the most useful templates of all the applications in this category included with their Gallery wizard. For this gallery, you'll use the Basic template. Here are the steps:

1. Select the files you want to use for your HTML Gallery in either the List view or the Thumbnail view.

2. Select Make > HTML Gallery.

3. In the HTML Options dialog box (see Figure 8.14), select the theme you want to use. You'll also name your gallery and set the thumbnail and image size on this tab. The Settings tab is where you'll select whether to include captions, what JPEG quality you want, and the file extension. Once you've made your selections, click Create.

> **Note:** The Index Table options change depending on the template you select. For templates that use frames, it's best to leave the settings at the default.

4. Select the location where you want the files located. Once you've made this selection and click OK, your gallery will be created.

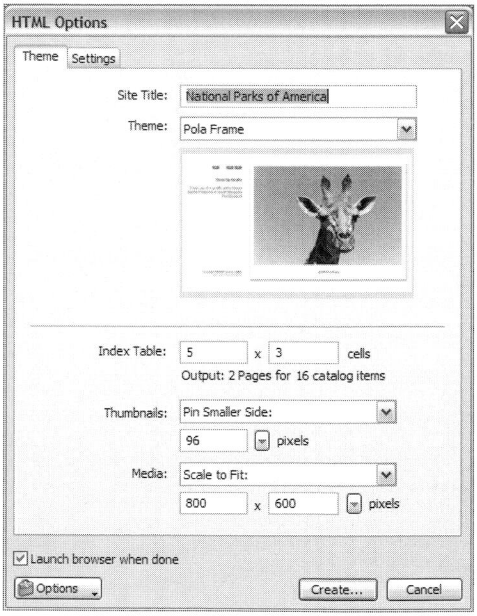

Figure 8.14 iView MediaPro has some of the best stock templates for web galleries.

Building Your Own Gallery

A quick gallery is an excellent way to see what you like and don't like, and to learn about what's involved in creating web galleries. If you happen to find one that suits your needs perfectly, then life is good. Usually, however, there is at least one aspect of the created output that you don't like. Now it's time to decide whether you want to modify the existing output or start from scratch. Typically, starting over is easier than modifying someone else's work, and that's the approach you'll take here. Using Dreamweaver MX, you'll create your own photo gallery using tables for the index page and a separate page for each image. You'll also create a simple frame-based gallery. You can find the templates for these galleries on the companion website. Feel free to use them as starting points for your own galleries.

Note: If you are using Studio MX 2004, you'll see that Dreamweaver has a Create Web Photo Album option available in the Commands menu. This command uses Fireworks MX (part of the Studio suite) to create an album similar to Photoshop CS. No template choices are available with this command, which makes it less than useful compared to the other quick gallery generators covered earlier.

Creating the Image Page Template

Once again, the use of a template page greatly reduces the amount of work required to create a consistent look for each of your images. You'll create a template in Dreamweaver MX that contains three editable regions: Navigation, Photo, and Description. Just follow these steps:

1. Create a new blank HTML page by selecting File > New (Ctrl+N Windows; Cmd+N Macintosh). On the General tab, select Basic Page as the Category, and then select the HTML template.

2. Create a table by selecting Insert > Table (Ctrl+Alt+T Windows; Cmd+Opt+T Macintosh) with one row and three cells. With the table selected, set the alignment to Center by clicking the icon in the Properties panel ≡ ≡ ≡ ≡ .

3. Make sure the table is selected and click on the width indicator, as shown in Figure 8.15. Select Make All Widths Consistent. This will keep all three cells the same width regardless of table width.

4. Resize the table to 300 pixels in width by clicking on the right edge of the table and dragging the mouse until the width indicator shows 300, or enter **300** in the Row Width field in the Properties panel.

5. Type **Previous** in the left cell; **Index** in the center cell; and **Next** in the right cell. These entries will be the labels for our navigation links.

6. With the table still selected, Select Insert > Template Objects > Editable Region (Ctrl+Alt+V Windows; Cmd+Opt+V Macintosh), and name the region **Navigation**.

Click here to display the dropdown menu.

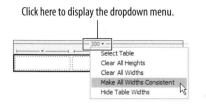

Figure 8.15 Click the table width indicator and set the cells to have a consistent width

7. Click outside the table and press **Enter** (Windows) or **Return** (Macintosh). Select Insert > Image Objects > Image Placeholder. Set the size to 600×400, and name the placeholder **Photo**. This is where our full size image will be displayed.

8. Click on the Image placeholder, and select Insert > Template Objects > Editable Region. Name this region **Photo**.

187

Note: The actual size you set for the Image Placeholder doesn't really matter. When you place the real image, the control will be resized to fit the image.

9. Click outside the placeholder, and then press **Enter** or **Return** again. Insert a table as in Step 2, with one column, one row. You're using a table here to keep everything aligned with the image. You can accomplish a similar effect by selecting Centered as the paragraph alignment, but you will lose the ability to control how wide the text display is.

10. With the table still selected, create another Editable Region and name the region **Description**.

11. Finally, save the template by selecting File > Save. Name the template **Image_Page**. The finished template should look similar to the one in Figure 8.16.

Creating the Image Pages

Now that you have a reusable template for your images, you'll create a page for every photograph displayed on your website. When finished, the image page will look similar to Figure 8.17.

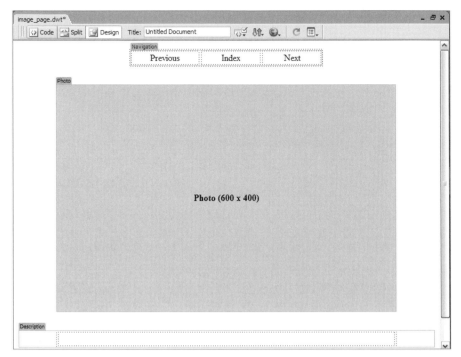

Figure 8.16 The completed Image_Page template is used to display the full-size images.

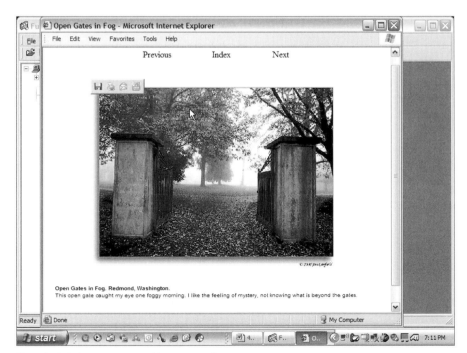

Figure 8.17 An image page created from our template

Use the following steps to create a page:

1. Select File > New, and then click on the Templates tab.

2. Select the template we just created, select Image_Page, and click Create.

3. Select the image placeholder by clicking on it. In the Properties panel, click the folder next to the Src field, and navigate to the image you want to use on this page.

> **Note:** If you found navigating to the image file a little slow, you'll be glad to know there are two faster ways to add an image to the placeholder. With the Files panel in Dreamweaver open, you can select the image and drag it onto the Src field. The second shortcut is to click on the target icon next to the Src field and drag it to the image in the Files panel. Both of these methods will update the placeholder with your image.

4. Enter the image title in the Alt field and in the title field at the top of the page. Remember that these two values are very important to search engines when evaluating the relevance of your page.

5. Select the Description by clicking on the editable region title. Enter a description for your image. Although you can get by with using only a name, a more complete description helps draw people into the image and gives them a sense of why the photograph was important to you.

6. The next step is to create the links to the index and other images. If this is the first image in the gallery, you'll want to leave Previous as plaintext or delete the text completely. Double-click on the text "Index" to select it. In the Link field of Properties, use one of the methods from Step 3 to select the photo gallery index page. You'll set the link properties for the Previous and Next links in the same way.

> **Note:** You can create links to pages that don't exist yet by entering the page name in the Link field. This method works well if you've decided on a common naming system for the image pages, such as `barn_image1.htm`, `barn_image2.htm`, etc.

7. Select File > Save to save your page.

Repeat this process for every image you plan to display on your website. In the next section, you'll create the index page that contains the thumbnails and link each thumbnail to the full-size image.

Using a Popup Window for Images

Creating image pages dynamically is very easy. However, you'll have less control over the result, and search engines will not be able to index your pages if you use that method. In Dreamweaver MX, when setting the link value in the Properties Pane, click the Target dropdown list and select _blank. This forces the image to open in a new window. Although this is a quick way to get your photo gallery online, the drawbacks make this a less-than-desirable option. If you want your images to display in a popup window, we highly recommend JustSo Picture Window3 from Valley Web Designs (www.valleywebdesigns.com/vwd_jspw3.asp).

JustSo PictureWindow3 is a Dreamweaver behavior, and it is accessed through the Behaviors panel. If Behaviors is not visible, select Window > Behaviors.

Note: In Dreamweaver, behaviors are JavaScript code that is placed in your web page and associated with a particular object, such as a hyperlink. When an event such as a mouse click is detected on the object the behavior is attached to, the behavior executes that code.

To apply the JustSo behavior to your image, do the following:

1. Select the image thumbnail on the Gallery page. At the bottom of the page, click on the <A> tag.

Note: If the behavior is grayed out when you try to select it, your thumbnail doesn't have a hyperlink set yet.

2. In the Behaviors panel, click the plus sign (+) and select JustSo Picture Window3. You'll see the dialog box shown in Figure 8.18.

3. Set the properties for the image. JustSo Picture Window allows you to set the title of the window, the Alt text, and optionally a description.

By default, the window will close on any mouse click. If you prefer to have the viewer click a Close button, or you want the window to close automatically after a set number of seconds, you can set these options on the Close tab.

Creating a Photo Gallery with Tables

Tables can be an extremely flexible way to create a photo gallery, and they work well for both index pages and image pages. Most of the photo gallery creation programs we covered earlier use tables to create the thumbnails page. For this example, you'll use the template page you created earlier in Dreamweaver. If you're using FrontPage or another method of creating web pages, the basics are the same. You'll create a 2×4 table that will contain thumbnail images. Each of these will link to the full-size image.

Note: We recommend keeping your thumbnails a consistent size. One hundred pixels on the longest side is a good compromise between screen space and identification. If you'll be using a large number of thumbnail images for a gallery, consider making the gallery index multiple pages rather than reducing the size of the thumbnails.

To get started, open a new copy of your template page in Dreamweaver. You're going to create your table in the Editable Region named "Content." Just follow these steps:

1. Click on the Content label to select it

2. Select Insert > Table (Ctrl+Alt+T Windows; Cmd+Opt+T Macintosh) to display the Table dialog box.

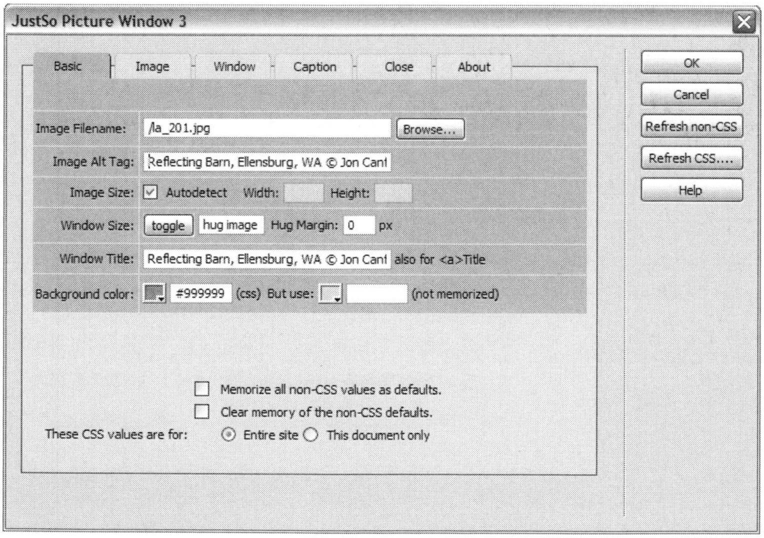

Figure 8.18 The JustSo Picture Window extension is an excellent way to create popup windows for your images, complete with captions and automatic sizing of the window.

3. We'll create a table with space for 12 thumbnail images. Enter 2 for Rows and 4 for Columns.

4. Table width has a couple of sizing options. You can create the table to be a percentage of the window size, which will enable it to grow or shrink with the browser window, or you can create the table with a fixed width. We recommend using a fixed width, as this prevents the window size from changing your intended look. Enter a width that leaves at least 30 pixels for the scroll bar. Because this website is designed for 1024×768, a width of 800 pixels will work fine (remember that the navigation bar takes up space as well, 160 pixels). The Table dialog box should look like the one in Figure 8.19.

5. To add white space around the thumbnails, set the Cell Padding and Cell Spacing values to 3. For this example, keep the Border thickness set to 0. This will keep the thumbnails from looking as though they are sitting in a table. Finally, set the alignment of your cells to Centered. If you have thumbnails of different widths, this layout will look neater to the viewer.

6. Leave the Header, Caption, Alignment, and Summary fields blank for now. Click the OK button, and you'll return to your page with the empty table inserted, as shown in Figure 8.20.

7. Click in the first cell of the table to select it, and select Insert > Image (Ctrl+Alt+I Windows; Cmd+Opt+I Macintosh). Navigate to the folder that contains the thumbnail images, as shown in Figure 8.21 (for both Windows and Macintosh), and select the thumbnail for this cell. Optionally, you can enter a text label to describe the image.

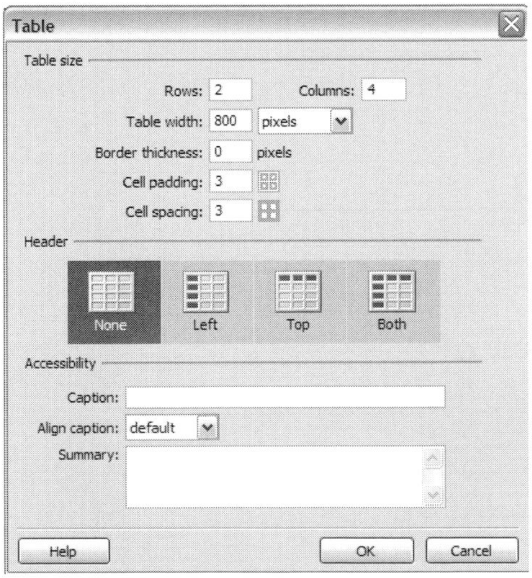

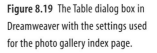

Figure 8.19 The Table dialog box in Dreamweaver with the settings used for the photo gallery index page.

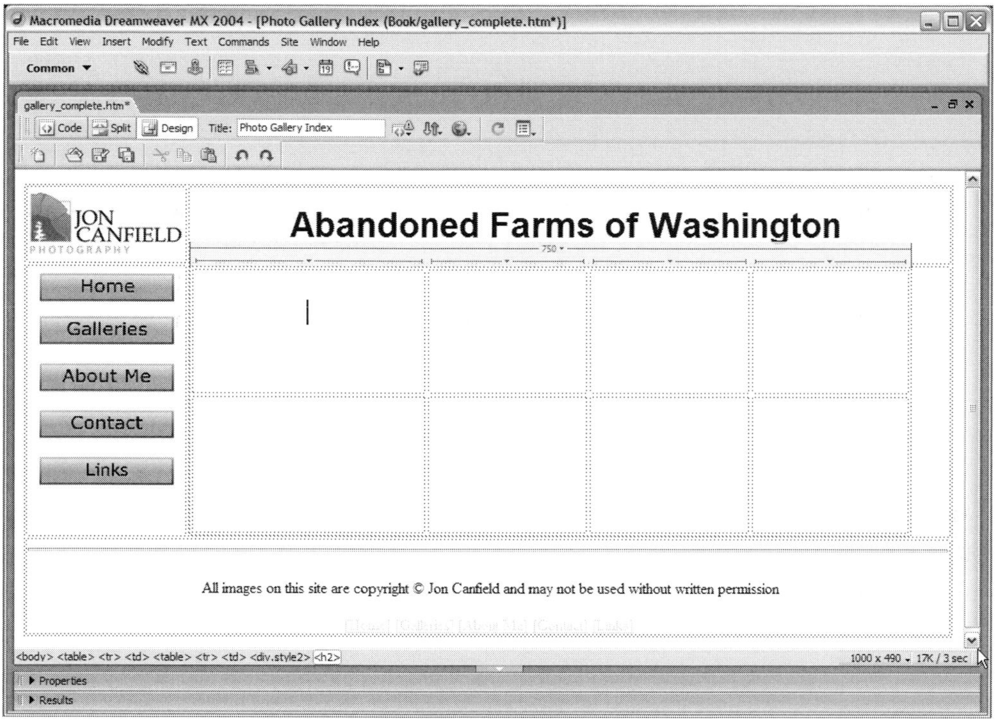

Figure 8.20 The photo gallery index page with the empty table, ready for thumbnails

8. In the Properties tab, set the Link to point to the full-size version of our image. Do this by clicking the folder icon next to the Link field and navigating to the file.

9. In the Alt field, enter a name for the image. As you've seen, the Alt field plays an important role in helping search engines index our site.

10. Repeat Steps 7 through 9 for each thumbnail on the page. When complete, your page should look similar to Figure 8.22.

Getting Seen

You've designed your pages and created your content, but being on the Internet with your beautiful website and incredible images won't do you much good if people can't find you. Promoting yourself in the digital age is perhaps more difficult and more important than ever. Global customers also mean global competition, and the winner is usually the one who is most easily found and seen. This is where search engines come into play. HTML provides elements (also available through web-authoring tools) you can use to help visitors find your site. By knowing what search engines look for, you can do things to encourage other sites to link to yours.

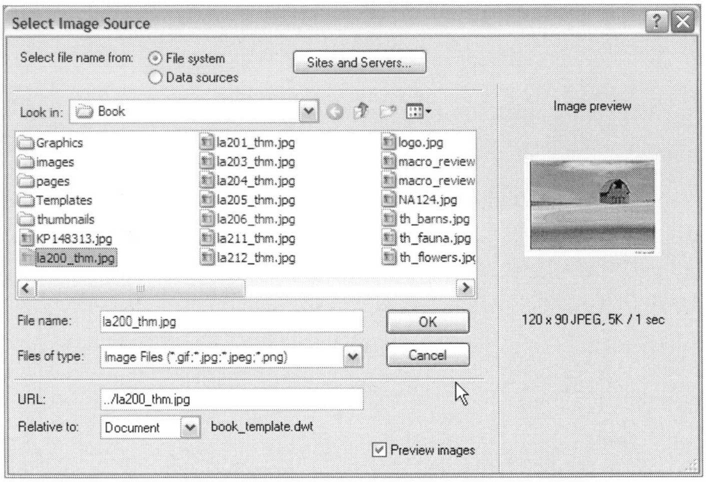

Windows

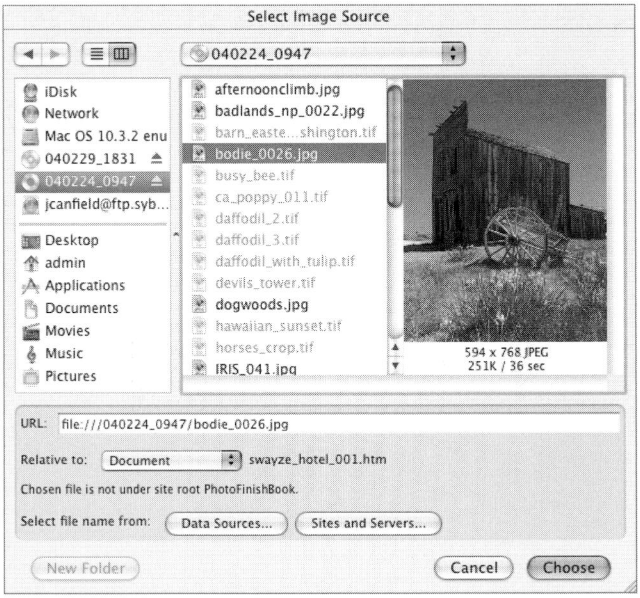

Macintosh

Figure 8.21 Inserting a thumbnail image into our photo gallery table

Setting Up Your Site for Search Engines: The Needle in the Haystack

Earlier we noted the importance of including alternative text (the alt element of the <img> tag in HTML) with navigation buttons to help search engines index your site. You saw how to include this text in Dreamweaver MX for both navigation buttons and photographs in your galleries. HTML provides two more elements that are equally important in making sure your site is found: the site title (the <title> tag) and descriptive keywords (the <meta> tag).

The Page Title and Description

First and foremost, you need to be sure the title of your page is relevant. The <title> tag is the single most important tag used by web crawlers, such as Google (www.google.com). Web crawlers index the title of every page they inspect and rate the search results based on how similar the title is to the requested information. Therefore, using titles that are meaningful and concise is important. In Dreamweaver MX 2004, you can enter a page title at any time in the Title field of the toolbar, as shown in Figure 8.23.

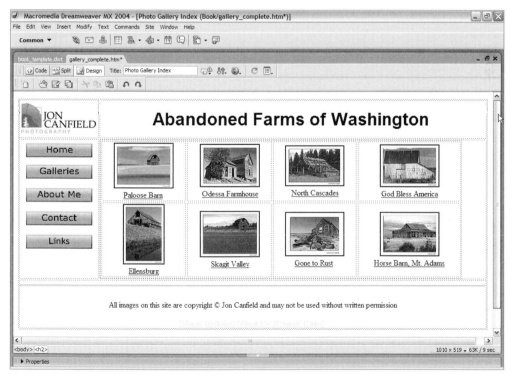

Figure 8.22 The completed photo gallery index page in Dreamweaver

Figure 8.23 It's important to give your pages a title to help search engines index the page (and avoid the viewer seeing "Untitled Document" in their browser).

This will generate a `<title>` tag. In FrontPage 2003, select File > Properties and use the General tab of the Page Properties dialog box to enter the title. Most photographers name their images, and the image name is a good candidate for the page title for that photograph. As an example, a page with a barn photograph might be titled "Abandoned Barn, Palouse, Washington."

Nearly as important to most search engines, the `description` META tag is used as a summary of the page contents. A good description will help a search engine zero in on your page. Using our title page as an example, a good description would read "This abandoned barn in the Palouse farming region of Eastern Washington sits in a field of wheat near Steptoe Butte."

When a potential visitor searches on "Eastern Washington barns" the search engine sees two word matches in the title and three matches in the description.

Keywords

While increasingly less important than page titles and the description tag, keywords still play an important role in how visible your website will be to someone searching the Web. Without the use of good keywords, no one will know how to find you. As an example, go to Google and type **Nature photography**. Sounds like a logical key word to use if you have a nature photography site, right? Well, about 4.5 million pages thought so too. What are the odds you'll be seen in that mess? For keywords to be successful, you need to try and place yourself in the top 10. Most search engines return the top 10 as their first set of results, and most users will find what they're looking for within this set. Obviously, you need to be more specific in your keywords.

Word-pair phrases, such as "Yosemite pictures" in keywords carry more weight than individual words. Ideally, you should have no more than 10–15 keyword phrases on a page.

In Dreamweaver, select Insert > HTML > Head Tags > Keywords, and type your keyword phrases separated by commas. For the barn example we used earlier, we might select "abandoned barn, Palouse region, Paloose region, Eastern Washington, wheat field, Washington farm, Steptoe Butte, Palouse Washington, barn picture, barn photograph." All of these word pairs are related to the content on the page and the description used. We avoided repeating the same words too many times; some search engines regard this as spamming to skew the search results. Using common misspellings as keywords can be effective too. In this example, we used both "Palouse" and "Paloose."

In FrontPage 2003, the same Page Properties > General tab used to enter a title also lets you enter keywords, which would be formatted the same way as our Dreamweaver example.

Killer Keyword Tips

Here's a summary of the most important tips for getting your website found by search engines:

- Give every page a title that matches the content. Titles have more weight than any other element on the page. The title should be brief and directly related to the content on that page.

- Use the `description` META tag to reinforce the page title. Especially for your index pages and home page, provide a good description of your site. The description should be used to expand on the page title and include the words used in the title to reinforce the importance of the subject to the search engine.

- Use the `<Alt>` element for all images. The `<Alt>` element should match the page title. If `<title>Abandoned Barn, Palouse, Washington</title>` is the title tag, the photo should use the same text in the `<Alt>` element.

- Use the `Keyword` META tag, but consider it a backup plan. Include less likely search words here. The keywords should use all the words in the description, with additional related words, such as in the example with "wheat field," "Washington barn," and "Steptoe Butte." If someone adds theses additional words to their search query, these additional words help to narrow down the results the search engine returns, thereby increasing the likelihood of making that first page of results.

- Use word pairs rather than single words. Each keyword phrase is separated by a comma. Search engines place more weight on word phrases than individual words. Ideally, a two-word phrase is best, such as "abandoned barn" rather than "abandoned" and "barn" used separately.

- Include common misspellings for keywords. For example, Palouse (correct), and Paloose (a likely misspelling for someone to use).

- Think like your target customer, not like a photographer. Your images may be photographs or images to you, but to many viewers they are pictures or photos.

- Avoid using frames if possible, unless you have experience optimizing framesets for search engines. Frames hide the title of the embedded page, thereby removing the best method by which search engines can find your page.

- Include text links on your pages. Web crawlers don't typically index Flash or graphics files. By using a set of text links at the foot of your page, you give the search engine something on which to index. If you do use Flash or graphics for links, remember the first tip: include the `<Alt>` element description.

- If your host service provides tracking reports, use them to see which pages are being visited most frequently. This can tell you where your visitors are coming from and help you tune your keywords for less frequently visited pages.

Note: You may not want every page on your website to be seen in a search result. Why? Typically, you want your visitors to start out at a home page or a gallery index page. If they link directly to your image of the barn, they may not know whose image it is, and more importantly, they may not see your other beautiful images. The easiest way to avoid this is by adding a META tag to the header of your individual image pages: `<META name="ROBOTS" content="NOINDEX">`. Most search engines, and all web crawlers, use "robots" to crawl through websites. When the robots see this tag in the header of a page, they skip the rest of the page and move on. Remember though that a page with this tag on it will not be indexed, and any pages linked from only that page will not be indexed either.

Getting Linked

In addition to building information to attract search engines into your site, you should try to get related sites to include links to yours. Most of the major photography sites will include links to your site on a reciprocal basis. For example, if you are a nature photographer, PhotoMigrations (`www.photomigrations.com`), NatureScapes (`www.naturescapes.net`), and the NANPA (North American Nature Photographers Association) site (`www.nanpa.org`) are all excellent places to start. Besides the intangible benefits of networking with your colleagues, getting linked externally helps potential visitors to find you directly as they surf, and it contributes to search engine placement. Search engines like Google and Inktomi are "web crawlers," which means they add links by following links already in their database. A link to your website from one of the popular sites can help pull up your rating.

Google and Inktomi also provide more direct ways you can improve your placement with them.

Google

Google is one of the most popular search engines today. In addition to inclusion through links, Google also has a Submit URL feature. (Submitting a URL isn't a guarantee of inclusion, but for someone just starting out with a website, it's certainly worthwhile to submit your URL.) To submit your URL, type **http://www.google.com/addurl.html** in your browser. In the URL field, enter the full URL for your website, including the **http://**. You can enter information in the Comments field as well. Google claims they do not use the comments when indexing your site, but we suggest adding the same text used in your site `description` META tag as it may be used in the future.

Inktomi

Inktomi (www.inktomi.com) is another major search engine. Yahoo, MSN, and other major websites use it. Like Google, Inktomi is a web crawler. Unlike Google though, you can buy your way onto its search listings. For an annual fee for the first URL, the Site Match program will review your submission for relevance and submit your URL into all the major search engines. The advantage to this method is that all the major search engines will carry your site. The disadvantage is the cost, but we feel that for the serious photographer selling on the Internet, this is a good way to get established with many of the major search engines.

Finding Links to Your Site

Most search engines will allow you to easily discover who is linking to your website once you have been listed with them. Remember that a website that is highly ranked in the search engines will help your own ranking. Not all links to your website are good though. You may occasionally find that someone is stealing your work by linking to an image on your site. If this is done without your permission, your copyright is being violated and you are, in essence, paying them to steal your work if your service provider charges for bandwidth. In Google, you can quickly see who is linking to your site by typing link:www.domain.com in the search field, replacing the www.domain.com with your own domain name.

Other Promotional Ideas

Link sharing and search engine placement all help users to find your website. However, they do require that the user knows what to look for. Sometimes, it's better to tell a potential customer they need your services.

Advertising

One of the most effective ways to generate interest in your website and photography is through advertising. For studio and wedding photographers, advertising is one of the best methods of promoting your services. Most major cities have at least one large bridal fair every year. Advertising on their website would be a great way to pull business to your website. Nature photographers don't have such an obvious outlet for our services though. Possible opportunities for nature photographers would be regional events, such as the outdoor show. If your work is specialized to a particular regional area, the local magazines or websites can be a great way to get your name and work seen. A great example of this is *Arizona Highways*.

Don't overlook the value of traditional advertising either. Always have a few business cards in your camera bag, and make sure they include the URL for your website. Curious bystanders can be an excellent source of business for images that remind them of a scene they visited.

E-mail Lists

Advertising in an e-mail mailing list can be a very cost-effective way to reach a targeted group of customers. Many large sites, particularly ones tied to traditional services (such as magazines, stores, etc.) send regular e-mails to customers. Buying space in these e-mails can be an affordable way to increase your exposure. This is not without its drawbacks though. Being associated with a mailing considered spam by the receiver might be viewed as a negative and actually hurt your chances of doing business with the receiver.

Snail Mail

Many magazines will sell their subscribers list for use in mailings. The response rate for this method is typically low. For all but specialized magazines, we don't feel that direct mailings are an effective use of time or money.

Setting Up for Internet Sales

One huge advantage the Internet has given photographers is the ability to easily sell our work anywhere in the world. There are services that will process credit card orders, online art galleries that will sell photographs for a commission, and the popular but traditional method of mailing in order forms.

Shopping Carts and Online Payment Systems

Also known as *eCommerce*, shopping cart systems are available from a wide variety of vendors. Most of us have purchased online using a shopping cart system. For a percentage of your sales, which varies by the number of transactions and average cost of item sold, these companies will assist you with setting up the needed security systems, transaction processing, and fraud protection. Expect to pay a pretty penny for the privilege, as these systems are designed for high volume sellers. MonsterCommerce (www.monstercommerce.com) is one of the most reasonable and full-featured of the eCommerce vendors, with prices starting at about $200 for the initial setup and around $80 per month. They, as do most eCommerce vendors, require that your site be hosted with them. For the average photographer, we don't think that eCommerce-style shopping carts are an effective way to sell on the Internet.

PayPal (www.paypal.com) has recently added shopping cart functionality, which we feel is a great way to set up business on the Internet. To get started, you'll need to have a PayPal account. Click the Merchant Tools link, and select the PayPal Shopping Cart link. After you fill in a few fields on the PayPal website, they will generate the HTML code for a Buy Me button.

Just paste the HTML into your web page by clicking on the page where you'd like the button to appear and clicking the Code button in the toolbar. Choose Edit > Paste (Ctrl+V Windows; Cmd+V Macintosh). When you switch back to Design view, you'll see the button on your page. The user only sees an Add To Cart button. When the user clicks the purchase button, PayPal creates a shopping session for the user with prices and order information that you supplied when PayPal created the button. This method is a great way to get started, and best of all, there's no additional cost beyond PayPal's normal transaction fees.

Other Options for Selling on the Internet

Another payment processing option is Verisign (www.verisign.com). For a reasonable monthly fee and a setup fee of about $180, Verisign will process up to 500 transactions. Customers can use checks, credit cards, or debit cards, all through Verisign's secure servers.

If you don't want to bother with handling sales at all, several large photo galleries online will display and process orders for your work. Expect to pay a high commission rate for this service, and most charge a membership fee. Because these sites tend to offer work from many artists, the only real advantage to using them is the immediate ability to get your work on the Internet. We'll cover this option in Chapter 14, "Displaying and Selling Your Images."

Publishing and Maintaining Your Site

Now that you are up and running with a live website, you can just sit back and watch the orders and accolades roll in. Right? Sorry, but it doesn't work that way! To be effective, websites (just like cameras, cars, and spouses) need regular attention.

Chapter Contents

Publishing Your Site
Checking Links
Updating Your Site Contents
Website Maintenance

Publishing Your Site

Now that you've created your pages, it's time to go live with them. Both Dreamweaver and FrontPage make publishing very easy with their built-in file transfer tools. You don't need to use these programs, though. As you'll see in this chapter, FTP client applications can be used to upload files. Finally, we'll cover checking links to verify that all of the buttons and hyperlinks take visitors to the correct pages.

Dreamweaver

If you didn't provide the website information when you first created your site in Dreamweaver (perhaps you didn't have a domain registered yet), you'll need to tell Dreamweaver where your site is and how to connect to it. Just follow these steps:

1. Select Site > Manage Sites.
2. If you have more than one site, make sure the correct one is selected and then click Edit. This will launch the Site Definition wizard shown in Figure 9.1.
3. Click the Advanced tab, and select Remote Info from the list.

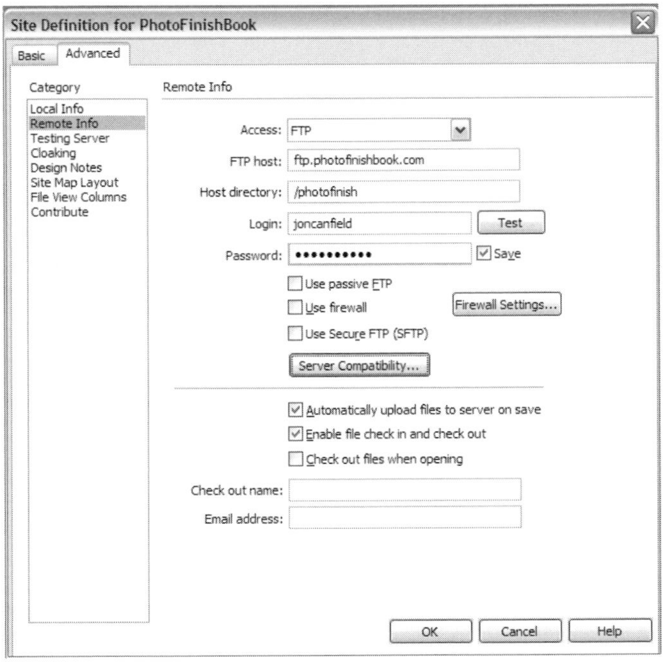

Figure 9.1 The Site Definition wizard in Dreamweaver will guide you through setting up the connection to your remote website.

4. Select FTP from the Access dropdown list, and provide the information your hosting service has provided for location, login, password, and any other required information.

5. Click the Test button to verify that you have provided the correct information. You should see a brief progress bar and then a success message. If you see a Failed To Connect message, recheck your provided information, and if needed, contact your host service for help. You may need to check the Use Firewall or Secure FTP checkboxes, depending on your ISP requirements.

Once you have a valid connection to your remote site, click the Put button in the Files Palette toolbar to copy your files to the web server. If no files are selected, Dreamweaver will ask if you want to copy all of the files to the website. If this is the first time you've uploaded, you'll want to click OK. If you're republishing changed files, the Synchronize option is a better choice, and we will cover this a bit later in the "Website Maintenance" section.

FrontPage

FrontPage has a very user-friendly interface for publishing files to the Web. As with Dreamweaver, you can publish individual files, a single file, or all of the changed files with just a couple of mouse clicks. Figure 9.2 shows the view presented when you select File > Publish Site.

From this one view, you can select which files to publish, synchronize the local and remote copies of your website, or republish the entire site if needed. Notice the question marks (?) and Conflict messages in the Local Web Site and Remote Web Site panes; they are the mechanisms by which Front Page signals that a file in one location does not match up with another.

If this is the first time you've published this website, you'll need to provide the host server information, as you did for Dreamweaver. Have your FTP server name, root directory, username, and password information ready. Once this information has been entered, FrontPage will connect to the host server and be ready to transfer your files.

Note: To quickly publish a single file or a group of files in the same folder, right-click the file in the Folder List in FrontPage and select Publish Selected Files.

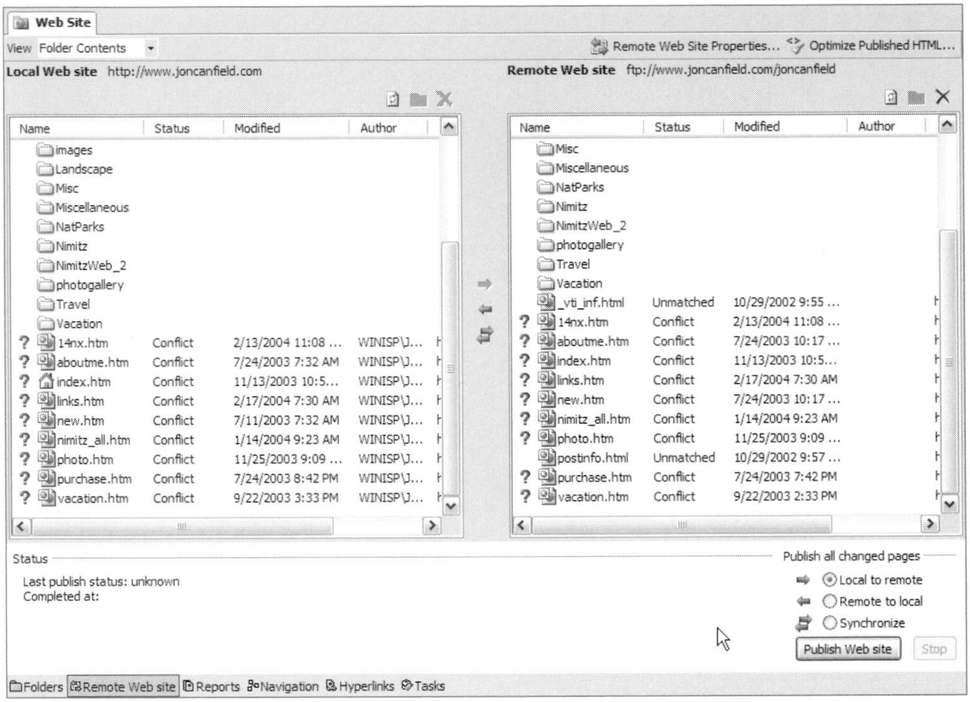

Figure 9.2 The Publish Site view in FrontPage shows both the local copy and the remote copy of your website. You can easily see which files have changed and need to be published.

Checking Links

Both Dreamweaver and FrontPage have very useful link-checking tools. Link checking will quickly identify any potential errors that visitors may run into. Any time your website is modified to add or delete pages, you should run a link check.

In Dreamweaver, select Site > Check Links Sitewide (Ctrl+F8 Windows; Cmd+F8 Macintosh).

FrontPage has a similar feature accessed by selecting View > Reports > Problems > Hyperlinks. Both of these link checkers work on the currently open website; therefore, it's a good idea to run them against the actual website, not just the local working copy.

A number of external link-checking tools are available. If your web-design program doesn't come with a link checker, we recommend the free Link Checker at http://validator.w3.org. The w3.org website is the Internet home of the World Wide Web Consortium (W3C), the standards committee for HTML, and it is a great resource for validation tools, information on HTML, and CSS.

Updating Your Site Contents

A static, unchanging website has very little chance of generating returning visitors or customers. Your goal as a website owner is to keep people coming back for more. Fortunately, photographers are constantly creating new images that are potential candidates for their websites.

Keep Your Home Page Fresh

If a home page has changed since the last time it was viewed, most visitors will assume there are other changes as well and will want to explore the rest of the site. Frequent changes and updates increase the possibility of being added to a visitor's Favorites list—something we all strive for.

There are several effective ways to keep a home page looking fresh without changing the actual layout of elements or the look and feel of the page. Figure 9.3 shows an example of a website that always has new content yet keeps the same layout. When a visitor comes back to the site, they'll focus on what's new, not how to browse the site.

Random Image Displays

Changing an image on your home page can be a very effective method of updating your site. By using extensions to Dreamweaver, you can select a set of images for your home page and change the image randomly on every visit or make a daily change. Expert Images and Advanced Random Images are both available from Kaosweaver (www.kaosweaver.com). Expert Images takes the random image feature a step further by including the ability to play a slideshow of your images, along with daily, weekly and monthly image changes.

Advanced Random Images, which can be downloaded for free with a requested donation, allows you to select a set of images for your home page. As shown in Figure 9.4, you can display a different image every day.

> **Note:** Unless you need to make wholesale changes, don't move elements such as navigation controls, menus, and graphics, or change color schemes. Returning visitors want to focus on what is new. Major design changes will draw their attention and may cause them to leave your site before finding the new content.

If you're comfortable working directly in HTML and other web-scripting languages, you can choose between hundreds of scripts for random image rotation that are available on the Internet. Most of these scripts will require some editing to adapt them to your site, and some require that your pages be in a particular format, such as ASP or PHP files that run the script on the web server and access the images from a database. You'll need to check with your ISP to see if your hosting package includes server scripting. If you're interested in the scripting method, you'll find links to some of the most popular ones on the companion website at www.photofinishbook.com. Searching Google for "random image rotation" will turn up thousands of possibilities.

Figure 9.3 Photographer and author Charlotte Lowrie regularly updates her home page (www.wordsandphotos.org), giving her site a fresh look that keeps visitors coming back for updates.

For ease of use and flexibility, however, the Dreamweaver extension approach can't be beat; and we recommend the extensions from Kaosweaver as great ways to add functionality to your website without adding complexity.

Figure 9.4 We used Advanced Random Images to display a new "Image of the Day" every 24 hours on our website. If a visitor clicks on the image, they are taken directly to the image gallery.

Updating Your Images

We all have favorite images that we've made and want to share, but our favorites may not be the most popular images with visitors. Deciding which images to change in a display is sometimes difficult. Most photographers have a tendency to continually add images rather than replace existing photos with new ones—thinking they're all great. Recall from Chapter 7, "Planning Your Site," that too many choices reduces the impact of all the images.

> **Note:** No change is permanent on the Web. Don't be afraid to try new image ideas. If you don't get the results you want (i.e., sales and webpage hits), try other ideas.

If you have sufficient storage space for your site, an effective way to implement these updates is to create a new gallery and simply update the link on your index page.

Featured Galleries are another excellent method of encouraging visitors to browse. Consider creating a link to a "Featured Gallery of the Month" on your home page and gallery index page.

The Gallery Show Analogy

Galleries tend to have showings that are theme based. Because your website is a virtual gallery, you can follow similar guidelines. What is a virtual gallery's biggest advantage over a conventional gallery? You have the whole gallery to yourself! Every visitor to your website sees the images you've selected to present with no competition from other photographers or artists. Of course, like any gallery showing, using a theme such as seasonal images and making regular changes to the images on display will keep interest up and visitors returning for more.

We've found it to be very effective to have a regular change of images every two to three months. A great example of this would be a gallery of seasonal images, as shown in Figure 9.5. You'll find more examples of thematic galleries in the color section.

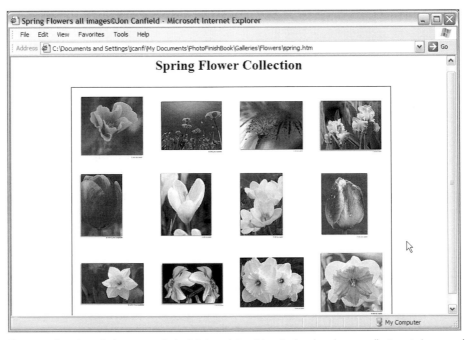

Figure 9.5 Changing galleries on a regular basis helps to bring visitors back and can be an excellent way to increase sales.

> **Note:** Having seasonal image displays is a great way to increase sales too. You should display images ahead of their actual season. Spring photos should be showcased during mid to late Winter, for example. This strategy works well for two reasons. People are usually more excited about the next season than the current one, and by viewing images ahead of time, potential customers have more time to consider ordering your work.

Your Latest Photo Shoot

Maintaining a photo gallery with images from your latest assignment or trip is a great way to continually update images. This works especially well for the photographer doing photojournalism or model work, but this strategy can be adapted to the nature or fine art photographer as well. Similar to the Featured Gallery, a link on your home page to your "Latest Work" or "Current Project" encourages browsing. The images in this type of gallery should be updated more frequently. Consider replacing the contents of this type of gallery every two to three weeks at most.

> **Note:** If you have a major shooting assignment or session planned, a Current Project link is a great way to let people know that new content is coming. If you have a Spring wildflower trip to California coming up, change the link to Coming Soon—California Poppies!, with information about your upcoming photo shoot.

Website Maintenance

Modern web-authoring tools have made website maintenance *reasonably* painless. Adding and removing files and pages from your website is easily done with the publishing features in Dreamweaver and FrontPage. Both of these programs offer version control, making it much simpler to upload all the changed files in one operation, as shown in Figure 9.6, while preventing you from accidentally overwriting newer files with older ones.

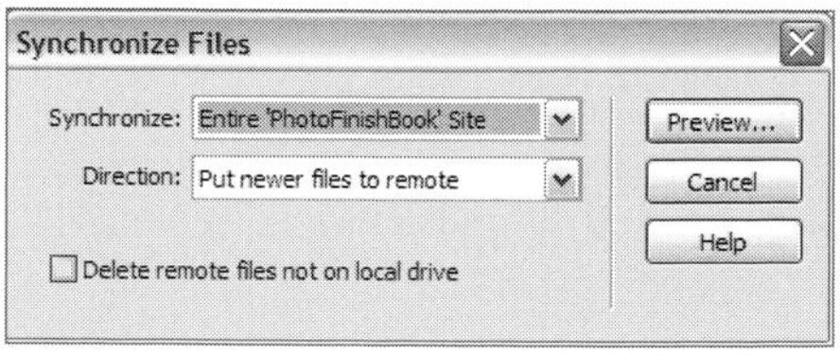

Figure 9.6 The Synchronize feature in Dreamweaver makes it much easier to keep your website updated by replacing only the files that have changed.

To upload all changed files in Dreamweaver, take the following steps:

1. Right-click (Ctrl+click Macintosh) the site folder in the Files panel. A context menu will appear.

2. Select Synchronize > Entire Site, and choose Put Newer Files To Remote in the Direction dropdown list. If you want to see what files will be uploaded, you can click the Preview button.

3. Dreamweaver will connect to your remote website, check each file on your local machine, and upload those files that are newer than the server copies.

If only one or two files have changed, you can click on the changed files to select them and click the Put button in the Files Palette toolbar (see Figure 9.7).

Figure 9.7 Select only the changed files in Dreamweaver and use the Put button to copy them to your website.

Note: To select multiple files, click on the first file, and then Shift+click on the last one to select all of the files between, or Ctrl+click (Cmd+click Macintosh) to select multiple files that are not together.

Using FTP to Post Updates

Sometimes, using an application like Dreamweaver or FrontPage to make simple updates is overkill for the task at hand. You can use a simple FTP client application such as CuteFTP (www.cuteftp.com/cuteftp/ available forWindows and Macintosh) or WS FTP Pro (www.ipswitch.com/products/WS_FTP/, Windows only) or Fetch 4.03 (http://fetchsoftworks.com, Macintosh only) when you need to quickly transfer a couple of files to your hosting service. Although FTP client applications aren't suitable for making large scale changes to a website, being able to upload images from a remote site is great when shooting on location. Both of the Windows programs use a familiar Explorer-style interface, so making file copies is easy to do from your hotel room and other away-from-home connections to the Internet.

Using CuteFTP as an example, select the files you want to upload from the local files list on the left and drag them to the remote list on the right. The selected files will be shown in the bottom window, along with the progress and success or fail status (see Figure 9.8).

Note: These lighter weight programs are excellent for quickly copying files, but they offer none of the safety features of the web-publishing applications. You'll need to verify that you are copying files to the correct remote directory.

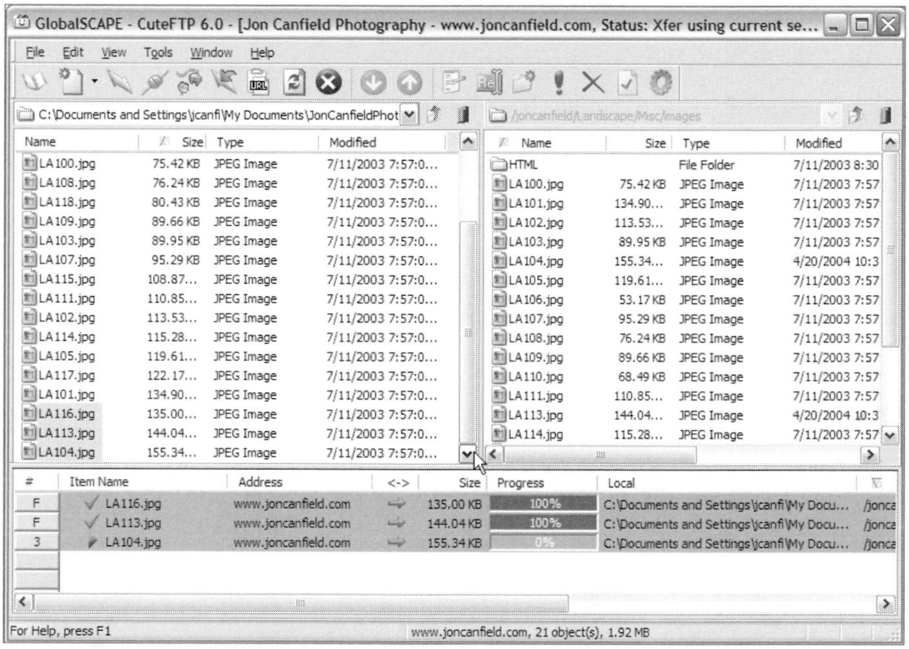

Figure 9.8 When you just need to upload a few files, particularly when you're on the road, lightweight FTP programs, such as CuteFTP, are good alternatives to the full web-design programs.

Adding Pages

As your website grows, you will add and occasionally delete pages. Not all additions are created equal. If you're adding a new gallery, you'll probably add the pages and images together in a new folder. To do this, create the new folder structure on the local copy of your website. Add the images and pages, as shown in Chapter 8, "Going Live."

If the additional pages are going to be part of an existing gallery, the approach changes. Depending on how the gallery was built, it may be easier to re-create the gallery completely by running the program used to create the HTML gallery.

If the gallery was created from scratch, you can easily add the new thumbnail images and links to the existing index table, just as you did when originally creating the page.

Some web gallery creation tools, such as inTensa Gallery from Kaosweaver (www.kaosweaver.com) make it easy to update existing gallery pages by adding individual images.

Reevaluate Site Layout

As your website knowledge and creation skills grow, reevaluating your site design and page layout is a good idea. Often, what appears to be a perfectly logical plan becomes less so when viewed with experience. A good point of comparison is our early efforts at photography —images that were once thought to be technically excellent can sometimes need to be improved when looked at with a more-experienced eye. It is likewise with a website.

Examining Site Reports

If your ISP provides reporting information (and most provide some level of reporting, typically more detailed as you move into the more complete service packages), you should examine them on a monthly basis to identify what interests your visitors. These reports, or *logs,* as shown in Figure 9.9, will help you identify which areas of your website are receiving the most hits (or *views*) and how much bandwidth your site is using. Here are a few things to track closely:

Page Hits   The ability to see which pages are the most popular makes it easier to determine what adjustments need to be made to layout and content. For example, if you have galleries for landscapes, wildlife, and flowers, you might decide to increase the number of images in your wildlife gallery or create subgalleries of bears, wolves, and deer, because those pages are viewed twice as often as your flower images.

Note: Most reporting tools require a database on the server to store the information. Setting up a SQL database is beyond the scope of this book (and most people's interest), but most ISPs provide packages that include database support. Register.com (www.register.com) offers web traffic reports with their entry-level hosting package for a small monthly fee.

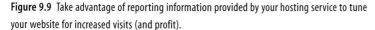

General Summary		
1.	Host name	photofinishbook.com
2.	Program start time	Mar 25, 2004 00:06
3.	Time of first request	Mar 17, 2004 16:11
4.	Time of last request	Mar 23, 2004 03:04
5.	Time last 7 days lasts until	Mar 25, 2004 00:06
6.	Successful server requests	76 Requests
7.	Successful requests in last 7 days	75 Requests
8.	Logfile lines without status code	24 Lines
9.	Logfile lines without status code in last 7 days	0 Lines
10.	Successful requests for pages	33 Requests for pages
11.	Successful requests for pages in last 7 days	33 Requests for pages
12.	Failed requests	38 Requests
13.	Failed requests in last 7 days	38 Requests
14.	Distinct files requested	45 Files
15.	Distinct files requested in last 7 days	45 Files
16.	Distinct hosts served	14 Hosts
17.	Distinct hosts served in last 7 days	13 Hosts
18.	Total data transferred	474.71 KBytes
19.	Total data transferred in last 7 days	474.11 KBytes

Figure 9.9 Take advantage of reporting information provided by your hosting service to tune your website for increased visits (and profit).

Bandwidth   The other statistic you'll want to pay close attention to is bandwidth usage. As your site grows more popular, you may find that more bandwidth is used than you anticipated. Depending on your ISP, this can cost extra each month. If your site is costing you more than you planned, it's time to consider upgrading your hosting package to allow for the higher traffic.

How Your Site Is Reached   Perhaps the most useful aspect of site reports is learning *how* people find a website. Most reports track the *referring URL*. In Chapter 8, we discussed search engine and keyword strategies. Examining where visitors are coming from can help you determine whether your keywords are effective. If a high number of visitors are being referred from search engines, you'll know that your keywords and descriptions are doing their job. If most of your hits are coming from link exchanges, you'll need to reexamine your keywords and descriptions to try and build traffic from these sources. Finally, if you're paying for advertising links on other sites, the referring URL reports will tell you how effective your ads are.

Producing Digital Slideshows

Not long ago, many of us were dealing with trays of slides that spilled, slides that were backward or upside down, music that was next to impossible to sync to our slides, and bulky, expensive hardware to handle transitions between slides.

Digital projectors, laptop computers, and affordable, easy-to-learn software have all but replaced the venerable slide projector in the last few years. As prices continue to drop, and features are added to make even more compelling presentations, it makes sense to consider moving into the digital world for both the hobbyist and the professional.

Choosing Slideshow Hardware

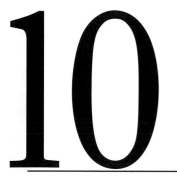

Slideshows aren't always presented to a group of people viewing a screen in the same room anymore. Individuals can now view them on computer or TV monitors, via the Web or a physical medium like CD or DVD. Still, for many photographers the classic standup presentation is the most common way to share a slideshow, and it's the method that requires specialized hardware—namely, the digital projector.

Chapter Contents

Choosing a Digital Projector
Other Display Options

Choosing a Digital Projector

Before selecting a projector, you need to identify your needs and budget. In this section, we'll cover all of the technical aspects of digital projectors and help you decide which is right for you. After a quick review of the basic features to look for, we'll look at the differences between LCD and DLP technologies and then focus on the crucial considerations of brightness and contrast, resolution, color fidelity, and price.

Basic Features and Considerations

Anyone who needs a digital projector for slide presentations should consider the following features. How important each one is will depend on how and where you'll be presenting your slideshows.

- Resolution, contrast ratios, and brightness all contribute to the quality of the projected image. Higher resolutions show more detail, while higher contrast ratios, which produce "blacker" blacks, display a broader range of tone from black to white. Resolution will be the single most-determining factor in price, while contrast ratios and brightness often differentiate cost between two projectors of the same resolution and feature set.

- Will you sometimes be presenting in small rooms? If so, you'll want to consider a projector with a zoom lens and a short "throw" or focus distance that allows the projector to be closer to the screen. Most budget projectors that include zoom lenses use manual zoom and focus, while mid-range and high-end projectors often include zoom and focus controls on the remote.

- Keystone correction is an important feature. The *keystone effect* occurs when the projected image is at any angle other than straight from the projector. Many projectors correct only horizontal keystone (caused when the image is projected from above or below a straight path), while some correct for both horizontal and vertical (caused by projecting from a side angle).

- Remote controls, particularly wireless remotes, make it much easier to give your presentation—especially when you're not able to be next to the computer. Many remotes include laser pointers and also allow you to adjust projector settings such as brightness and color.

- Wireless connections can be very useful when setting up the computer near the projector isn't feasible. Wireless connectors are becoming more common in higher-end projectors. However, if your projector doesn't include this feature, products such as the WiJET (www.otcwireless.com) are available. WiJET uses standard 802.11b, or Wi-Fi (Wireless Fidelity), wireless networking to transmit images from your computer (or multiple computers) to a projector from up to 50 meters away. These devices are not suitable for video use though, because the data transfer rate is too slow (although 802.11g promises to address this issue when it becomes widely available).

Note: In addition to Wi-Fi, devices that use Bluetooth and HomeRF (Radio Frequency) are also available. Neither of these methods is a good choice for presentations. Bluetooth is limited in range to about 10 meters, and it has $1/10$ the data transfer rate of Wi-Fi, HomeRF suffers from interference problems and is also much slower than Wi-Fi. Because of these deficiencies, we strongly recommend using Wi-Fi if you go wireless.

- If the projector will be used for multiple purposes, such as presentations and home theater, you should look for a projector with output options for s-video, composite video, component video, and support for rear projection.

- Not all LCD projectors are compatible with both Macintosh and Windows systems. Macintosh users may need to purchase an optional adapter for the video connection.

- If you'll be presenting in large rooms, poor resolution will be more noticeable. Higher-resolution projectors will show better detail, which is particularly important when projecting to larger sizes. Larger rooms also require projectors with higher brightness (lumens) ratings in order to maintain image quality when the projector is farther from the screen.

- Projector lamps have estimated life spans of 2,000 to 3,000 hours. Given the high cost to replace a lamp (usually $200 to $400), a longer life span is certainly better.

If You Travel

Two more considerations are particularly important if you're taking your slideshow on the road:

- If you travel internationally, a universal power supply that works with both 110 volt and 220 volt should be a requirement.

- If you travel often, weight and size will be important as well. Most of the portable projectors in the 5 pound and under category will sacrifice some features and tend to have lower brightness (lumens) than larger projectors.

Travelling without Your Projector

If you take your show on the road, many venues have their own projection systems. Check in advance with the organizer or location. What should you ask about?

1. Is a projection system installed?

2. What type of projector is used?

3. What is the resolution?

4. What size is the room?

Regardless of the answers, bring your own projector as well. At best, it's a safe backup plan. At worst, it's the difference between a show and a blank screen.

LCD or DLP?

Two common technologies are currently used with digital projectors: LCD (liquid crystal display) and DLP (digital light processing). As you can see in Figure 10.1, both types look very similar on the outside. Like the familiar analog projectors, both types use a lamp to generate the light and a lens to focus the projected image. What happens in between—how the image is formed from the digital information— is how they differ.

Figure 10.1 Although the HP DLP-based projector on the right is only half the size of the NEC LCD projector on the left, it offers higher resolution, a brighter image, and is more portable.

LCD

LCD, or Liquid Crystal Display, is the established display technology in digital projection. It's also the main technology in laptop displays and flat panel desktop displays. LCD comes in two flavors: active matrix and polysilicon. Active matrix (laptops and flat panels typically use active matrix, often backlit) uses a single panel for all pixels: red, green, and blue. Polysilicon uses three panels, one for each color.

The biggest advantage to three-panel displays is an increase in saturation and brightness. Most current model LCD projectors have moved to the polysilicon variety. LCD is a "transmissive" light source and works by turning individual pixels on or off to generate the correct color. An LCD panel consists of a grid of cells that are mapped to pixels in the bitmap image received. The liquid-crystal material in each cell is electrically charged so that it either blocks light from the source or passes it through to form the complete image. A series of mirrors and prisms breaks up the white light from the lamp into red, green, and blue light that is transmitted through the LCD panel. In the panel, individual cells mapped to red pixels in the bitmap let the red light through and block the other colors, and so on. You'll find an illustration of the process in the color section.

Using this technology, LCD projectors display all three colors at once. This gives it a brightness and saturation advantage over DLP, which (as you'll see next) displays red, green, and blue in rapid succession.

Side by side with a DLP projector of equal resolution, LCD images will appear sharper, although this is more of a concern for text than images. (In fact, the slightly smoother image produced by DLP can be an advantage for photography presentation because it reduces the stair-step appearance along contrast edges in the image.)

DLP

DLP, or Digital Light Processing, is a relatively new technology that offers some distinct advantages over LCD (but, as with everything, there are some tradeoffs as well). Most DLP projectors use a single chip, called a DMD, or Digital MicroMirror Device, with up to 1.3 million micro mirrors. Like the cells in an LCD panel, the mirrors in this grid are mapped to pixels in the bitmap image.

These mirrors are used to modulate, or control, the light from the projection lamp and direct it through the lens by wobbling back and forth on a hinge, allowing more, less, or no light to reach the lens. If a mirror is more frequently in the On position, the pixel will be lighter. Darker shades are created by having the mirror in the Off position more frequently. DLP is a "reflective" light source, and as such isn't as bright as LCD.

In order to create color, these single chip projectors use a spinning light wheel with red, green, and blue panels between the projector lamp and the chip to create the color display shown on the screen. The color wheel acts as a filter, separating the light into red, green, and blue. A mirror mapped to a red pixel will be positioned to reflect light during the red phase of the wheel's cycle, and so on. The wheel spins fast enough that the colors appear to be displayed simultaneously, but there is some loss of saturation and brightness compared to LCD. The combination of the mirror position in conjunction with the color wheel generates the hue and lightness/darkness of each pixel. Using a single color wheel, DLP projectors are capable of producing over 16.7 million colors.

See the color section for an illustration of DLP technology.

Note: A third display technology is gaining ground. LCOS, or Liquid Crystal On Silicon, is gaining in popularity. LCOS projectors are beyond the range of most users now, but they offer extremely high resolution with SXGA (1280×1024) as the starting point. Considered the best of both worlds, LCOS has a more-analog, or less-pixilated, look to its projected images, resulting in smoother pixels and higher saturation. Current models have lower contrast ratios though, and lamp life is shorter than with other projector technologies.

The Advantages of LCD

- LCD is more light efficient. Transmitted light is inherently brighter than reflected light. You can judge the difference for yourself quite easily. Hold a print next to your computer monitor with the same image displayed. The image on the monitor will be brighter than the one on paper. This increase in brightness can be an important factor if your presentations are typically in large rooms.

- LCD has better color saturation. Because it can light all three colors at one time, images viewed with LCD projection are capable of higher saturation. For photographic images where saturation is an important issue, this can be a deciding feature.

- LCD produces a sharper image. If your presentations vary from photography to text, LCD projectors will have the advantage.

- DLP displays are subject to the "rainbow effect." Because DLP uses a spinning color wheel to create each color, it has the potential to produce visual artifacts. Technically, DLP displays only one color (red, green, or blue) at any instant. Because the wheel is spinning so fast, most people do not detect any color change. However, the level of annoyance ranges from irritating to intolerable for a small percentage of people who can see the change.

The Advantages of DLP

- DLP wins in contrast range, producing richer blacks. While a good LCD projector may have a contrast range of 500–800:1, DLP projectors are typically 1000:1 and higher.

- DLP projectors are typically lighter and more compact. If you travel for presentations, this can be an important factor in your decision. While a typical LCD projector may weigh 5 to 7 pounds with a dimension of 4"×12"×10", a comparable DLP projector will be in the 2 to 4 pound range with a 3"×8"×6" size.

- DLP projectors have less pixilation than LCD projectors. Again, this is more of an issue for text or video, and it shouldn't be a driving factor in your purchase decision unless you also plan to use the projector for a home theater setup. For photographs, this creates a smoother transition from one pixel to the next. For text and video, it creates a slightly softer image.

- LCD display quality deteriorates over time much faster than DLP. Because LCD uses organic components (the Crystal in LCD), it is more susceptible to wear, particularly in the blue channel. LCD components are also more expensive to replace. DLP uses no organic components, and most displays consist of a single chip, which is less expensive to replace. Texas Instruments (the sole supplier of DLP technology) recently published a report showing that DLP showed little change in image quality after 4,700 hours, while LCD displays were showing significant color shifts, particularly in the blue channel, and contrast changes in about half that time.

Both LCD and DLP will do fine jobs of displaying images, especially when those images have been optimized for the display. Jon prefers DLP projectors for their wider contrast range and compact size, and Tim prefers LCD projectors for their more vibrant colors.

Brightness

Brightness in digital projectors is measured in ANSI lumens. Brightness and resolution will be the two largest factors in determining the cost of any given projector. One of the difficulties in deciding which projector best meets your needs is figuring out where you'll be using it most. If your shows are normally in a small darkened room, you can get by with a projector that puts out about 1,000 lumens. A large room with brighter lighting might call for a projector with upward of 3,000 lumens. Table 10.1 will help you determine how much you need.

▶ **Table 10.1:** Brightness Requirements by Room Size and Lighting

Lumens	Room Size	Room Lighting
700–1,000	Small meeting rooms, classrooms	Dark
1,000–2,000	Mid-size conference rooms	Dim
2,000–3,000	Large conference rooms	Normal room light
3,000+	Auditoriums, theaters	Normal room light

As photographers, we have an advantage in our brightness needs because we normally use reduced lighting during a presentation. Still, don't skimp on the brightness when you are shopping for a projector. Your projector is a long-term investment, similar to your camera and lenses. We recommend a projector with a lumens rating of 1,500 as sufficient for most users and situations.

Resolution

The sharpness and clarity of the projected image on the screen is determined to a great extent by the projector's resolution. Resolution is the other major factor that affects price. Typically, the resolution on projectors is expressed in the same fashion as computer display resolution. Of course, few of us actually know what all the actual resolutions are when we see the letters. Table 10.2 shows the basic resolutions and their classes.

▶ **Table 10.2:** Basic Computer Display Resolution and Class

Resolution	Class
800×600	SVGA
1024×768	XGA
1280×1024	SXGA
1600×1200	UXGA

Most budget projectors have a display resolution of 800×600 (SVGA). Although not optimal for a really impressive presentation, SVGA can be effective for photo presentations, particularly in small rooms. As the room size grows, the screen size grows along with it. The SVGA display that looked good at 50 to 75 inches (diagonal) is going to start looking pixilated as you move up to 100 inches or more. We consider the XGA class projector to be a good compromise between resolution and cost. If you'll occasionally be presenting in a large room, it might make sense to rent the SXGA or UXGA projector when needed.

Note: Projector rental fees vary from region to region; however, for a higher-end projector, you can expect to pay $250 or more per day. It doesn't take many rentals to justify the purchase of a projector. Most of the camera stores that cater to professional photographers have rental departments, and many have expanded into the digital market. Their products are usually less expensive to rent than a similar rental item from a hotel or convention center.

Projector specifications will often show multiple resolutions. The only one that really matters is the native resolution. Just like a computer LCD that supports multiple resolutions, the displays are optimized for the native resolution. Regardless of the resolution, an LCD or DLP projector has a set number of pixels that defines the native resolution. Any change from this requires the image to be interpolated, usually with a loss of quality.

Note: The optical quality of the lens used in the projector will make a dramatic difference in the quality of the projected image. When looking at zoom lenses, optical zoom is the important factor. Digital zoom always degrades image quality. Multicoated optics, such as those used in camera lenses, improve color rendition.

Color Fidelity

Most digital projectors offer no color management support, and display quality from one projector to the next can vary dramatically. This is more of a problem when the presentation must be made using a projector provided by the site.

Some of the high-end projectors support the sRGB color space (the same color space used for most on-screen display including the Web), as well as the ability to adjust brightness and contrast. Most often, you'll need to make adjustments to your images for proper display through a projector though. We'll cover how to optimize your images for projection in Chapter 11, "Optimizing Your Images for Slideshows."

Note: Profiling a projector is possible. GretagMacBeth's Eye-One Beamer (www.i1color.com/products/i1_pro_with_i1beamer.asp, about $1,600 for Windows and Macintosh) is designed to calibrate both digital projectors and displays. For more information on profiling projectors and other output devices, check out Tim's book *Color Confidence* (Sybex, 2004).

What about Screens?

Digital projectors may have changed the way we present images, but we still need a screen to project those images onto. Portable screens haven't changed a great deal over the years, and a good quality screen will last much longer than the average projector. We highly recommend projection screens from Da-Lite (www.da-lite.com).

When looking for a screen, keep these guidelines in mind:

- **Size.** Portable screens are available in sizes from 40" up to 96". Be sure to buy one large enough for the room you'll be using for your presentation. To determine how large the screen should be, use the following formula: distance to last row of seats × .15. If the back row of seats is 30 feet from the screen, you'll need a screen approximately 54" tall.

- **Border.** A black border around the screen area will add pop to your images by increasing the apparent contrast and brightness.

- **Surface color.** For most LCD and DLP projectors, matte white or high contrast matte white is the best choice, with the high contrast screen being well suited for the budget projectors. The matte white screens have good uniform reflectivity, and they don't create color shifts in the projected image. Glass-beaded screens, with high reflectivity, are another option, but they tend to give projected images a cool color cast.

Price

Projector prices are dropping, and features are improving constantly. However, you may be in for sticker shock when you start looking at projectors. Products in today's budget range would have been considered high-end just a couple of years ago. The prices shown here are estimates as of Spring 2004, and as with most hardware, they can be found at significant discounts. A number of options are available that fall into three main categories.

Budget A number of excellent products are available in the budget range, and it seems that more are entering the market monthly. Some of our favorites in this category are the Epson Powerlite S1 (LCD), the Dell 2200MP (DLP), and the NEC VT46 (LCD).

Resolution: SVGA (800×600)

Brightness: 500 to 1,000 lumens

Contrast: 400:1 contrast ratio (LCD); 1500:1 contrast ratio (DLP)

Price Range: Under $1,000

Mid-Range In the mid-range category, we highly recommend the Mitsubishi XD50U (DLP), and we've been impressed with the Dell 4100MP (DLP).

> **Resolution:** XGA (1024×768)
>
> **Brightness:** 1,500 to 2,500 lumens
>
> **Contrast:** 700:1 contrast ratio (LCD); 2000:1 contrast ratio (DLP)
>
> **Price Range:** $1,000 to $2,500

High End We should all be fortunate enough to *need* a projector in this category. If you are, it's hard to beat the Sharp PG-M25X (DLP) with its built-in color management support for sRGB, the Epson PowerLite 7800P (LCD), or the Canon LV-7215(LCD).

> **Resolution:** XGA (1024×768) or higher (resolutions up to 1600×1200 are possible if you're willing to pay the premium price).
>
> **Brightness:** 3,000 lumens
>
> **Contrast:** 900:1 contrast ratio (LCD); 3000:1 contrast ratio (DLP)
>
> **Price Range:** Over $2,500

Table 10.3 summarizes the features available in the major price categories.

▶ **Table 10.3:** Digital Projector Features and Price Categories at a Glance

Feature	Budget	Mid-Price	High End
Resolution	800×600	1024×768	1024×768 or higher
Brightness	500 to 1,000 lumens	1,500 to 2,500 lumens	3,000 lumens
Contrast	400:1 LCD	700:1 LCD	900:1 LCD
	1,500:1 DLP	2,000:1 DLP	3,000:1 DLP
Price Range	Under $1,000	$1,000 to $2,500	Over $2,500

Other Display Options

Presentations aren't always about showing images to a group of people. A slideshow can be viewed on a monitor or television by an individual at any time. The input source for monitor viewing may be a CD or DVD. However, with the improved connection speed many people have, slideshows on the Internet are now a viable option as well.

Slideshows on CD/DVD

Affordable CD and DVD writable drives and the growth of home DVD players have made it possible to create slideshows that can be enjoyed on a television or the viewer's computer. A slideshow on CD is an excellent way to distribute your portfolio as well.

Most current DVD players for the home will work with both DVD writable media and VCD (Video CD). For quality purposes, DVD is the better option for the photographer. When slideshows are created for either DVD or VCD, they are converted to MPEG files, which is essentially a movie with still images. VCD uses the MPEG-1 format, which has a screen resolution of 352×240 pixels, which is certainly not optimal for our beautiful images!

DVD on the other hand uses MPEG-2, which increases resolution to 720×480 pixels, which is four times the size of the MPEG-1 format. DVD also increases the amount of space available for files from about 600MB to over 4GB. DVD writers are becoming more affordable all the time. If you're considering purchasing one, we recommend getting the dual standard DVD+R/-R drive. Sony and TDK both make excellent products that support the dual standards.

Note: There are two standard formats for DVD writable media. DVD+R, supported by Philips, Ricoh, and Sony among others, and DVD-R, primarily supported by Pioneer and used in most Macintosh computers. DVD-R discs are not compatible with DVD+R drives. If you already have a DVD writer, check the format and buy only the appropriate media. If you're shopping for a writer, get the dual format model and stop worrying about which media to buy.

The Web and E-Mail

With broadband connections, viewing slideshows on the Internet with reasonable quality is now possible. Most of the web gallery creation tools we covered in Chapter 9, "Publishing and Maintaining Your Site," also include a slideshow feature. In reality, a typical web slideshow is nothing more than image pages that refresh with new content after a predetermined amount of time.

The Advanced Random Images extension from Kaosweaver (www.kaosweaver.com/extensions/, free download), which was used in Chapter 9, can be set to show images as a slideshow by selecting the list of images to use, setting the Action to Slideshow, and setting the Slideshow Timer to the number of seconds to display each image.

A PDF presentation is a great way to share a group of images via e-mail, and it can provide a measure of safety against having your images copied. Chapter 12, "Putting a Slideshow Together," shows how to create a PDF presentation in Photoshop, along with other ways to build a slideshow.

OTHER DISPLAY OPTIONS

Optimizing Your Images for Slideshows

11

Regardless of the method you use to display your photography, you should always strive for the best quality presentation possible. Your output will dictate many of the decisions you make, including how much saturation or sharpening is needed. In Part I, "Printing on the Desktop," we covered optimizing your images for printed output. This chapter will show you how to optimize your images for on-screen display.

Chapter Contents
Perfecting the Image
Color Management
Optimizing for the Screen

Perfecting the Image

In some ways, life was easier in the conventional film days. If you wanted a larger image on a screen, you just moved the projector farther back. Optimizing for the screen typically meant blowing the dust off and making sure the slide wasn't backward or upside down. After all, slide projectors used a daylight-balanced light bulb, and the image was a finished entity—developed film.

Today, numerous options for presenting your images are available to you. Whether you use a digital projector, distribute your shows via the Web, use DVDs, or create shows for your home computer, specifically optimizing your images for the intended display medium will present your work in the best light. Adjusting the saturation, sharpness, and image size for each intended use will help your photographs "shine."

Color Management

Before you make any image adjustments for any output medium, make sure you calibrate your monitor. Without a known reference point, any adjustments that you make will be little better than a guess. You might get lucky, but the odds are against you. Guessing wrong can be embarrassing. For specific information on calibrating your monitor, refer back to Chapter 2, "Preparing the Image." For more in-depth coverage of monitor calibration and specific products to help you set up a color-managed workflow, we recommend Tim's book *Color Confidence* (Sybex, 2004).

Setting the sRGB Color Space

For all the output options discussed in this chapter, your image should use the sRGB color space. It is the default color space for monitors, the Web, and most projected images, and it will give your images the widest compatibility and consistency across viewing devices. This color space tends toward brighter, more saturated colors. Some digital cameras today offer multiple versions of the sRGB color space, usually tuned to even higher saturation than the default setting.

You can check which color space your image is using, and convert it to sRGB if needed. Just follow these directions:

1. In Photoshop, select Image > Mode > Convert To Profile to display the window shown in Figure 11.1.

N o t e : Photoshop Elements does not support assigning specific profiles as Photoshop CS does. To set the correct space in Elements, choose Edit > Color Settings (Windows) or Photoshop Elements > Color Settings (Macintosh) and select Limited Color Management - Optimized For Web Graphics. This will force your image to use the sRGB color space.

2. If the Source Profile is set to anything other than sRGB, you'll need to set the Destination Space by clicking the dropdown list and selecting sRGB IEC61966-2.1. If your Source Profile is already set to sRGB, then no changes are needed. Under Conversion Options, we find that Relative Colorimetric works best as the Rendering Intent. Make sure the Black Point Compensation and Use Dither boxes are checked. The Rendering Engine should be left to Adobe ACE. For more about profiles and color spaces, Tim's book *Color Confidence* is an excellent reference.

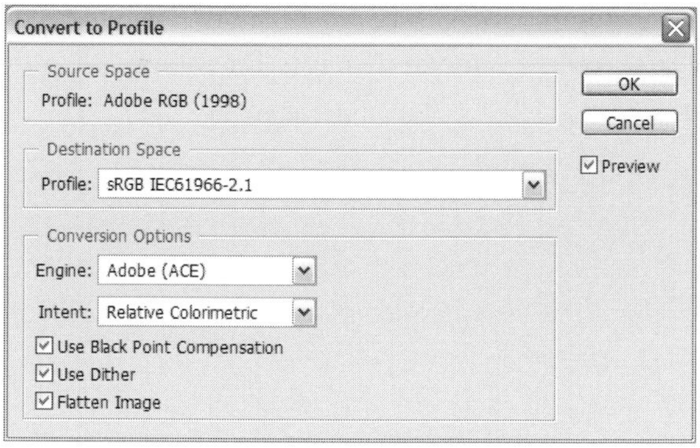

Figure 11.1 For on-screen display, set the color space of your image to sRGB. This ensures the broadest compatibility with other viewers and output devices. The color space can be changed in Photoshop by using the Convert To Profile dialog box.

Optimizing for the Screen

Preparing photographs for screen display is a series of compromises, all of which affect the quality of the image. The primary goal is to optimize an image for a specific use, whether that use is in a Web display, e-mail, or a projection-based presentation (our focus in this chapter). The color space used for screen display is a smaller color space, or *gamut*, than the print color space. (See the example in the color section.) The resolution of the screen display image is typically reduced and, in many cases, shadow and highlight detail must be adjusted.

Because you will be, in effect, throwing away detail and information, the very first step in optimizing an image for a screen is to make a working copy of your work. Never use the original! Screen-based displays usually have a smaller resolution than the original image, and by working on a copy you won't end up with a file that is too small for print use.

Evaluate on a Monitor

Once you've backed up the images you want to present in a slideshow, the process of optimizing them begins with a close look at how they appear on screen. Examining your images on a monitor can help you determine whether an image is suitable for the intended presentation. Some images, particularly those with high contrast or that show extended shadow detail, do not translate to the screen as well as they do to printed media. These images will likely need adjustment, particularly to the output levels to keep the contrast of the image within acceptable ranges. The safest way to do this is through adjustment layers in Photoshop, which we'll cover later in this chapter.

Color Saturation

When it comes to landscape or nature photography, many people prefer an image with higher saturation, or more vibrant color. If you've ever used a consumer-type digital camera, you've probably noticed that the images tend to be more saturated than those from a high-end digital SLR. (In fact, many people, when first using a DSLR, complain about their images appearing washed out, with less color. The reality is that the camera is capturing a more accurate representation of the scene.) Thanks to film like Fujichrome Velvia, and the glossy magazines with their rich color, we've become accustomed to highly saturated images.

Portraits and other images that have very defined expectations for accuracy don't have this problem. People will often remember a tree as more green than it actually was or the sky as a deeper blue, but if your skin tones are off, everyone notices. These types of colors are what are known as *memory colors,* because viewers intuitively know when the color is right or wrong. Therefore, most of this advice about boosting color is directed at photographs that don't include people.

Fortunately for us, most color changes need to be done only twice. Printed images have their own requirements and are covered in Part I of this book. The same modifications made for the Web will also be fine for slideshows on television and images sent in e-mail or viewed on a computer. Preparing images for a digital projector poses the primary problem. If you'll always be showing images using your own projector and screen, this isn't issue. However, if you make presentations where you have little control over the equipment provided, you need to prepare yourself to make some image adjustments to optimize for the hardware on hand. Luckily, this can be accomplished very quickly in Photoshop through the use of Actions. The companion website at www.photofinishbook.com has several sample Actions to get you started.

Digital projectors tend to oversaturate photographs because they are tuned to PowerPoint presentations where bold, solid colors are desired. Because projectors typically have a narrower contrast range and are dimmer than conventional monitors, this all adds up to images that need a little extra help. As we discussed in the previous chapter, the contrast range is typically lower on LCD displays, which means blacks are less black and whites lose detail sooner. It's also common to see a color shift due to oversaturated reds. Many of the better projectors have adjustments for this, but entry-level projectors might not give you any control, requiring you to make all adjustments in Photoshop (or your preferred image editor).

Using Adjustment Layers in Photoshop

Because display quality varies so widely with projectors, the best way to deal with the changes needed is to work with adjustment layers. By making your edits on a separate layer, it's a simple matter to change the amount of adjustment as needed to a copy of the image, all the while maintaining the original image data for future modifications.

Before making any changes, connect the projector to the monitor and view your images. In particular, you'll want to evaluate the images with the most contrast and strongest colors. The most common adjustments to be made for projectors are levels and saturation. Take these steps to adjust for a projector with a narrower contrast range:

1. With your image open in Photoshop, select Layer > New Adjustment Layer > Levels.

2. Name the adjustment layer something descriptive, such as **ProjLevels**. Click OK.

> **Note:** Including the layer style in the name makes it easier to quickly identify what type of layer it is. In this example, ProjLevels is shorthand for Projector Levels.

3. In the Levels dialog box (see Figure 11.2), adjust the Output Levels sliders on the bottom by dragging the black pointer to the right and the white pointer to the left. Alternatively, you can enter values for the black point and white point. On average, you will raise the black point by 10 to 20 and drop the white point down 20 to 30. These values will vary from one projector to the next, so consider these recommendations as guidelines and not hard and fast rules.

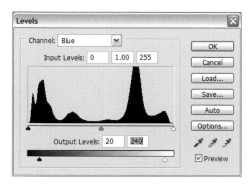

Figure 11.2 Changing the output levels decreases the contrast range in the image, keeping more of the shadow and highlight information within the range of the output device.

Creating a saturation adjustment layer is very similar. Just follow these steps:

1. With your image open in Photoshop select > Layer > New Adjustment Layer > Hue/Saturation.

2. Name the adjustment layer something descriptive, and include the saturation in the name. Click OK.

3. Frequently, red is the only color channel that is oversaturated, so in the Hue/Saturation dialog box (see Figure 11.3), select the Red channel from the drop-down list. Drag the Saturation slider to the left to reduce saturation, as shown in Figure 11.4. Small changes are often all that is needed. A range of 5 to 25 will work for many nature type images, and a range of 3 to 10 will work for people. If changes to the saturation affect the overall hue of the image, make a very slight adjustment (in the range of 1 to 5 typically) to correct the hue.

Note: Hue affects the actual color, such as red, green, yellow. Saturation affects the strength of that color.

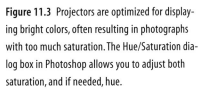

Figure 11.3 Projectors are optimized for displaying bright colors, often resulting in photographs with too much saturation. The Hue/Saturation dialog box in Photoshop allows you to adjust both saturation, and if needed, hue.

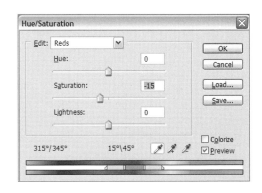

Figure 11.4 Adjusting the Red channel in the Hue/Saturation dialog

Once you've made any adjustments needed, it's a simple and quick fix to drag the adjustment layer onto each image in the slideshow. To do this, keep your adjusted image open, and open each additional image to be adjusted. Drag the adjustment layer from the adjusted image by clicking on it in the Layers palette (see Figure 11.5) and dropping it onto the new image. This can be easily handled by recording an Action in Photoshop. If you've placed all your images in a new folder as we suggested, you can run the Action as a batch command on every file in the folder. We've placed a sample Action on the companion site to demonstrate this.

Figure 11.5 Dragging an adjustment layer onto a new file is a quick and effective way to apply changes to the other images in a slideshow.

Matching Image Size and Resolution to the Output Device

Wouldn't it be nice if you could set one size and resolution for your images and have it work everywhere? The reality is far different though. Every intended output for your images will have different size and resolution needs. Some are dictated by the format being used. Images, whether in slideshows or for individual use, that are displayed on a television will be limited in size by the media being used. Projectors, as do all LCD devices, have an optimal native resolution that works best with them. For images on the Web, you need to worry about how large the image is in order to keep the download times reasonable.

Regardless of the intended output, we recommend that you do your image resizing in Photoshop. Resizing your image should be your final step prior to sharpening, and it will give your photos the best appearance possible.

Resolution means different things for different media. Display resolution is expressed in width and height; that is, the total number of pixels horizontally and vertically. With print media, image resolution is expressed in dots per inch (dpi). On a monitor or projector, the notion of dpi is largely irrelevant. Macintosh systems typically use a resolution of 72 dpi, and the standard on Windows is 96 dpi. A photograph with a resolution of 360 dpi will not look any different on screen than the same image (uninterpolated) with a resolution of 72 or 96 dpi.

For screen display, the only number you really need to focus on is the number of pixels in each dimension. For example, Figure 11.6 shows Photoshop's Image Size window for the same image sized on the left for screen display and on the right for print. In both of these examples, the pixel dimensions, or size on screen is the same—1152×768. The image file size on disk is also the same—2.53MB. The only change is document size. If you were to print this image at 360 dpi, you'd have a print just over 3″×2″; and at 72 dpi, it fills a 16″×10″ page.

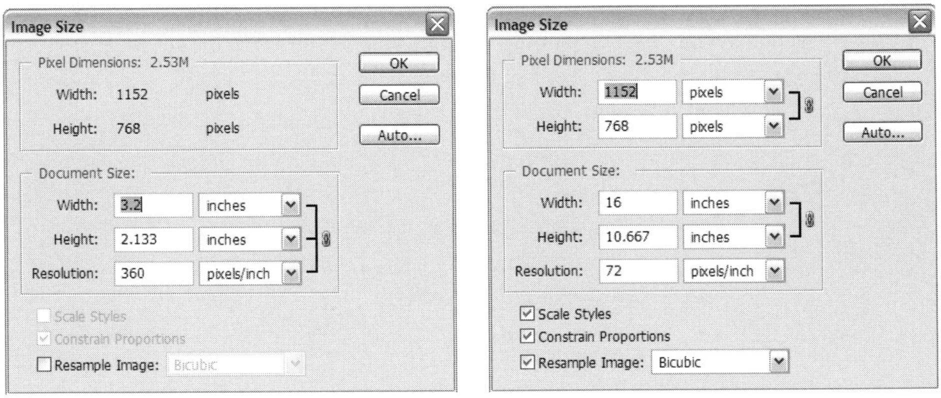

Figure 11.6 For screen display, it's all about the number of pixels in each dimension. Both of these images will display the same on screen.

Projectors

In Chapter 10, "Choosing Slideshow Hardware," we talked about the main categories of digital projector resolution. If you always use your own projector, sizing the image for display is much easier. If you have a SVGA resolution projector, setting your images to 800×600 pixels will work fine. XGA projectors are designed to work with images 1024×768 in resolution.

If you'll be presenting images on a variety of projectors, we suggest sizing your images to the largest size you may encounter. Typically, setting the resolution to 1280×1024 pixels will give you the most flexibility.

Note: Most presentation software does a good job of reducing the image size. By setting the resolution at or slightly higher than the projector resolution, you'll avoid upsizing your image with the resulting pixilated look.

Computer Monitor

Creating slideshows for computer display gives you the greatest freedom in sizing your images. Most of the slideshow creation software we cover in Chapter 12, "Putting a Slideshow Together," includes the option to create an executable, or stand-alone, file that contains all of the images and music. When creating an executable show, a player application is built into the show and used to play back your creation. Creation of an auto-play CD is also a common feature.

For computer display, we find that a resolution of 1024×768 pixels is an excellent compromise between image size and monitor capabilities. However, if you will be primarily viewing on your own computer, or at a known resolution, you can size your images for the native resolution of that computer.

Television

Image size for television display will be dictated by the media format used. Three main formats are supported by many home DVD players. Your slideshow software will typically size images for the intended media when the show is burned to disc.

> **Note:** Two different standards are used for televisions. NTSC is used in the United States and some other countries, and PAL is used primarily in Europe and Asia. When burning your show to CD or DVD, you'll need to identify which format you're using.

- **VCD.** This is the lowest resolution format at 352×240 (NTSC; 352×288 PAL) pixels. If your show is recorded to standard CD-R, this is the default resolution.
- **SVCD.** SVC also records to standard CD-R, but thanks to better compression algorithms, image resolution is increased to 480×480 (NTSC; 480×576 PAL) pixels.
- **DVD.** Images recorded to DVD are 720×480 (NTSC; 720×576 PAL) pixels in resolution, four times the resolution available with VCD.

Because the software used for producing the slideshow will resize the image based on the output media, you'll get the best results by doing all of your image resizing in Photoshop prior to creating your slideshow. Photoshop has better resizing methods than any of the slideshow programs we've seen; therefore, taking the time to size appropriately up front will keep your image quality at its best.

What about Video Output from a Camera or Computer?

Many digital cameras include video output connectors, allowing you to view the photos in the camera on your television. With this type of connection, you'll have no sizing options or issues. The camera will send the photograph to the television, which will then display it. Essentially, you've connected a single frame video camera or VCR to your television.

Many laptop computers also have video output in addition to their external monitor ports. If you plan to display your slideshow on television directly from a laptop, formatting the slideshow for DVD will give you the best results.

You should size your images according to their longest dimension. If the image is in landscape orientation (longest side is width), size the image to the first dimension. In the case of DVD, this would be 720 pixels. For portrait orientation, you'll size according to the second dimension. Again, for DVD, this would mean setting the height of your image to 480 pixels.

The increase in quality with DVD is apparent. With the continuing drop in prices, along with the increased compatibility we discussed in Chapter 10, we highly recommend creating your shows on DVD if you plan to show them on televisions with a DVD player.

Web

Image display via the Web shares many of the same design factors as image display on a local monitor, the primary difference being bandwidth. All those bytes have to go over a wire, and the fewer bytes that need to be sent, the faster the image will transmit. In Chapter 8, "Going Live," we recommended sizing your images to fit within a resolution of 800×600 pixels. This works well for photographs viewed individually, and the download time is reasonable. For slideshows, however, the delay in download time can ruin your carefully constructed show. Transition effects, music, and images need to be optimized for the slower connection speed in order to stay synchronized.

Unless you want to optimize your show for broadband (DSL, cable, etc), we recommend keeping image sizes to 600×400 pixels. If you plan to include music with the show, you may need to reduce this image size further as sound increases the amount of data the website must send to the viewer.

Sharpening

Nearly all digital images need some level of sharpening, which is handled in Photoshop by a tool with the unlikely name of Unsharp Mask. Chapter 2 showed how to use this tool to optimize images for print. Depending on the intended output, the amount of needed sharpening will vary. Screen displays, with their smaller image size, require less sharpening than the same image destined for the printer.

Unsharp Mask works by finding contrast changes in your image and selectively lightening or darkening these areas. The amount of change is controlled through the Amount, Radius, and Threshold sliders. Amount sets how much of a change you want, and the Radius value determines how wide of a selection to apply the changes to. Lower numbers affect a narrower band in the image. The Threshold slider determines how much difference there needs to be in contrast between adjacent pixels. A setting of 3 would require pixels to have at least three levels of difference. The default setting of 0 will affect every pixel in the image. The sharpening process is very similar to the one used for printing in Chapter 2. The settings will differ though, because we're working with a smaller file.

Although most digital cameras offer built-in sharpening, especially for JPG images, this is normally not the best approach. Typically, three or four different levels of sharpening are available (low, medium, and strong, with strong being the most common). This is akin to buying new shoes but only having three sizes to choose from—one of the sizes might work, but it probably isn't going to be the best solution.

Oversharpening an image creates undesirable artifacts such as halos, and in some cases color shifts. Once done, it can't be undone. If your camera includes the option to turn off in-camera sharpening, you should do so. Sharpening is seldom the same from one image to the next, and requirements for print differ from screen display. Therefore, sharpening should be done as the last step in your image-editing process.

In most cases, you can handle your image sharpening much better with Photoshop's Unsharp Mask filter. Most image-editing programs contain an unsharp mask feature; it may have a different name, such as sharpen, but the functionality is similar. Just follow these directions:

1. With your image open in Photoshop, select Image > Duplicate. Close the original file, and then flatten all layers in the duplicate. Finally, resize as needed to the correct dimensions.

2. Select Filter > Sharpen > Unsharp Mask to display the window shown in Figure 11.7. Set the preview to 100 percent

3. Drag the Amount slider to the right, setting it to 75 to 125 percent as a starting point.

4. Drag the Threshold slider to the right. The amount will vary depending on image type. Highly detailed images will use a lower number, typically less than 4. Portraits will use a higher number, such as 5 to 12 to keep skin tones smooth.

5. Adjust the Radius slider until the halos around the defined edges in your image are acceptable. For low resolution projector images, this will typically be in the range of 0.2 to 0.7 pixels.

6. Adjust the Amount if needed until the image has the appropriate overall sharpness, and halos and other artifacts have been removed.

7. Finally, use the Threshold slider to reduce noise or sharpening artifacts in smooth areas such as sky.

By creating a duplicate layer for sharpening, you can easily reuse the image for other purposes. Simply delete the layer used for sharpening, and repeat the USM process for the new use.

Figure 11.7 Use the Unsharp Mask filter in Photoshop to enhance the sharpness of an image.

Note: The Unsharp Mask dialog retains the settings from the previous use. If you are sharpening a group of similar images and want to use the same settings, Amount, Radius, and Threshold will all have the previous settings when the dialog reopens. If Unsharp Mask was the last filter applied, you can bypass the dialog entirely. Select Filter > Unsharp Mask (Ctrl+F Windows; Cmd+F Macintosh) to reapply the same settings. Better yet, automate the entire process by adding this to the adjustment Action suggested earlier.

Putting a Slideshow Together

The digital revolution has made it easier than ever to create presentations with transition effects, synchronized music, and multiple display options that have left your old carousel slide projector collecting dust in the closet. One thing that hasn't changed though is the need to carefully prepare your shows for the intended audience. In some ways, the wealth of software tools choices, combined with the ease of use of these programs, has actually made it more difficult to create a presentation that focuses on the photography and not on the technology. In this chapter, we'll show you how to plan, create, and present a digital slideshow that puts your images in their best light.

Chapter Contents

Planning an Effective Show

Effective slideshows have always been best when planned carefully. The goal is to tell a story through images. The true measure of success is having a finished presentation that conveys the message and leaves the viewer wanting more. Ruthlessly culling images that are less than your best is critical to a slideshow—perhaps even more important than culling them for a web presentation. On the web, viewers can simply click another image. At a presentation, they may start fidgeting in their seats or simply get up and leave.

Telling a Story

A slideshow is a visual story. As with any good story, it should have a logical beginning, a story line, and an ending. Many of us have sat through an incredibly boring vacation slideshow more than once (and vowed to never do it again) with countless images of places and people that in reality do nothing more than document the fact that someone was at a particular place.

When you tell a story through photographs, every presentation has a purpose and your goal should be to convey that purpose, whether it is to give a sense of place, teach a technique, or document a subject. Title slides should be used sparingly to set the viewer up for what is about to be shown, rather than using a title on every image.

A show about the Grand Canyon will be much more effective and enjoyable by presenting your viewers with scenes that show the location in a unique way. For example, you might start with a wide angle shot of the canyon with warm morning light, and then transition to more detailed images, such as individual rock formations showing rich color banding, shapes, and textures. Next, you could show smaller details in the scenes, such as a stunted tree clinging to life on the edge of the canyon, wildflowers growing in a crevice in the canyon wall, or a waterfall that flows into the Colorado River. If your show is about the entire park, this is where you'd place images that show other aspects of the park, such as the forests, wildlife, and other features that are not obviously part of Grand Canyon to the viewer, yet make up a large part of the park. To close out the story, images of the canyon with its changing weather patterns and their dramatic skies would be appropriate. To really tell a story about the Grand Canyon, you might want to include images that show the crowds and commercialism to which the park has been subjected. Regardless of your subject, you want to organize it in a way that makes visual and logical sense with coherent transitions from slide to slide and section to section.

Selecting the Photos

Careful photo selection is key to an interesting slideshow. On the Web, viewers can skip images that don't interest them. With a slideshow presentation, you hold them hostage to your image choices. They must view your images in the order you want them to be seen and for the length of time you determine.

You'll find it very difficult to select the right photos without some planning up front. Prior to making any selection, you should know what the overall theme of your show will be, the target audience, and the amount of time you'll have. Will you be speaking with each slide? If so, the number of images you'll be able to show in the allocated time will be reduced.

Once you've set the theme for your show, think about the sections you'll divide the show into and begin collecting potential images. At this point, your goal is to gather images that fit the overall theme, giving you a better idea of the choices available. Once you've collected these images, it's time to start reviewing them more critically. Make a first pass on these images, looking for images that are very similar, or that have repetitive content. Examine each image closely to select the best image with the most impact, both technically and aesthetically.

> **Note:** Create a new folder for your show and copy images to this folder. Use a descriptive name for the folder, and be sure to copy your images. Don't just move them. This will help prevent accidental deletions or modifications to the source, or original, image. If you use an image management application such as ACDSee or iView Media Pro, you can create a new category or gallery for these images.

Know Your Audience

If you know your audience, you can select images that will meet and even exceed their expectations. As an example, consider a slideshow on flowers. If you will be presenting this show to a mixed group of people, you'll probably select images that show color and shape, perhaps opening with scenes of a large formal garden in full bloom. Change the audience to a group of horticulturists, and the focus of your images might be on technically perfect shots of individual flower specimens, perhaps concentrating on a variety of one flower, but going into great detail with stages of growth, different color variations, and environmental images.

The same subject presented to a group of photographers would be more effective by showing images that present the flowers in unique, artistic, and dramatic ways. Macro shots concentrating on form and color in a variety of lighting conditions and abstract patterns will be effective to this audience.

Timing

As you build the show, keep your timeframe in mind. We've found that keeping your show to 20 minutes or less is optimal. Most people begin to lose interest after this amount of time. For typical presentations, 5 to 10 seconds is generally an appropriate amount of time to spend on each image. Of course, not every show will have the same needs or requirements. Instructional presentations typically last much longer, but because you'll be speaking, and at times in detail, about the subject, the number of slides shown will be considerably less than an artistic type of slideshow.

Note: Although 5 to 10 seconds may not seem like much time to spend on an image, spending more than this on an image will tend to break up the flow of the presentation. Unless you're speaking about the subject in the image, 5 to 7 seconds is a good guideline. For images with more detail, or title slides, 10 seconds is a good choice.

With this round of editing done, you're still likely to have more images than you can use. If you have a set amount of time for your show, you can estimate how many images you'll have time to use. Using our guideline of 5 to 10 seconds per image, a 15-minute slideshow would contain 90 to 180 images, including title slides. If you're speaking with the images, the total might drop down to 50 to 75 slides or less.

Using a Script

If you'll be speaking during the slideshow, rehearse what you plan to say for each image. We find it works best to write your planned comments and run through this script several times to work out duration and timing for slides.

Although a script is very helpful in practicing your presentation, and getting the timing right for slide durations, avoid reading from a script during the actual presentation. Reading from a script sounds stiff and can make your audience (or the presenter) uncomfortable or nervous. Rehearse the main points until you feel comfortable adlibbing and throwing in a few off-the-cuff remarks. Finally, if you are speaking during the presentation, speak about each slide while it is displayed and not during a transition from one slide to the next.

Transitions

Most of the slideshow applications available have hundreds (or thousands) of transition effects available. Unless you're going for that "ransom note" look from the early Macintosh days when documents were created using every font on the system, the most effective and compelling shows will use simple transitions throughout the show. We like to use a dissolve effect, while other photographers prefer a fade or wipe. The important thing here is consistency and keeping your audience focused on your images, not the special effects between them.

Soundtracks and Music

Music can be very effective when used with thought and in moderation. At all costs, you want to avoid having a soundtrack compete with your images for the audience's attention. For this reason, you will usually want to be careful when you are using vocal music (although it can be very dramatic and enhance the presentation when the subject of the vocal music is carefully selected to coincide with the subject of the slides). Music should suit both the mood of the subject and the topic being shown. New age and light classical music work very well with nature presentations; think of Peer Gynt with a slideshow on flowers, and light guitar or harp music with a show on birds. Of course, a slideshow covering a football game or a fashion shoot would work best with a faster paced, louder style of music that suits the subject matter.

Perhaps the most difficult aspect of selecting music for your slideshow is synchronizing segments of the soundtrack with sections of images. Most dedicated presentation software includes the option to automatically synchronize music with images.

Copyright permission for commercial music is legally required for any public presentation. Consider how you would feel if your photographs were used without your permission before you think about pirating someone else's work. For information on licensing commercial music for your presentation, the best place to start is BMI, Broadcast Music, Inc. (www.bmi.com). You'll find complete information on song use, licensing fees, and available titles.

Obtaining permission for the use of commercial music has led to the rapid growth of royalty-free music. A number of websites offer downloads, and several sell collections of music on CD. SmartSound (www.smartsound.com/music) sells themed music on CD; the price depends on whether you are using it for personal/educational or commercial purposes. Freeplay (www.freeplaymusic.com) allows their music library to be used at no charge for noncommercial purposes. They charge a reasonable license fee to use their music for commercial purposes.

A final alternative is to create your own music. Macintosh users can use a great application, GarageBand (see Figure 12.1); available as part of the iLife 2004 package (www.apple.com/ilife, about $50, Macintosh OS X only). GarageBand lets you create your own soundtracks, regardless of your musical talent (or lack of it). If you enjoy music, this application is almost enough to justify owning a Macintosh by itself.

GarageBand includes thousands of sounds and instruments that you can combine in multiple ways to create the type of music you want. Additional royalty-free sound loops are available for download from the Apple website.

Windows users also have a number of options for creating their own soundtracks, including Acid (http://mediasoftware.sonypictures.com/products/acidfamily.asp, starting at about $70, Windows only) and Cakewalk HomeStudio 2004 (www.cakewalk.com/Products/HomeStudio, about $130, Windows Only). Both products allow you to create soundtracks from recorded loops, or you can create your own if you're musically inclined.

Using the Available Tools

An incredible number of programs that allow you to create and share digital slideshows are available. Your options run the gamut from basic utilities that may be included with image cataloging applications to dedicated presentation software with numerous transition effects and other dedicated features. We've selected some of the most popular to use as examples on both Windows and Macintosh systems.

Figure 12.1 Apple's GarageBand is an incredibly powerful and easy way to create your own music for presentations.

Pitfalls to Avoid

Even with spectacular images, your slideshow can still be less than perfect. Here are a few things to avoid that we've learned through experience:

- If possible, don't alternate portrait and landscape orientation images. Your show will flow smoother with all landscape or all portrait images grouped together.

- Beware of major brightness changes from one image to the next. The eye doesn't react well to large differences in brightness, and recovering from unexpected bright light can take a while.

- Use borders that suit the images. A black border might help your images stand out more prominently. If your images are mostly darker colors, a white border is a good choice and provides the same effect.

ProShow Gold

Photodex ProShow Gold (www.photodex.com/products/proshowgold, about $70, free trial version available for download, Windows only) is one of the most full-featured slideshow programs available for Windows. ProShow Gold handles most common image formats, including JPG, TIFF, and PSD. The program automatically converts and resizes your images to fit the output options you set. It includes a large selection of transitions, the ability to synchronize audio and slides in multiple ways, and "Ken Burns" motion effects (in which the camera pans across a still image like the historical photographs in Burns' documentaries). Your completed show can be output to many formats, including DVD, various video CD formats, self-running executables, e-mail, streaming shows from your website, and screensavers.

Photodex also offers a standard version of ProShow for about $30. This lower-end version doesn't support many of the DVD and CD output options, and it is more limited in the captions and other effects.

ProShow Gold is widely used by photographers to create slideshow programs no matter what the output medium will be. To build a slideshow with ProShow Gold, we typically use the following steps:

1. Copy all of the images you'd like to use in the slideshow into a single folder, so they'll all be in one place. You don't need to resize the images or save them in a particular file format. ProShow Gold will resize your images for the intended output, and it can handle many standard image file formats.

2. Launch ProShow Gold.

3. Select File > New (Ctrl+N), or click the New slideshow button in the toolbar to create a new blank show.

4. In the Folders list, navigate to the folder you created in Step 1. The Folders list works like Windows Explorer and shows all the available drives and folders. The Thumbnails list directly below the folders will display all image files in the selected folder (see Figure 12.2).

5. Select the images by clicking on the thumbnails and dragging them onto the empty placeholders in the timeline. (You can Shift+click to select a range of files, or you can Ctrl+click to select noncontinuous multiple files. Edit > Select All [Ctrl+A] will select all the images in the folder). Images can be reordered at any time, so it's not critical to drop them in order at this point.

6. Click the Transition button ![Transition button] between the slides you want the transition applied to in order to open the Transitions dialog.

7. Set the transition effect you'd like to use between the images for your slideshow (see Figure 12.3). As you can see, 280 different effects are available. The thumbnail image in the lower-left corner of the dialog box shows a preview of each effect as you move the mouse over it. Most of these effects are not appropriate for a professional show, and we prefer to use a simple dissolve or fade effect.

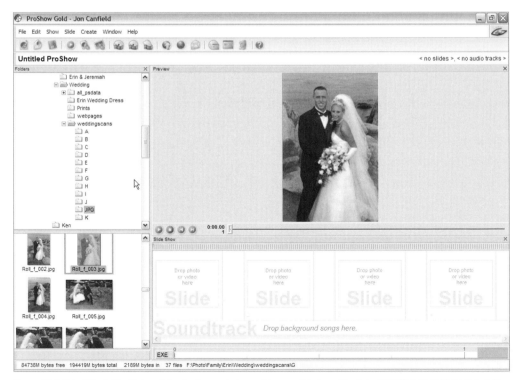

Figure 12.2 Select the folder that contains the images to be used in your slideshow. (Photodex® ProShow™ Gold 2.0. Copyright © 1994 – 2004 Photodex Corporation. Photodex and ProShow are trademarks of the Photodex Corporation.)

8. To add a soundtrack to your show, double-click the Soundtrack area of the time-line, or select Show > Show Options (Ctrl+H) to open the Show Options dialog. Click the Soundtrack button (see Figure 12.4). Click the Add button, and navigate to the folder containing your sound file. ProShow Gold supports MP3 and WAV audio files. In this example, we've added Pachelbel's *Canon in D Major* to our slideshow. You can add, delete, and reorder additional soundtracks at any time

9. Now that your slides are added to the show, you can add captions or title slides. Title slides are most effective when used to introduce the show and to announce major changes in subject matter. We believe titles and captions should be kept to a minimum for most artistic photography shows because concentrating on both text and images at the same time is difficult. Instructional shows, such as equip-ment comparisons, will differ and likely require text to be most effective. To cre-ate a new title slide, click on the slideshow timeline where you want the slide to be created and select Slide > Insert Blank Slide (Ctrl+I). You can also right-click on the slideshow timeline where you want to create the title slide and select Insert Blank Slide from the context menu.

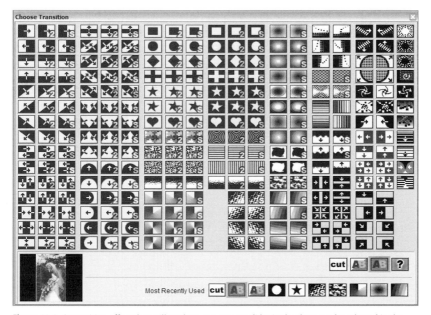

Figure 12.3 A transition effect that will apply to one or more slides in the show can be selected in the Transitions dialog. (Photodex® ProShow™ Gold 2.0. Copyright © 1994 – 2004 Photodex Corporation. Photodex and ProShow are trademarks of the Photodex Corporation.)

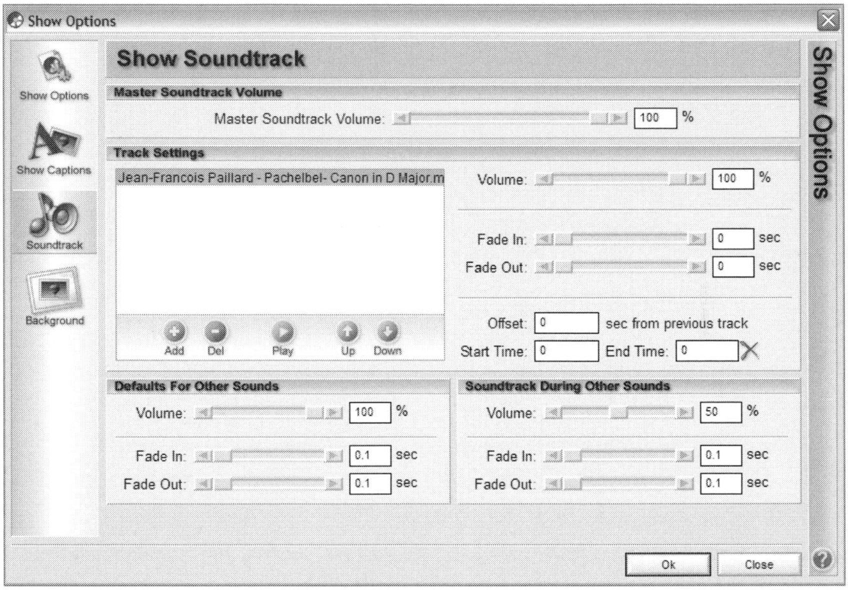

Figure 12.4 ProShow Gold supports multiple music tracks with several options for controlling volume and fades. (Photodex® ProShow™ Gold 2.0. Copyright © 1994 – 2004 Photodex Corporation. Photodex and ProShow are trademarks of the Photodex Corporation.)

ProShow Gold offers an extensive set of controls for text placement and effects. Select Show > Show Options (Ctrl+H), and click the Show Captions button (see Figure 12.5). Text effects can be set for entrance (Fly In), exit (Fly Out), and Normal. If you want to use text effects, we suggest a simple fade in or fade out.

Note: The Show Options dialog can be left open while you select individual slides, saving time if you'll be doing several changes. Double-click on the new slide to select it, and the slide will be shown in the preview window of the dialog box. To move from one slide to the next in order, click the forward or back buttons in the lower-left corner of the dialog box.

10. As a final step in assembling the basic slideshow, you might need to synchronize your slides to the length of your soundtrack. The same Show Options dialog offers a quick way to do this. Clicking the Sync Show Length To Soundtrack button will automatically adjust the length of time each slide is displayed so that the entire show fits the length of the soundtrack. If your show is close to the right length, this can be an easy way to synchronize slides and music. ProShow Gold also has controls to allow you to manually record slide timing by selecting Show > Record Show Timing (see Figure 12.6) or synchronize a selected set of slides to a particular piece of music.

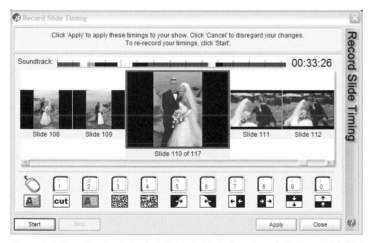

Figure 12.5 Captions and effects are also set in the Show Options dialog. (Photodex® ProShow™ Gold 2.0. Copyright © 1994 – 2004 Photodex Corporation. Photodex and ProShow are trademarks of the Photodex Corporation.)

Figure 12.6 Recording the timing for individual slides is done through the Record Slide Timing dialog. (Photodex® ProShow™ Gold 2.0. Copyright © 1994 – 2004 Photodex Corporation. Photodex and ProShow are trademarks of the Photodex Corporation.)

11. Once you've assembled your slideshow, it's time to generate it for a particular output medium. To select a medium, choose Create > Output Options. In Figure 12.7, we've chosen Web Show as the Output Option. Web shows can use menu screens for the viewer to select from multiple shows, which is useful when you have a series of related but separate shows. To protect the show, a registration key can be required to view the show, or you can limit the show to a set number of days or runs.

ProShow has a multitude of features and output options. The software is very straightforward and easy to learn, and it allows you to put your shows together quickly. Once you have the main options set, you can easily make adjustments and output to web, DVD, executable file, or e-mail.

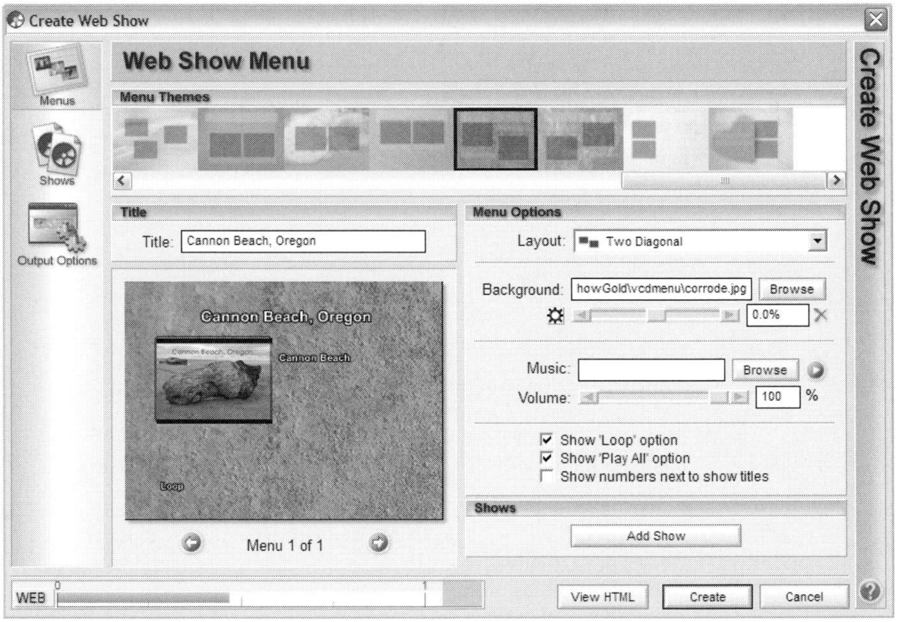

Figure 12.7 The output options for creating a web slideshow include menu pages for multiple shows, image size, and security settings. (Photodex® ProShow™ Gold 2.0. Copyright © 1994 – 2004 Photodex Corporation. Photodex and ProShow are trademarks of the Photodex Corporation.)

SmoothShow

SmoothShow Pro 2.1 (www.smoothshow.com, about $70, free trial version available for download, Windows only) provides an easy way to create digital slideshows from images in a variety of file formats with a wide range of transitions between images with synchronized music. One of the strengths of SmoothShow is the automation in handling a wide variety of image file formats and resolutions, converting the images as needed for use within the show. SmoothShow Lite is available for about $20. It offers most of the same key features as the Pro version, although batch conversion, web export, audio conversion, and some file formats are not supported.

Adobe PDF

Photoshop CS and Photoshop Elements include the option to create a PDF presentation (see Figure 12.8). A PDF show can be viewed by anyone with the Adobe Acrobat Reader software on Macintosh and Windows, which is a free download from www.adobe.com/products/acrobat. While the number of options available is much more limited than the dedicated presentation programs, PDF is a good option when posting or sending images because it offers protection from image copying or printing.

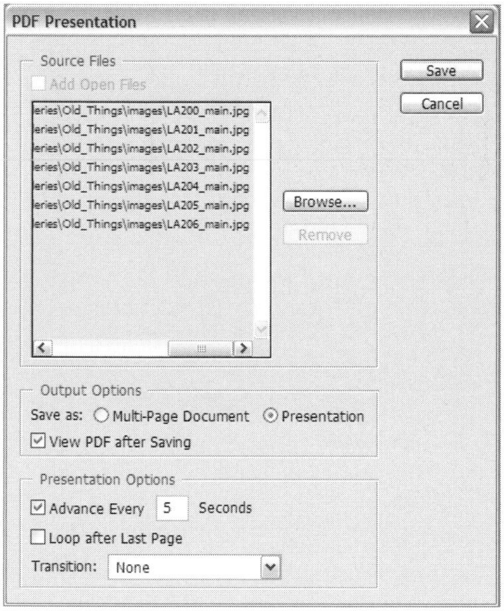

Figure 12.8 Saving your slideshow as a PDF file puts your images in an Adobe Acrobat format, complete with transitions and controls. You can link your slideshow from your website so your visitors can view it in their browsers.

To create a PDF Presentation in Photoshop, follow these steps:

1. Select File > Automate > PDF Presentation.

2. Select the images you want to include, either from the open images or by clicking Browse to find your images.

3. Select Presentation as the Output Option.

4. Under Presentation Options, click the Advance Every _ Seconds checkbox and enter the number of seconds you want each image to display.

5. If you want the slideshow to continually repeat, click the Loop After Last Page checkbox.

6. If you want transition effects between images, select one from the Transition dropdown list.

7. Click Save, and provide a name for your slideshow.

8. In the PDF Options dialog box, we recommend setting Encoding to JPEG with a quality level of 8 (see Figure 12.9). The JPEG format will typically result in much smaller file sizes (a reduction to $\frac{1}{5}$th the size is not uncommon) at a minimum loss of image quality, particularly useful when e-mailing or placing on the Web for downloading.

9. Clicking PDF Security opens an additional dialog box that enables you to prevent viewers from copying or printing images in your presentation (see Figure 12.10).

10. Click OK to save the presentation. If you selected View PDF after saving, your new slideshow will automatically launch.

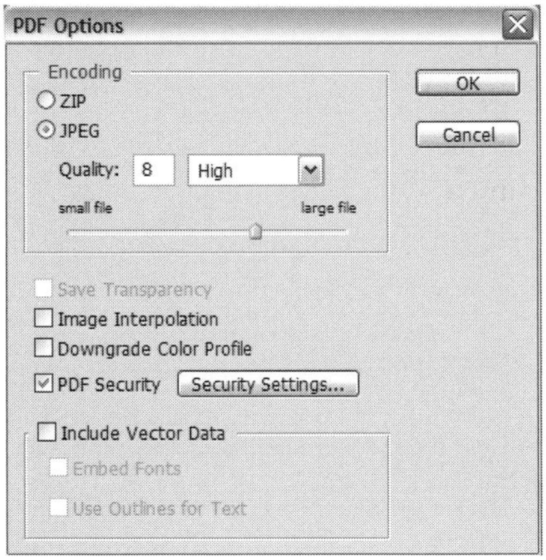

Figure 12.9 Setting the encoding type to JPEG will generate a much smaller file, which is especially useful for e-mailing your presentation.

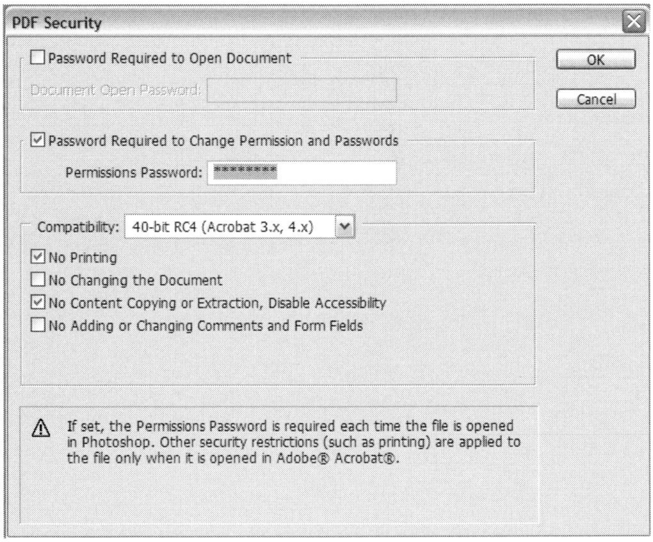

Figure 12.10 Setting security options for the PDF presentation restricts how much access viewers have to your images and gives a measure of copy protection.

PowerPoint 2003

Although it was originally designed to deliver business presentations with charts and text, many professional photographers have used Microsoft PowerPoint (www.office.microsoft.com/home, about $200, Windows version 2003) for years as their slideshow-presentation software of choice. Recent versions of PowerPoint for Windows have recognized this and do an even better job of building image-based slideshows. The easiest way to build a slideshow in PowerPoint is to use the Photo Album Wizard. To get started, select File > New (Ctrl+N).

1. In the New Presentation panel, select Photo Album.

2. In the Photo Album Wizard (see Figure 12.11), click on File/Disk and navigate to the folder containing your images. You can select single or multiple images in the file dialog. Clicking Insert will add the images to the Pictures In Album list. Image order can be changed by clicking the up or down arrows, and simple image adjustments can be made to brightness and contrast along with image rotation. Because PowerPoint gives you no control over the amount of change, we recommend doing all of your image editing work in Photoshop or your favorite image editor.

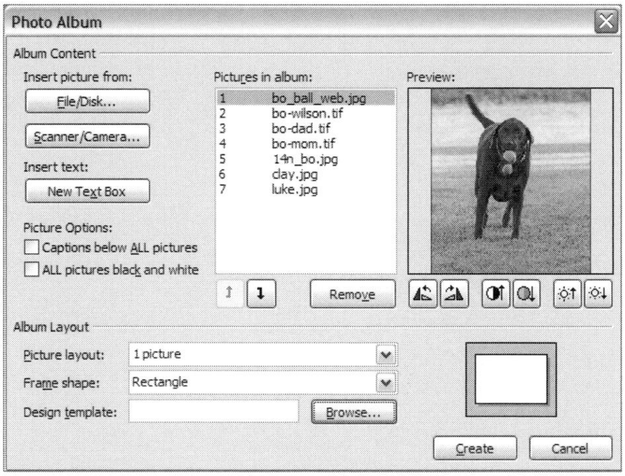

Figure 12.11 Using the Photo Album Wizard in PowerPoint is a quick way to create a basic slideshow.

3. Album Layout offers options to fit your pictures to slide or set images to a particular size. We prefer to size the images prior to inserting them into PowerPoint and, therefore, recommend the 1 Picture option, with the Frame shape set to Rectangle. This keeps your images at the planned size and gives room for a border color.

4. Click Create. PowerPoint will import all your images and create a new slide for each, along with a starting title slide. At this point, you can customize the layouts for border colors and other options.

Note: Although PowerPoint allows you to capture your JPEG or TIFF images directly from a camera or scanner, we have yet to see images in a slideshow that didn't benefit from some level of editing before adding them to a show.

5. To set the background color for your slides, choose Format > Background, or select Format > Slide Design to select from all available templates. Figure 12.12 shows both windows.

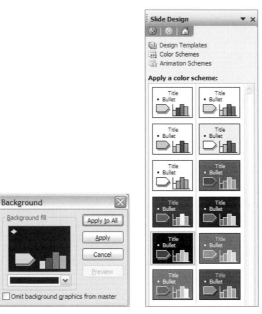

Figure 12.12 Background colors for slides are set in either the Background dialog box or the Slide Design panel.

6. To edit the Title slide, select it in the Slide list, double-click the default text "Photo Album" to select it, and replace the text with the name of your show.

 Note: You can delete all text by clicking in the text box and pressing delete. Pressing delete a second time removes the text box.

7. To apply an effect to your text, select the text, then select Slide Show > Animation Schemes, or select Animation Schemes from the Slide Design panel, and select one of the ready-to-use options. We suggest using a simple Fade effect to keep your show from looking too busy.

8. If none of the ready-made animation effects suit you, PowerPoint offers a wealth of custom animation options allowing you to build your own effects (see Figure 12.13) for entrance, emphasis, motion, and exit.

9. If you want to apply a transition effect between slides, select Slide Show > Slide Transition (see Figure 12.14). As with the animation effects, all transitions will apply to selected slides. Additional options include setting the transition speed, using a sound between slides, and whether to move to the next slide automatically after a set number of seconds or to advance on mouse click.

10. Once you've completed your slideshow, you can either save it as a PowerPoint presentation or package it for play on CD or as a web show. For CD, select File > Package for CD (see Figure 12.15). PowerPoint will copy all the needed files, including a viewer application to a folder or directly to CD. Selecting Save As Web Page creates a presentation that can be viewed in a web browser.

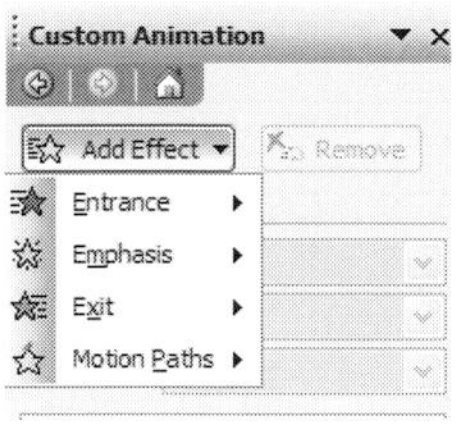

Figure 12.13 You can build your own animation effects using the Custom Animation option in PowerPoint.

Figure 12.14 Select a transition for all slides by selecting them in the Slide list and then choosing the transition from the Slide Transitions panel.

Note: If you choose to output as a web page, you have two options. The default is to save as an MHT, which places all your images in one file and can be quite large. Saving as HTM creates an index page along with a folder that contains all the images, web pages, and navigation controls as separate files. This option improves performance, but it offers less protection from copying.

Note: The Macintosh version of PowerPoint (www.microsoft.com, about $200, Macintosh OS X) has a very similar feature set to the Windows version. The main difference between the two applications is the lack of the Photo Album Wizard in the Macintosh version. The Macintosh version has a Save As Movie option in place of the Windows Package for CD.

Figure 12.15 PowerPoint can package your show for CD, including a viewer application and password protection.

Keynote

Keynote (www.apple.com/keynote, under $100, Macintosh OS X only) is a relatively new application that takes full advantage of the Macintosh OS X system. Figure 12.16 shows its interface. Similar to PowerPoint (in fact, it imports and exports to the PowerPoint format), slides are built individually. Keynote has several advantages that make it a worthwhile choice for photographic presentations:

- Quartz graphic engine handles image resizing and rotation extremely well.
- Anti-aliased text for smooth edges at any size.
- Alpha channel support for transparency. Photoshop and TIF files retain transparent properties when used in Keynote. Keynote also supports layered images with control over the transparency of objects, letting you create frames, translucent text, and other effects that can enhance your presentation.
- Easy-to-use transition "builds" for elements on a slide, and both 2D and 3D transition effects between slides.

- Dual monitor support. If you'll be narrating your slides, the laptop screen can show the speakers notes while the slides are projected to the large screen.

- Exports to QuickTime, PDF, and PowerPoint, making it easy to share your presentation with Windows users.

To create a slideshow in Keynote, just follow these steps:

1. Select File > New. The Theme Selection window is displayed (see Figure 12.17). For normal presentations, we start out with the simple White template. Select the theme you want to start with, and click Choose Theme. The templates displayed with images use layers with cutouts for your images. For a fun or casual show, one of these templates can make a great starting point. You'll also set the size for your show in this window by clicking the Presentation Size popup list.

2. The Master Slides list on the left side of the window allows you to select the slide style you want to use. Starting with the Title slide, follow the onscreen directions to replace the text with your show title.

3. Click the Inspector button in the toolbar. Almost all aspects of your show are controlled through the Inspector panel, including modifications to the master slides, layer transparency, text attributes, transitions, and sound. To start, click the Build button to the right of the Text icon. You'll see the window shown in Figure 12.18.

Figure 12.16 Keynote offers a simple-to-use interface with nice transition effects and excellent image display for Macintosh users.

4. From the Build In tab, select a transition style from the Build Style popup. Build In controls how elements, in this case the title text, will be displayed when the slide is shown. Build Out offers the same options and controls what happens when leaving the slide.

5. Create a new slide by selecting Slide > New Slide (Shift+Cmd+N). To set the slide to Blank, click the Masters icon in the toolbar and select Blank. You can also select the Blank slide thumbnail in the Masters Slides list and drag it onto the new slide.

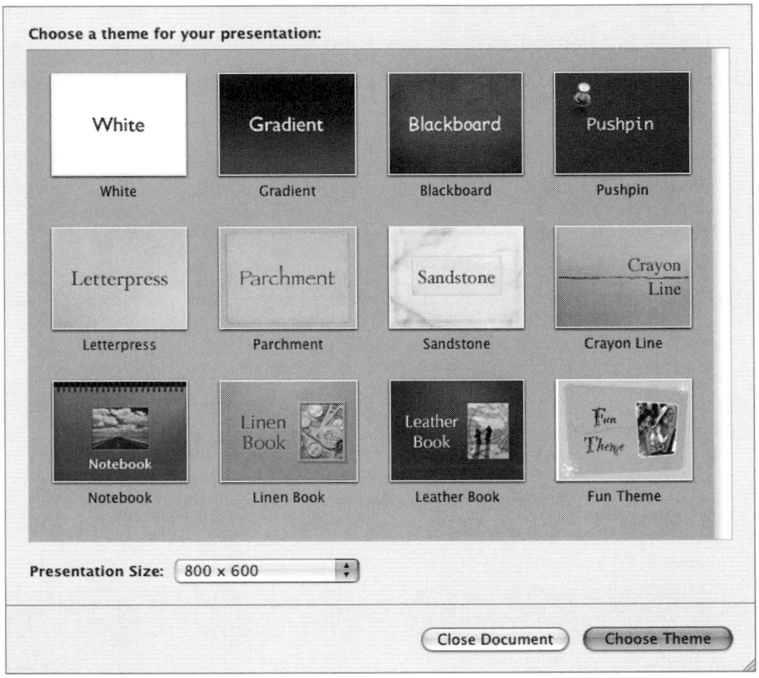

Figure 12.17 Keynote includes several themes, including photo themes with cutouts.

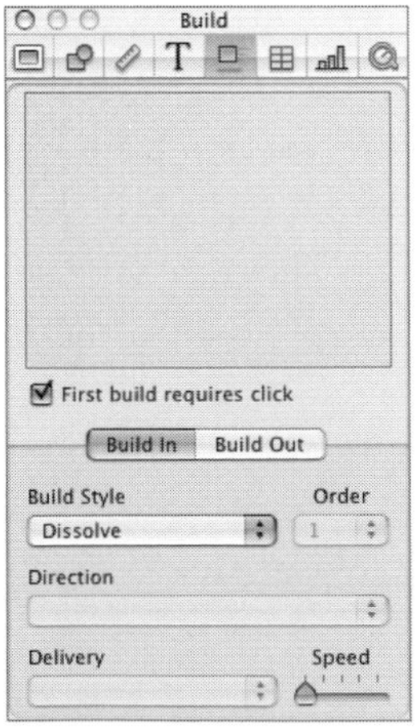

Figure 12.18 The Inspector panel controls most aspects of your slideshow entrance and exit transition effects for text or images on the slide.

6. To place an image on the slide, select Edit > Place > Choose (Shift+Cmd+V) to open the Macintosh file browser window. Alternatively, you can drag and drop the image from another application such as iPhoto.

7. In the Inspector panel, click on the Ruler icon.

8. If you need to resize your image, set the longest dimension to the proper size and leave Constrain Proportions checked.

9. Repeat Steps 5 through 8 for each slide in your show.

Transitions for the entire show can be set through the Master & Layout Inspector (see Figure 12.19). All changes made here will be applied to each slide of that type in the show. Each of the slide types can be selected by clicking the triangle next to the slide preview or by selecting the slide in the Master Slide list.

When the slideshow is completed, select File > Export to create a show that can be shared with others. Keynote exports to QuickTime movie, Adobe PDF, and Power-Point formats.

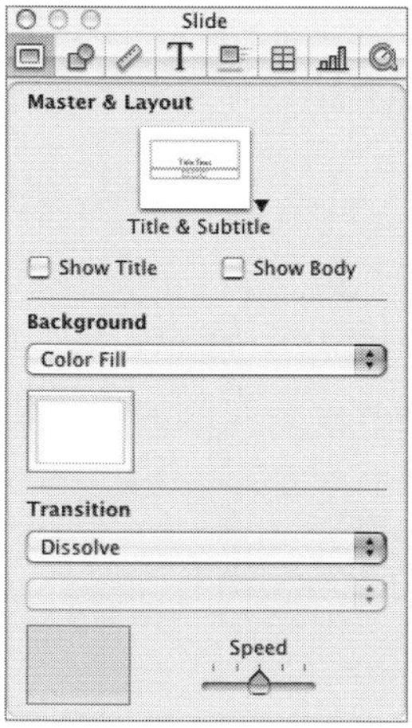

Figure 12.19 Transitions and backgrounds can be applied to all slides by selecting the Master & Layout Inspector.

Note: For more information on Keynote, try *Presenting Keynote* by Erik Holsinger (Sybex, 2003).

iPhoto

Apple iPhoto (www.apple.com/ilife/iphoto, under $50 for iLife, Macintosh OS X only) is part of Apple's iLife package of programs, which includes GargageBand for mixing your own music, iDVD to create a DVD of your finished slideshow, and iMovie for video editing. It's currently shipped with all new Macintosh computers.

Mac users will find that iPhoto offers a very simple interface for creating a slideshow. It includes fairly basic options for controlling display time, transitions, and adding a musical soundtrack. Figure 12.20 shows its Settings and Music tabs. The completed slideshow is saved as a QuickTime movie. You also have the option of publishing the finished slideshow to the .Mac shared service, where anyone you notify can view it.

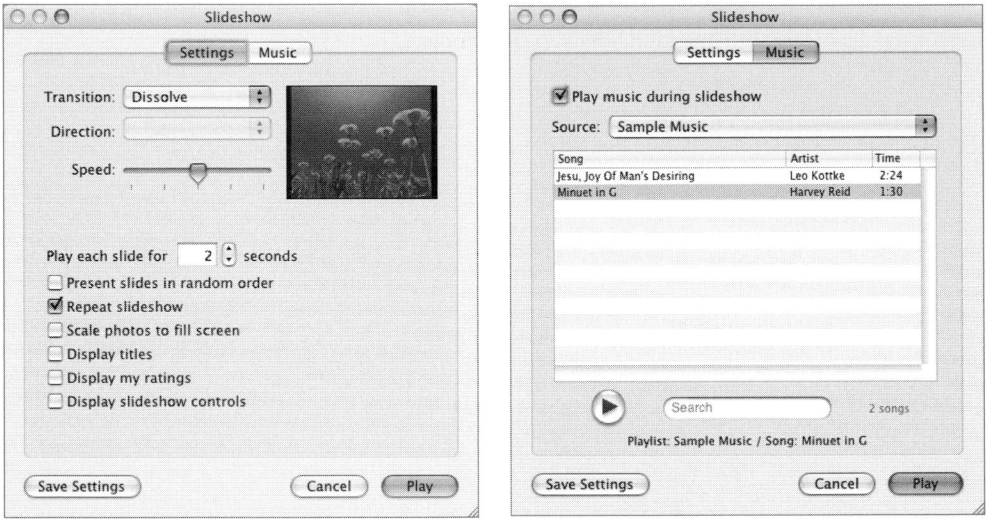

Figure 12.20 iPhoto offers a simple set of controls for playback, transitions, and adding music.

A Quick Comparison

Table 12.1 summarizes the major differences between the types of applications discussed in this chapter (as well as some Web gallery tools introduced in Part III) to help you determine which will work best for you.

Sharing Your Slideshow

One of the biggest advantages to the digital slideshow is being able to share your images with people who would otherwise never see them. In addition to a "live" stand-up presentation, you have the options of publishing your show on the Web, sending it out on CD or DVD for viewing on a television or computer, or even sending your masterpiece in e-mail. Earlier chapters have shown how to prepare your images for these various media; here are some final tips.

Giving a Live Presentation

Practice! The more time you spend rehearsing your presentation, the more confident you'll be. Confidence translates to knowledge, and your audience will notice. Whether you'll be introducing a show or speaking about each slide, reviewing your script and doing practice runs will result in a more polished presentation.

Set up early if possible, and test the equipment. Make sure that your images look correct on screen, and if needed, make adjustments to brightness, lens focus, sound volume.

▶ **Table 12.1:** Features of Common Slideshow Presentation Tools

Application	Windows	Macintosh	Soundtrack	Self running	Manual advance	Stand-Alone Shows
ProShow Gold	Yes	No	Yes, multiple tracks. Synchronizes to slides.	Yes	No	EXE, CD, DVD, Web, e-mail
SmoothShow	Yes	No	Yes, multiple tracks. Synchronizes to slides.	Yes	No	EXE, CD, DVD, Web
PowerPoint	Yes	Yes	Yes, but limited. No synchronization to slides.	Yes	Yes	Package with player, Web
Keynote	No	Yes	Yes, but limited. No synchronization to slides.	Yes	Yes	PDF, QuickTime, Web
iPhoto	No	Yes	Yes, but limited. No sync to slides	Yes	Yes	QuickTime, .Mac slideshow
ACDSee, ThumbsPlus, Adobe Photoshop Album	Yes	No	Yes, but limited. No synchronization to slides.	Yes	No	Web, CD, EXE

Bring business cards with your web address. A presentation is an opportunity to create new business and opportunities.

Use a laser pointer to highlight aspects of your slides. When feasible, consider moving around rather than standing stiffly behind a lectern. Make certain your audience can adequately hear you and your music. Using a microphone when necessary can make the show much more enjoyable to those in the back of the room.

CD and DVD Considerations

Most current DVD players will read the various Video CD formats, and almost all will read DVD discs created on the computer. CD-based presentations have several limitations that make them less than ideal for your slideshow. Chief among these are lower capacity (700MB for CD versus 4+GB for DVD) and lower resolution for your images. Table 12.2 lists the major differences between the various formats.

▶ **Table 12.2:** Format Differences

Format	Capacity	Resolution	Compatibility	Notes
VCD	70 minutes	352×240	High	Most compatible CD format
XVCD	60 minutes	352×240	Medium	Slightly better frame rate for video
SVCD	30 minutes	480×480	High	Better resolution, frame rates, high compatibility
DVD HQ	60 minutes	720×480	High	Best resolution, compatibility, and quality
DVD SP	120 minutes	720×480	High	Doubles capacity with slight drop in quality
DVD LP	180 minutes	720×480	High	Quality is slightly lower than DVD SP
DVD EP	240 minutes	720×480	High	Quality is slightly lower than DVD LP

For most uses, the higher compression used by the SP, LP, and EP versions of DVD are not readily visible. DVD SP is a good compromise between capacity and quality.

If you expect users to run the CD or DVD from a computer rather than a dedicated player, saving your slideshow as an EXE file is the way to go. This offers security, because the images are contained within a single file and the CD is usually created to autorun. When inserted in the users disc drive, it begins to play automatically.

CHAPTER 12: PUTTING A SLIDESHOW TOGETHER

On the Web

With the faster connection speeds that many users now have, sharing your slideshow on the Web is a real possibility. Programs such as ProShow Gold can create a web show that includes a viewer that plays in the visitor's browser window. You can host a show on your own site, or Photodex will host it for you on their site.

PowerPoint and iPhoto also have web output options. PowerPoint can create HTML pages (as discussed earlier), and iPhoto can create shows that can be saved to the .Mac service for viewing by others or that can be used as screensavers.

Showing and Selling Your Images

Although slideshows and websites are great ways to get your work in front of large numbers of people, neither of them has the impact or intimacy of a print that has been mounted and matted. The size, richness of color (or tonal ranges for black-and-white prints) simply can't be matched any other way. In this part of the book, we'll show you how to present your work professionally with well-chosen mats and frames, and how to get these masterpieces onto gallery and ultimately buyer's walls.

Finishing Your Prints

A photograph that has been properly mounted, matted, and framed takes on new importance. Mounting the print protects the image and serves as support and backing. The mat is designed to both enhance the appearance of the print and protect it. The style of frame you choose can make a tremendous difference in the presentation of your images. In this chapter, we'll show you how to take your photograph from the printer to hanging it on the wall and what options are available to you.

13

Chapter Contents
Mounting Your Print
Matting Your Print
Framing Your Print

Mounting Your Print

Whether you frame your print or simply mat it, you'll need to begin by attaching it in some way to a mounting board. Several common methods are used to mount photographs for presentation; these methods are categorized as either *permanent mounting* or *conservation mounting*. If you're not familiar with them, these terms may seem confusingly similar. The difference is that conservation mounting aims to conserve the physical print for the long-term, in archival storage or display. This means mounting in such a way that the print can be removed from the mounting without damage. By contrast, permanent mounting methods affix the print to the mounting material permanently, so that it usually can't be removed without damage.

For work you will be selling on your own, especially work that is not a limited edition or custom piece, permanent mounting is not only fine, but in many cases preferable because it is less fragile to handle. Conservation mounting on the other hand is best for prints that have high monetary or personal value, such as limited edition prints and family heirlooms, or that will be displayed in galleries. Most of the traditional photomounting processes work for most inkjet prints. The key here is the word "most." Not all inks and papers react in the same way to mounting adhesives, so it's best to know up front what your options are. The most popular methods are dry, hot, cold, and laminated. We'll cover the strengths and weaknesses of each of these methods so you can make the best choice for your needs.

Note: Regardless of the method used to prepare your photograph for display, inkjet prints need time to dry. As the inks dry, they emit gasses. This *outgassing* can cause discoloration and spotting or fogging of the glass used in the frame. Give all prints at least 24 hours to completely dry before mounting, matting, or framing them.

Conservation Mounting

Conservation mounting of photographs requires that all mounting materials be acid free, lignin free, and pH neutral. In order to be considered truly conservation quality, all materials must be removable with minimum exposure to adhesives. To be truly archival, an image should be printed with archival quality inks, such as the UltraChrome pigment inks used in some Epson printers as discussed in Chapter 1, "Choosing the Printer and Medium." Mounting boards for conservation mounting will be 100 percent cotton rag mat. Cotton is used because the lignin in paper pulp breaks down and creates an acid that yellows, becomes brittle with age, and will actually ruin photographs. The photograph should be attached to the mounting board with Japanese paper hinges.

Paper for hinges is available from most conservation suppliers under a variety of names. To make sure the paper is conservation quality, look for 100 percent kozo fibers. As shown in Figure 13.1, the paper hinges are attached to the back of the photograph, using a rice or wheat starch paste, and then attached to the mounting board. The paper hinges expand and contract with humidity and temperature variations, preventing the photograph from tearing or buckling. Detailed instructions for this method are widely available on the Internet; point your search tool to "Japanese paper hinge" to find numerous articles.

Japanese Paper Hinge

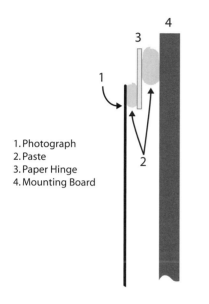

1. Photograph
2. Paste
3. Paper Hinge
4. Mounting Board

Figure 13.1 Attaching a photograph to a mounting board with the Japanese-paper hinge method

As an alternative to paper hinges, corner mounts or side strips that are attached to the mat will hold the photograph in place with no adhesive touching the actual photo paper. The 3M #415 Film Tape (about $10 for 100 strips) works well for making corner mounts. They are self adhesive and come with prescored marks for folding.

Conservation mounting is much more time intensive and the materials used are more costly. You'll want to be sure and figure these additional costs into the price of your print.

Note: Some galleries require that all displayed work be mounted using conservation techniques. Be sure to check with a gallery before preparing your photographs for display.

Permanent Mounting

When you don't need to worry about preserving the individual print, more mounting options become available. Permanent mounting methods all use an adhesive to attach the print directly to the mounting material. When the adhesive is a tissue, acetate, or aerate rubber-based cement, the method is described as *dry mounting*; when the adhesive is paste, spray adhesive, or liquid, it's called *wet mounting*. When heat as well as pressure is used to create a bond between the photograph and the mounting board (with either dry or wet adhesive), it's called *hot mounting*; when pressure alone is used, it's called *cold mounting*. Both hot and cold methods can be either dry or wet. We recommend dry methods, as wet methods tend to be messy and often error prone.

For best results, hot mounting requires the use of a specialized press, although it can be done with a household iron. (Do not use steam!)

For cold mounting, you can buy mounting boards with adhesive backings that allow you to place the photograph on the board and reposition as needed. The advantage to these boards is that they require no special press. Once the position is correct, use pressure to set the photograph to the mounting board. Several manufacturers make adhesive-backed mounting boards. We prefer 3/16″ thick Foam-Cor. It is available with low-tack or high-tack adhesives in sizes from 11″×14″ to 48″×72″.

3M markets PMA (Positionable Mounting Adhesive), which can be used as an alternative to the ready-made mounting boards. PMA is available in rolls from 11″ to 24″ wide starting at about $50 per roll and can be pressure set with a roller system or the included squeegee.

A Few Basic Cold-Mounting Techniques

With either the PMA or peel-and-stick mounting boards, the process is nearly the same. Just follow these steps:

1. Cut the mounting board to the desired size, and mark the location where the photograph will be mounted.

2. If you're using PMA, cut a piece just larger than the dimensions of your photograph.

3. Wipe the back of your photograph to make sure there is no dirt or hair. Anything on the back of the print will show through as a bump or crease when the photo is pressed into place.

4. Peel the protective backing off the mounting board, or one side of the PMA.

5. Lightly place the photograph onto the adhesive surface. If you're using PMA, once the photograph is in the proper position, use a squeegee or roller to create

a bond, and then trim the excess PMA from the photograph. Next, peel the backing from the other side of the PMA and place the photograph onto the mounting board.

6. Apply firm pressure, using a squeegee or roller to create a bond to the mounting board.

In the wet process, adhesive spray or contact cement is used. 3M Photo Mount spray adhesive is a single surface spray that is pH neutral. To use Photo Mount, follow these steps:

1. Wipe the back of your photograph to make sure there is no dirt or hair. Anything on the paper will cause a crease or bump when the photograph is mounted.

2. Spray an even coating of Photo Mount on the back of your photograph. (Be sure to do this in a well-ventilated room.)

3. Lightly place the photograph onto the mounting board, repositioning as needed until you're satisfied with the placement.

4. Apply even pressure to activate the bond.

A third option for cold mounting is the Rollataq Adhesive System (about $30 for the hand applicator model). This method uses an applicator that rolls a $2^1/2''$ strip of adhesive.

Although some of the cold mount systems are acid free, as are the mounting boards such as Foam-Cor and Gatorboard, they are not true archival mounting methods, because the photographs may be damaged if you try to remove the image from the mount.

Dry Hot Mounting

Dry hot mounting is a permanent process that uses a tissue type adhesive or acetate to glue your photograph to a mounting board, usually Foam-Cor, by applying heat and pressure.

Dry hot mounting is best used for prints that do not have a high monetary or personal value. It is not appropriate for signed, limited edition prints because the mounting process is permanent, in most cases not archival, and it will decrease the value of expensive collectibles. Many framing shops that offer mounting services use a hot press. The primary advantage to hot mounting is cost, which is typically 25 to 30 percent lower than cold mount materials.

To dry hot mount a print, place the adhesive tissue between the mounting board and the photograph. This sandwich is placed into a press that heats up the tissue to activate the adhesive while applying pressure. A protective cover sheet is used to prevent the ink from sticking to the press.

 Note: Dry hot mounting can also be done using a standard household iron, although we generally don't recommend it. This isn't as well suited to large prints because even pressure and specific times at a specific temperature are the basic ingredients in a successful mount. Irons can be used to great effect with small prints, but irons are the most suitable for tacking the mounting tissue to the print before placing it into the press.

There are two styles of dry hot mounting: border and bleed. Border mounting requires more preparation, as the mount board must be cut to the exact dimension of the finished size. Bleed mounting uses a mount board slightly larger than the finished size and is trimmed to final dimension after the photograph is mounted.

Dry mount presses are not an inexpensive proposition. The entry level Seal 160M currently sells for over $1,000, but it works quite well with the Epson UltraChrome inks. If you have only an occasional need for this type of mounting, you can use a framing store. Most of them offer this service.

The biggest drawback to dry mounting systems is the permanence. Once you've mounted your print to the mounting board, it's there for good. None of the dry mount processes are true archival options, so longevity is an issue for limited edition prints.

Laminating

Another alternative to mounting your images is lamination. Lamination is usually one of two styles, pouch or roll. The pouch style is better suited to smaller print sizes and thinner mounting boards. The lamination pouch is usually sealed on one side and the inside of the pouch is coated with a heat-activated film. As the pouch is run through the laminator, the heating element activates the adhesive, sealing the photograph between two layers of film.

Because of the increased capacity, both in size and thickness, roll laminators are more common for photographic purposes. Roll lamination uses two sheets of laminating film and can have either heat-activated or cold-pressure adhesive on one side. This film is much thinner than the familiar laminate film used for ID cards, and it is available in gloss, luster, and matte finishes. The mounting board and photograph are placed between the sheets of laminating film, which is then run through rollers to create a seal. Cold laminate systems are also available using a similar technology. Perhaps the biggest advantage to lamination is that some films have UV protective properties. UV coatings can increase the display life of photographs considerably.

As with the hot mount and cold mount processes covered earlier, laminating is a permanent process. The laminating films with UV protection are a good way to protect prints that will be exposed to sunlight, but the materials used are not archival quality.

For photographs that won't be mounted in a traditional frame behind glass, laminating provides protection from the elements by completely sealing, or encapsulating, the photograph and mounting material. Lamination also provides a measure of protection from moisture, which is more damaging to inkjet prints than traditional photographs.

As with hot mount presses, a hot roll laminator will run about $1,000 and up. The cold roll laminators are much more affordable in sizes up to 12″ wide. Roll laminators are available in widths up to 80″. Clearly, this is not a process for the occasional user, but most printing shops offer laminating services.

Lamination is an excellent option when print sizes make standard framing with glass or acrylic impractical or cost prohibitive.

Matting Your Print

Placing a mat around a photograph can make an amazing transformation. The photo goes beyond a mere image and becomes a focus point. When selecting a mat, you have many options, including the amount of open space around the print to color, accent lines, and multiple mats.

For most photographs, simple is best. The idea behind a mat is to draw attention to the image. Colors, accent lines, and fancy cuts should be used to accentuate the print and not pull the viewer's eye from the image. Too many distractions can all detract from the real purpose. One popular method of dressing up the presentation is to use a double mat, with white on white, white and black, or white with a small color strip visible that complements the photograph.

Matting serves three main purposes:

- It separates the photograph from its surrounding frame and creates a space that helps viewers focus their eyes on the photograph, giving it a stronger presence.

- It acts as a buffer space between the photograph and the glass that will be used if the print is also framed. A print that is pressed against the glass in your frame will deteriorate quicker with spots on the print and fogging on the glass.

- It makes your photograph more marketable. A matted print is ready to be framed and hung. By matting your images, you save customers the time and expense of having this done.

Samples of matting and framing styles can be seen in the color section.

Mat Cutting Tools

Mat cutting tools can be a simple as a razor blade and straight edge or as complicated as a computer-driven cutting system that costs nearly $50,000. Neither of these is the best option for most of us. Mat cutting setups, such as the Alto's 4501 (www.altosezmat.com) can be found for about $130. It uses a simple adjustment system and allows for straight or beveled cuts (see Figure 13.2). The Alto's cutter can handle mats up to 30″ and adjusts in 1/8″ increments up to 6″ wide borders. Alto's also has oval and circle cutters available.

Figure 13.2 The Alto's 4501 is an affordable mat cutting system that produces excellent results. (Image courtesy of Alto's EZ Mat, Inc.)

Higher in quality, and able to cut larger mats, the Logan Framer's Edge 650 (www.logangraphic.com) has a list price of about $700. It can handle sizes up to 40″ square (see Figure 13.3), with a maximum border width of 5½″. Unlike the Alto's system, the Logan is fully adjustable (no 1/8″ increments) with a cutting blade that runs in a track rather than a separate holder. The Logan also features stops that can be set to prevent over or undercutting and wasting mat boards. This is particularly helpful when cutting a series of mat boards to the same size. For smaller work, the Simplex 750 line offers the same construction as the Framer's Edge for about half the price. The Logan system also allows you to make straight or beveled cuts.

Similar in design to the Logan system, the Fletcher MatMate and Fletcher 2200 Mat Cutting System (www.fletcher-terry.com) cutters are used in many museum matting classes and start at about $1,000. They can handle mat boards as large as 60″. If you're serious about the quality and quantity of mats you cut, these systems are hard to beat.

At the very high end, computer-driven systems such as the Wizard CMC (www.wizardint.com/matcutter.asp, about $16,000) can cut a variety of mats using provided templates, or they can be programmed to create custom designs on boards up to 40″×60″.

Cutting a mat, regardless of the cutter used, follows the same basic approach:

1. Cut the mat board to the correct finished size if needed. The correct finished size will be the size of the print, minus ½ inch for mat overlap of print, plus the width of the mat on each side. So an 8″×10″ print with a 1½″ mat border would be cut to 10 ¾″×12″.

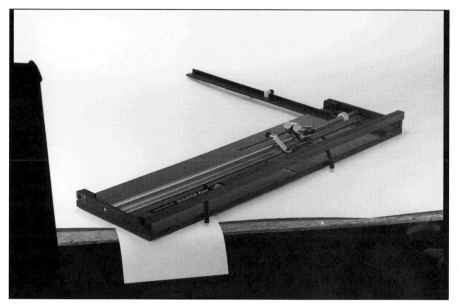

Figure 13.3 The Logan Framer's Edge is a high-quality mat cutting system that handles mat sizes up to 40″.

2. Measure the photograph to be matted, and then subtract ¼ inch from the length and height measurements to allow room for the mat to cover the print.

3. On the backside of the mat board, mark the opening to be cut using a pencil. The corners are the only critical marks needed for the cutting systems. If you'll be cutting freehand with a rule and razor, mark all the lines. (Image courtesy of Alto's EZ Mat, Inc.)

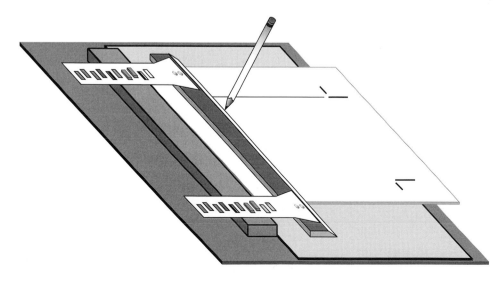

4. Place the mat board on the cutter, and adjust the rule for the proper size.

5. Cut along the guides, turning the mat board for each cut. If your border widths are the same, all four sides can be cut with no resetting of the rules. (Image courtesy of Alto's EZ Mat, Inc.)

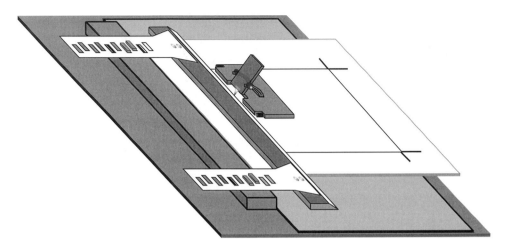

Ready or Precut Mats

The standard method of sizing a mat is to use the next largest print size as the finished mat size. For instance, an 8″×10″ print would be matted in a 11″×14″ mat board. When selecting mat sizes, it's better to go larger than smaller when deciding between two sizes. Many digital cameras don't shoot images with the same proportions as the film cameras they are replacing. This requires cropping to fit into standard sizes, or cutting custom-size mats. If your print size is actually 10″×12″, your print will look better in a 16″×20″ mat and frame than it would if you tried to fit it into 11″×14″ mat and frame. Increasing the size of the mat creates negative space around a print and increases the feeling of importance (see Figure 13.4), because there is additional space between the print and the frame or the wall, leaving less to distract the eye. With a large mat, you basically see nothing but the image.

Standard sizes for ready-cut mats are 8″×10″, 11″×14″, 16″×20″, and 20″×30″. These sizes are readily available at most craft-type stores, as well as framing-supply stores. If you need a nonstandard size mat or opening, framing stores and online suppliers such as www.pictureframes.com and www.matcutter.com can cut custom mats for you. However, you'll soon find that cutting your own is a great cost savings. We recently priced a custom-cut mat at a local framing shop with a 12″×18″ opening in a 20″×30″ rag mat board. The cost was over $80. Cutting our own cost less than $25.00. When we were finished, the center cutout was large enough to be cut into an 8″×10″ mount. By recycling the cutout, we saved even more!

Figure 13.4 The same image size matted to 8″×10″ (top) has a very different feel when matted to 11″×14″ (bottom) to set it off from its surroundings.

How Thick Should Your Mat Be?

As the dimensions of the frame and photograph increase, the use of a thicker mat board will add to the impact of the presentation. Typical precut mat boards that you find in a craft store are 2-ply, or $1/32''$ thick. Four-ply mats are $1/16''$ thick, and should be considered the minimum for conservation matting. For large prints in the 16"×20" range, 6-ply or 8-ply mats should be considered. Such mats are available in solid core or with contrasting colors. The thicker mats are quite a bit more expensive than the thinner ones, and cutting them accurately is more difficult. Before cutting your own, practice on scrap material.

How Much Mat?

If you need to cut to a nonstandard size, you'll generally want to follow the same relative proportions used with standard sizes—but you also have the freedom to vary the proportions a little. Mats often look best when the top and bottom borders are larger than the sides. As an example, the standard 11"×14" mat used with an 8"×10" print would have $1^1/2''$ border on each side with a 2" border top and bottom. Leaving slightly more border at the bottom of the mat is also effective. Using the previous example, we could cut $1^1/2''$ borders on the sides and top with a $1^1/2''$ border on the bottom. The extra weight at the bottom of the mat gives the image more visual appeal. The actual choice of dimensions used for a border area is subjective, and you should consider these tips as guidelines and not hard rules.

On average, a border width of $2^1/2''$ or less is used, but larger pieces will look good with a wider border of up to 5". Border width is a personal preference, but avoid overpowering the photograph with too much mat. In some cases, particularly gallery showings, all photographs must be framed to the same dimensions, regardless of image size. Your gallery will have full mounting and matting requirements to guide you.

Double matting is an option to give a photograph more depth and space between photograph and glass. When using double mats, the outer border will be narrower, allowing the inner border to show with a small edge. Typically, a $1/4''$ narrower border on the outer mat will give a pleasing layered look to a finished print.

Selecting a Color

Mat color should never compete with the photograph, and for similar reasons should not be selected to match a room color. While white (or one of its many shades) is universally acceptable as a mat color, black and neutral shades can be effective as well.

Color, if used at all, should enhance the photograph. For portraits, one way to accomplish this is to select a mat color that is complementary to the subject's eye color. Landscapes will look best with neutral tones in most cases.

> **Note:** Many museums and galleries require that photographs be mounted with single white or off-white mats only. When double mats are requested, white on white or black with white is commonly used.

To help select a mat color, look for complementary colors within the photograph and avoid looking for an exact color match. Most framing stores also sell mat boards and have corner pieces to check colors. If going into a store isn't convenient, Photoshop and your browser can provide an alternative. Many websites that sell matboards, including Dick Blick Art Materials (www.dickblick.com), have online color samples you can view. You can simulate the appearance of matting a photograph with one of these colors by applying it as a border in Photoshop. The various art supply sites differ in the way they present color samples, so we can't give you a single "universal" method for saving a sample into a form with which Photoshop can work. If you'd like to try the Photoshop border technique without having to create your own color sample, download one of the color chart files from the www.photofinishbook.com website. For example, Crescent_Museum_ Grade.tif is a sample we created from the Crescent Museum Grade Matboard colors on the Dick Blick site. If you want to select from a different set, you'll need to create your own sample.

Once you have your color samples, take these steps to create a test border:

1. Open *filename* (the image file you'll be matting).

2. Select Image > Canvas Size (see Figure 13.5) and increase the size of the canvas by the border size you've decided to use. In this example, we're taking an image that is slightly less than 5″×7″ and enlarging the canvas to 8″×10″. We leave the anchor point set to center.

> **Note:** Alternatively, you can check the Relative checkbox in Canvas Size and enter the desired border size, such as 2 inches.

3. Open the color sample file (either the Crescent_Museum_Grade.tif that you downloaded from our website or one you created) and arrange the two windows side by side, as in Figure 13.6.

4. Use the Eyedropper tool ![eyedropper] to sample a color from the sample file. For the grayscale portrait in Figure 13.6, we've chosen a dark grey.

5. Select the Paint Bucket tool ![paint bucket], and click on the canvas area. Figure 13.6 shows the result.

Framing Your Print

The final and finishing touch for your print is the frame (see Figure 13.7). Whether you plan to purchase ready-made frames, make them yourself, or have the frame made professionally, a number of options in materials, color, size, and style are available.

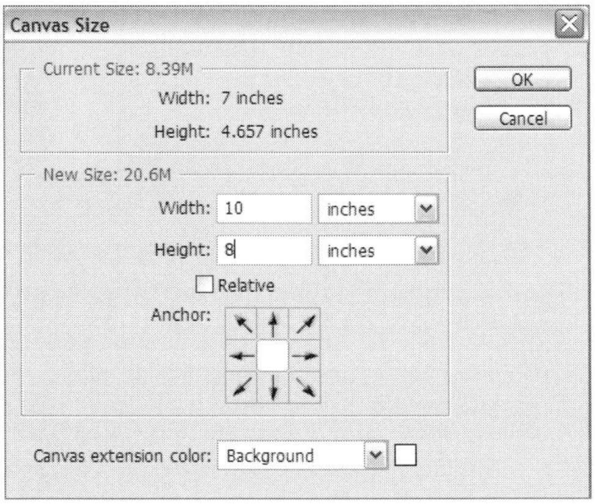

Figure 13.5 Enlarging the canvas around an image in Photoshop will provide a quick preview of the matted print.

Figure 13.6 Once you've selected a color from the sample file, you can fill in the canvas border area with the Paint Bucket tool to simulate the mat color.

In our opinion, if the print is worth mounting and matting, it's worth the extra expense and effort to frame it as well. The exception to this is a print that goes into your portfolio, which we will cover in Chapter 14, "Displaying and Selling Your Images." Inkjet prints are susceptible to fading and color shifts when exposed to light for long periods of time. The protection offered by framing with UV glass will add years to the life of your images. If framing is not an option, due to weight concerns or just aesthetics, a laminated print with matting is an alternative.

Museum and gallery display usually means simple black metal frames. You'll want to verify framing requirements with your gallery. Museum-style framing adds an elegant and formal look to most photographs, and it works well with nearly every subject. For portrait framing, some people prefer a heavier frame that suits the environment where the portrait will be hung. As with mat size, frame choices are a matter of personal taste.

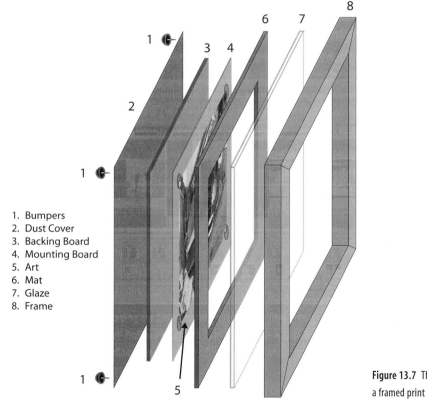

1. Bumpers
2. Dust Cover
3. Backing Board
4. Mounting Board
5. Art
6. Mat
7. Glaze
8. Frame

Figure 13.7 The elements of a framed print

Glass or Acrylic?

Glass has been the typical choice for use as a protective layer in framed prints, and it is still a valid one depending on your needs. Acrylic, or Plexiglas®, is often a better choice for several reasons:

- **Weight.** Especially in larger sizes, the weight difference between acrylic and glass is significant.

- **UV protection.** Acrylic can be UV coated to block up to 97 percent of ultraviolet light, nearly twice as effective as regular glass. Several types of UV glass are available. Some have a color cast that may be objectionable, so be sure to check in advance.

- **Shatter resistance.** Acrylic is much more durable than glass, although significantly more susceptible to scratching. Acrylic can have a duller appearance, especially the anti-glare type.

Some subjects lend themselves very well to unique frame styles. As an example, the photograph of an abandoned farm house (see Figure 13.8) is framed using wood from the house itself. Jon obtained permission from the property owner to use boards that had fallen off the house in exchange for a copy of the print.

Figure 13.8 The frame used for this photograph is made of wood taken from the subject.

Professional Framing

Even though ready-made frames come in a variety of styles, custom frames offer many more choices. With odd-size prints, professional framing is your only option unless you want to make your own (which we will cover next). Professional framing and mounting typically runs double the price of ready- or self-made framing and mounting.

PictureFrames.com (www.pictureframes.com) offers custom framing and ready-made frames, as well as a very cool "Personal Frame Shop" that lets you interactively create your frame and mat online with your own image (see Figure 13.9). As you select each option, the pricing is updated, and a simple click on the Add To Cart button submits your order.

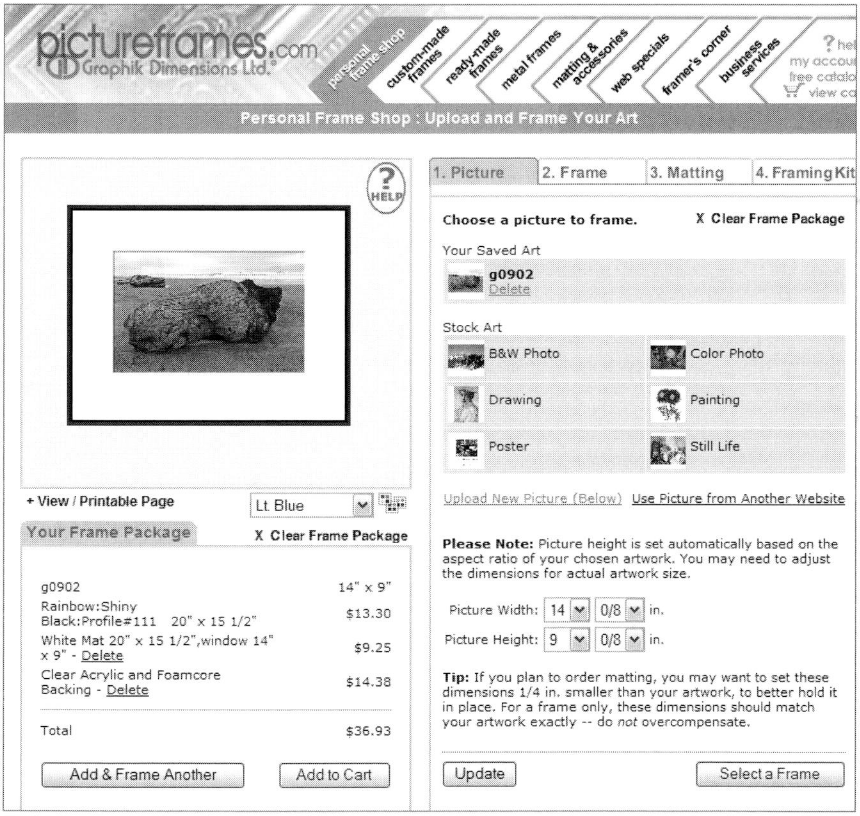

Figure 13.9 The Personal Frame Shop (www.pictureframes.com) lets you preview what your frame and mat choices will look like with your image.

Making Your Own

If you've matted your image to standard dimensions, a frame kit is an excellent option and will usually be more cost effective than buying the individual components needed. Light Impressions (www.lightimpressionsdirect.com) offers several styles of frame kits that include the frame, UV acrylic, archival mat, backing board, and mounting hardware. Light Impressions (and many other companies) also offer frames custom cut to any size you specify that come with the necessary hardware. You will need to order the glass/acrylic separately. This gives you the option to create a custom-sized mat that specifically enhances your photo no matter how unique the size and still purchase a reasonably priced frame to fit. We've included a list of companies on the companion website.

A final option, for photographers with the appropriate tools and shop skills, is to build your own frame. This can be a satisfying experience, and one that gives you complete control from image capture to final presentation. Metal frames can be made with a minimum amount of equipment (a miter box and saw, corner brackets, and spring clips). Wood frames are a bit more involved, usually requiring a rabbet cut with a saw or router into the back of the frame as a recess for the glass, mount, and mat. In addition, a point driver to hold the image in place is used.

Attractive wood frames can be built from common mouldings as well, giving you a large selection of profiles, and more can be fashioned using a router.

Regardless of the style of frame, the important dimension is the inside opening. Standard framing uses a $1/4''$ recess, covering as little of the image and mat as possible. If you're framing a $16''\times20''$ piece, the inside frame dimension will be $15\,1/2''\times19\,1/2''$, allowing for $1/4''$ on each side.

Excellent resources are available if you're interested in building your own frames from wood, including *Matting and Framing Made Easy* by Janean Thompson and *Making Picture Frames in Wood* by Manly Banister. If you really get into building your own frames, you should check out *Picture Framing Magazine* (www.pictureframingmagazine.com) for ongoing ideas, tips, and equipment reviews.

Displaying and Selling Your Images

The pinnacle of success for many photographers is their first gallery showing. Getting your work exhibited is very rewarding, but it requires planning, research, and hard work. Very few of us get a call out of the blue begging for our work to be shown when we're starting out—it's usually the other way around. Although art galleries are the obvious outlets for exhibiting your images, other options exist, and they can help open gallery doors. We'll cover these options in this chapter.

Chapter Contents
Exhibiting
Getting into Galleries
Selling on the Internet

Exhibiting

So far, we've focused on exhibiting electronically. Part III, "Displaying Images on the Web," and Part IV, "Producing Digital Slideshows," made some analogies to gallery showings. Many of the same guidelines used in those parts apply regardless of the medium used to present your work. For example, carefully selecting your best work for displaying prints on a gallery wall is just as crucial as it is for displaying JPG files on your web gallery. There are significant differences to consider as well. First and foremost is that, unlike creating a website, exhibiting your work in someone else's venue—whether that's a neighborhood café or a prestigious gallery—is not a "do-it-yourself" operation. Before you can impress the general public with your work, you first need to convince someone else to display it for you. That means creating a portfolio designed to demonstrate that your work meets their standards and enhances their space. With a web gallery, you want to create a small selection that will invite viewers to see more; however, when proposing an exhibit, you have a much smaller group (in many cases a single individual) that needs to be impressed enough with your work.

One of the best ways to get started exhibiting is through smaller local venues. Your community probably has many nontraditional locations where you can display your work. Locations such as restaurants, coffee shops, bookstores, banks, libraries, art framing shops, and other locations frequently display works from local artists. Typically, these locations will display work that has local interest. They may or may not allow you to sell your photographs, but they can help establish a reputation for yourself within a community. Having such displays on your resume will improve your credibility with galleries, will improve your confidence, and will help familiarize potential customers with your work.

As an example of this type of exhibit, the local Borders bookstore near Jon's home in Washington has a monthly rotation of artwork. The artist is responsible for all work involved in displaying their work including matting, framing, labeling, and setup/removal. (The artist is responsible for arranging to hang and remove their work after hours.) To be considered for display, the artist makes an appointment with the store representative to bring in a small (five prints maximum) portfolio for review. While the store is open to a wide variety of subjects, they prefer images that have a local or regional connection. Pacific Northwest landscapes are a better subject here than Hawaii landscapes. Once approved, a one month period is reserved for the showing.

Most of these venues will not sell your work directly, so you should provide business cards for potential customers to contact you directly.

An excellent option that does allow direct sales is the arts and crafts fairs that many cities and communities hold. These shows range from the very casual where any work is welcome, to shows that are judged and restricted in entry. Typically booth space is rented out, with a 10′×10′ booth being a good size. A simple stand to hold framed pieces and tables with matted prints in various sizes works well. Matted prints should be in clear bags and clearly priced. Framed prints should be kept to a minimum and be your most compelling images, designed to catch the viewer's eye and pull them into your booth. To find fairs in your area, www.craftlister.com is a good starting point, and searching on "art fairs" will return a number of results.

Do Your Homework First

Using a little common sense goes a long way toward making a good impression and can make the difference between exhibiting your work and being rejected. Here are a few guidelines:

- Visit your prospective location to see if they currently display work from local artists/ photographers. If they don't, be prepared to sell them on the idea.

- Call to make an appointment. Never just show up with your portfolio expecting them to drop what they're doing for you.

- Know what you want from an exhibit before you approach a location. What is your goal? Sales? Exposure? Experience? All of these? If you plan to sell, have an idea of the amount you need to charge to cover expenses, including the commission the gallery will charge. These fees, along with others associated with the costs of producing your show, including announcements and their costs, and artist's reception, can sometimes be negotiated with the gallery.

- Don't approach a location unless you already have the images. If you get an approval, you need to be ready to mount and mat your photographs now, not in three or four months. More typical though is to have a gallery schedule your showing for six months or more in advance. Depending on the content of your show, you can prepare photographs for display as you approach the show date. (If a gallery requests only your most current work, this method of spreading out the work and associated costs won't work for you.)

- Customize your portfolio for each location. You should bring images that will fit into specific locations. For instance, flower or wildlife photographs won't do as well in a sporting goods store as climbing or kayaking photographs that generate excitement for the lifestyle and products they promote. Tailoring your presentation for the store increases your chances of having your work shown (and sold!).

- Dress appropriately when presenting your portfolio. In many ways, this is a job interview and should be prepared for the same way. Your attire should fit or be slightly more formal than what the employees are wearing.

Creating a Portfolio

Your portfolio is the key to influencing a gallery or store to exhibit your work. Portfolio images should be printed to the same high standard that a framed photograph would have.

To create your portfolio, we recommend printing your images to 8″×11″ and mounting with white rag mat to 11″×14″. Using photo corners as mentioned in Chapter 13, "Finishing Your Prints," will allow you to change your images to suit the presentation without requiring new mounts and mats. Another approach is to use protective pages for each unmatted image, placed in a standard portfolio case.

Keeping your portfolio in a carrying bag, such as the ones sold by Light Impressions (www.light-impressionsdirect.com), will protect the images and the mats from bent corners and dirt, as well as give your portfolio a more professional appearance.

Selecting Images

It should be obvious that only the absolute best of your work should be put on display. The number of images selected will vary from location to location and from one exhibit type to the next. An exclusive show in a large gallery may require 25 or more photographs, while the coffee shop may have room for only five or six.

In many cases, gallery owners will want to review a selection of your work and select the final set of photographs themselves. If you've done your research (see the sidebar "Do Your Homework First"), you should have a good idea of the subject matter that will be appropriate for the exhibit, making it easier to narrow down the list of candidates for your portfolio and ultimately exhibited images. As an example, Jon recently exhibited images from Eastern Washington. His portfolio images included images of agriculture, the geology of the region, and abandoned farm buildings. After review, the exhibit director specified images of the agriculture and farm buildings in the area.

Sizes, Mats, and Frames

Occasionally, presentation requirements will be set by a gallery with little or no control on your part, although it's typical for galleries to leave many of the specifics up to the photographer with some general suggestions on what they would like to see. If your show is being presented as a series of related images, a gallery will typically require all images to be framed to the same size, whether that is 11″×14″ or 16″×20″ with mat sizes cut to fit. As with image selection, a gallery has almost total control over image size, mat style and color, and frame style. Chapter 13 deals with mounting, matting, and framing your photographs.

Normally, you will be responsible for all aspects of the presentation including the mat and frame. Exceptions to this are exhibits representing several photographers. In this situation, the gallery will often specify size and mat requirements but will handle the framing themselves for consistency. (You will still normally be responsible for the costs involved with the framing.) In general, galleries will specify conservation mounting. Keep this in mind when you estimate sales prices, as conservation quality materials and framing will add as much as $100 to the cost of a 16″×20″ framed print.

Many of the local venues we discussed earlier in the chapter won't have rigid requirements. They may not have answers for you if you have questions. They sometimes depend on you as the photographer to present your work in a size and style that suits the location and images. For smaller locations, 11″×14″ is a good frame size to use due to the space constraints and typical viewing distances.

One approach that many photographers use to great success (and increased sales and profits) is to use a variety of sizes, featuring one larger photograph, such as a 16″×20″, with the remainder in a smaller size such as 11″×14″. Another method of increasing sales is to offer matted but unmounted prints if possible.

Getting into Galleries

Photographers capture images in large part because we want to share our vision of the world with others. Usually, we want to share that vision with as many people as possible. A gallery show helps photographers reach a somewhat larger audience and provides a setting where they can show the images they put so much effort into capturing, optimizing, and preparing for the perfect presentation. Even for photographers who don't necessarily want to make a living at photography, getting images into a gallery is a common goal.

Chances are you won't get a show in the first gallery you approach. Many galleries schedule their shows months or even years in advance, and there is no shortage of photographers or other artists anxious to have their work displayed. Understand up front that you will face rejection from many galleries. Don't let that discourage you. Each gallery has their own taste, and most galleries are approached by far more artists than they could ever accommodate. There is only so much space on the walls, so galleries are always looking for art that they know will sell well. If you focus on producing the best images possible, present them professionally, and are persistent in your efforts, chances are good you'll be able to get your images into a gallery.

Note: When you do get your first gallery show or exhibit, you should add information about the show to your website. This provides more credibility to your work and also increases the exposure and potential attendance (not to mention sales!) at your show.

Finding the Right Gallery

You may be tempted to approach every gallery you can locate in an effort to get your images accepted. However, you'll greatly improve your chances of success and limit the frustration of rejection if you do your homework and find galleries that are most appropriate for you and your work.

The first step is finding which galleries are even available. No doubt you already know about some local galleries, and probably have a few favorites. You may even have one gallery you dream will someday display your images. Look beyond these galleries for others that might be appropriate. You may even want to look for galleries in other communities rather than focusing only on those close to you. You can locate galleries by checking in your phone book, by checking out the arts section of local newspapers, and even using the Internet to search. Also, when you're driving around town, keep an eye out for galleries you might not otherwise discover.

Talk to other photographers to see if they have recommendations on galleries you should consider. You might also want to talk to the local framing shop to see if they have any recommendations. They deal with many photographers and other artists when preparing images for gallery display, so they often have a very good idea of which galleries are best suited for particular types of photography, and they may be able to provide helpful information about some of the galleries.

Networking in this manner may also lead to contacts who can introduce you to gallery owners. This provides a tremendous advantage over simply walking in the door at a gallery. If someone else recommends you and is able to help arrange a meeting with the gallery owners, you'll have a much better chance of getting your work accepted.

When you have a list of possible galleries based on the information you have gathered, visit each of them as a customer. This is an opportunity to learn more about the gallery to see if it might be an appropriate match for you and your photography. When visiting, consider the following:

- **Type of Work on Display.** Many galleries focus on a particular type of work. Some may not display photography at all, and you may not be able to convince such a gallery to consider your photographic images. Other galleries may have a more eclectic display, welcoming a wide variety of presentations. Try to imagine some of your images hung on the wall, and consider whether they would fit in based on the subject matter and presentation.

- **Quality of Work.** Honestly evaluate your own images, and compare them to the quality of work displayed on the walls. This can be the most difficult part of the whole process. It isn't easy to admit that your images might not be quite up to the level of the work displayed at a particular gallery, but knowing where you stand will improve your chances of success. If you only attempt to get your images displayed in galleries with the highest of standards, you may get frustrated. Don't aim low, but rather try to be realistic about which galleries seem appropriate for the quality of your images.

After visiting a number of galleries, you should have a pretty good idea of which you should approach. You can even prioritize them based on those that are most appropriate for your particular images and that are most likely to accept your work for display.

During the process of trying to find the right gallery, don't forget about the nongallery options discussed earlier in the chapter. Again, these alternatives can build both your own confidence and your credibility with gallery owners.

Approaching a Gallery

Having done your homework, it is time to approach the gallery you've targeted. You can do this over the phone or in person. At first, you want to make a simple inquiry about getting an appointment to show your portfolio. If you arrive in person, we recommend leaving your portfolio in the car. The gallery owner may be busy, and walking in with portfolio in hand may be perceived as rude. Instead—whether on the phone or in person—ask if you can schedule a meeting with the owner so you can present some of your work. They may have particular policies about submitting images, and this is your chance to learn about them.

If you are there in person and the owner indicates that you can arrange a meeting any time, mention that you have your portfolio with you and would be happy to present it now if that is convenient. If not, schedule an appointment to share your portfolio.

The meeting is your chance to sell yourself as a photographer and artist. Present the images in a professional manner, provide some background on your work and any exhibitions you've already had for your images, and explain how you feel your images would fit in with this particular gallery based on the homework you did earlier.

Chances are you'll get a very clear indication of whether the gallery will consider your work. If they are interested, inquire about scheduling a show. If not, thank the owner for taking the time to view your images, and start thinking about the next gallery you'll approach. If the owner won't commit right now but has left open the possibility of a future show, ask when an appropriate time would be to follow up to possibly schedule that. Be sure to follow up in a timely manner.

As we mentioned earlier, you need to understand that you'll likely be rejected for one reason or another by several galleries before you get an opportunity to show your work. The simple fact is that there are many more photographers who would like to display their work than there is space on the walls in the galleries. Work toward developing a relationship with the owners of the galleries you feel are most appropriate for your images, and be persistent.

Pricing Your Work

Setting appropriate prices for your images can be a real challenge, and the process often seems to be very arbitrary. When working to establish prices for the images you'll hang in a gallery, consider the following factors:

- **Production Cost.** Besides providing a public venue for your images, getting a chance to share your vision with the world, and gaining pride in your photography, you are probably looking to make some money with a gallery show. Therefore, you'll need to price your images high enough that you are covering your basic costs for printing the images, and having them matted and framed. Calculate these costs to come up with the base price for your images.

- **Gallery Commission.** The specific percentage will vary from gallery to gallery, but obviously the gallery expects to get a commission for displaying and selling your work. The average seems to be around 50 percent. Some charge relatively low percentages around 10 to 20 percent, but that is somewhat unusual. Find out what commission will be, and factor it into your price. If it costs you $200 to have a particular image printed, matted, and framed, you will need to set the price at $400 just to break even if the gallery is taking 50 percent.

- **Effort and Uniqueness.** Besides considering the direct expenses involved with preparing the image for display, consider the special effort that went into each image and whether the image is particularly unique. You can't exactly split the cost of that two-week safari to Africa among the dozen or so prints on display in the gallery, or your prices will be astronomical. However, you may be able to charge a premium for images that will resonate with viewers or that required special effort to capture or that are unique in some way.

- **Pricing Comparison.** Considering what images of similar size and subject matter are selling for can be particularly helpful. When visiting galleries, note the prices for photographic prints at various sizes that are matted and framed similar to how you will present your images. This will give you a good idea of what the "going rate" is for photographic images in the area, making it easier to set your own pricing and to keep your work from being overpriced. If you price your work at $400 and the average sale is only $300, you'll find yourself bringing most of your work home with you (and eating the costs in image preparation).

> **Note:** Once you price the cost of having your photographs mounted, matted, and framed, you'll quickly see the advantage of doing this work yourself. Buying your materials at discount suppliers, such as those mentioned in Chapter 13 and listed on the companion website (www.photofinishbook.com), can recoup some of the profits lost to gallery commissions.

Selling on the Internet

In Chapter 8, "Going Live," we discussed setting up for direct sales from your website and using shopping carts and merchant services, such as Paypal and Verisign. While these services are easy to set up and use, they are only available if you have a website. Other options that don't require setting up a presence on the Internet are available, and while none offer the level of control you have when selling on your own, they are viable alternatives for selling your photographs to a world-wide market.

Using these alternatives has several advantages, including the immediacy of getting your work online and the convenience of having sales handled for you, as well as the increased exposure to potential customers offered by an established online gallery. Finally, the imprimatur of having "expert" approval of your work lends more credibility in the eyes of both individual purchasers and potential gallery owners.

Of course, as with most things that save you time, there are drawbacks as well. The largest of these is the costs involved. Not all of your costs will be monetary. Your costs can include the loss of control over the presentation of your images to potential customers or the competition of being on a website with a number of other photographers, all trying to stand out from the crowd for the viewers attention and money.

Online Galleries

There are several online galleries that act as intermediaries for photographers. The services available range from a reference collection of photographers grouped by subject matter to full brokerage sites that handle sales for you.

Profotos.com

Profotos (www.profotos.com) bills themselves as "All photography all the time" and offers memberships for a small monthly fee (memberships start at $5 per month for the first 10 images displayed on the site). According to Profotos, only one in five photographers who apply are accepted for membership and allowed to post images. Profotos doesn't sell your work directly; it serves as a showcase with images organized in categories such as nature, stock, wedding, portraiture, and fine art. If a buyer is interested in your work, Profotos will send you an e-mail. The site also includes links to your website if you have one. (See Figure 14.1.)

The biggest advantage to a service such as Profotos is the sheer number of visits they receive (currently, they claim over 3 million hits per month).

Figure 14.1 Profotos.com serves as a showcase for photographers.

YourArtSource.com

YourArtSource.com (www.yourartsource.com), previously Investment-Art.com, acts as a true online gallery for the sale of artwork. As with Profotos, acceptance by a jury is required to be exhibited on the site. YourArtSource will exhibit three images at no charge and up to seven additional images for a monthly fee for each image. (See Figure 14.2.)

> **Note:** Because the cost of additional images is expensive (as of Spring 2004, $50 per image for six months), we suggest starting out with the free exhibit to see if the service will generate sales for you.

YourArtSource charges a 40 percent service fee and handles the transaction for you. When a photograph sells, they'll send you the sale and shipping information. (You need to be ready to pack and ship your work within three days of a sale.) Once the transaction is completed, they'll mail you a check.

Figure 14.2 YourArtSource.com is a true online gallery handling sales for your images.

Stock Agencies

Although the Internet and digital imaging have changed the stock photography market tremendously, companies such as Corbis and Getty Images still exist and accept work from new photographers that meet their needs and criteria. The stock photography world is competitive. Breaking in and earning an income within it is very difficult. Doing so requires a very large library of images. The average photographer earns an about $1 per image on file.

With the expansion of royalty-free image libraries and an increase in the number of stock agencies that have Internet sites, this figure will probably drop even further. It doesn't take a math wizard to realize that a huge number of images will need to be on file to earn a reasonable income. Most successful stock photographers have 10,000 or more images on file with agencies, and they continually add new images to their stock list. Other photographers, particularly those with established names such as Art Wolfe (www.artwolfe.com), Art Morris (www.birdsasart.com), and John Shaw (www.johnshawphoto.com) run their own stock photography businesses, eliminating the middle man and increasing profits.

If you're interested in pursuing the stock agency approach to marketing your photographs, we suggest visiting Corbis (www.corbis.com) and Getty Images (www.getty-images.com) to get an idea of the type of imagery that is selling today. Doing a search on "**stock photography agencies**" will return a large list of agencies, including very specialized ones that may be a good fit for your style of photography.

Wrapping Up

Throughout this book, we've presented a number of ideas, tips, and techniques to help you take your digital images past the capture and editing phases of photography. We've shown you how to create dramatic prints on fine art papers, how to give your prints unique border treatments, and how to use backlit frames. We've discussed creating websites that showcase your photography and allow you to sell your work worldwide, and we've shown you how to create slideshows that inspire viewers individually and in groups of family and friends. We hope that you'll be inspired to try these options for yourself to see what works best for your needs.

This book has been a labor of love. We both enjoy teaching and helping others expand their skills, and we'd love to hear about your successes, including gallery showings, creating your first website, and making your first print sale. Send e-mail to feedback@photofinishbook.com, and be sure to include your website URL.

Index